Recognizing People in the Prehistoric Southwest

Recognizing People
in the Prehistoric Southwest

JILL E. NEITZEL

With contributions by

ANN L. W. STODDER
LAURIE D. WEBSTER
JANE H. HILL

THE UNIVERSITY OF UTAH PRESS
Salt Lake City

The Defiance House Man colophon is a registered trademark
of the University of Utah Press. It is based on a four-foot-tall
Ancient Puebloan pictograph (late PIII) near Glen Canyon, Utah.

21 20 19 18 17   1 2 3 4 5

LIBRARY OF CONGRESS CATALOGING-IN-PUBLICATION DATA

Names: Neitzel, Jill E., editor, author.
Title: Recognizing people in the prehistoric Southwest / [edited by] Jill E. Neitzel ;
    with contributions by Ann L.W. Stodder, Laurie D. Webster, Jane H. Hill.
Description: Salt Lake City : The University of Utah Press, [2016] | Includes
    bibliographical references.
Identifiers: LCCN 2016033173| ISBN 9781607815297 (pbk. : alk. paper) |
    ISBN 9781607815303 (ebook)
Subjects: LCSH: Indians of North America—Southwest, New—Antiquities. |
    Archaeology—Southwest, New.
Classification: LCC E78.S7 R335 2016 | DDC 979/.01—dc23
LC record available at https://lccn.loc.gov/2016033173

Cover image: Ceramic effigy head with dotted facial designs, Pueblo Bonito,
Chaco Canyon, northwest New Mexico. Courtesy of the Division of Anthropology,
American Museum of Natural History, cat. # H/5243.

Printed and bound in the United States of America.

The journey has begun.
From over at Shadow Spring,
along the leaders' consecrated path,
we have set out on our journey to you,
coming this way.

—from Hopi song "Soyohímkatsinmuy Taawi'an,"
Hopi Katsina Songs, by Emory Sekaquaptewa, Kenneth C. Hill,
and Dorothy K. Washburn

Contents

List of Figures   ix

List of Tables   xi

Preface and Acknowledgments   xiii

Introduction   1
Jill E. Neitzel

1 Physical Variation   13
Ann L. W. Stodder

2 Clothing   35
Laurie D. Webster

3 Ornaments   71
Jill E. Neitzel

4 Hair   103
Jill E. Neitzel

5 Facial Decoration   131
Jill E. Neitzel

6 Language   149
Jane H. Hill

Conclusion   173
Jill E. Neitzel

Appendix (Tables)   179

Notes   197

References   221

Figure Sources and Permissions   255

Contributors   259

Index   261

Figures

I.1. Map of the North American Southwest — xvi

I.2. Map of site locations — 2

I.3. Desert Hohokam man's reconstructed head — 4

I.4. Sedentary-period Hohokam man — 4

I.5. Map of prehistoric culture areas, AD 900–1150 — 6

I.6. Map of prehistoric culture areas, AD 1300–1450 — 7

I.7. Period names discussed in this volume — 8

1.1. Male and female stature by cultural group — 16

1.2. Male stature by period — 18

1.3. Female stature by period — 20

1.4. Male orbital and nasal indices — 22

1.5. Male and female femur robusticity through time — 25

1.6. Male and female femur robusticity by cultural group — 26

1.7. Mountain Mogollon cranial modification — 30

2.1. Ancestral Pueblo braided sash — 39

2.2. Weave structures — 42

2.3. Ancestral Pueblo decorated blanket — 45

2.4. Ancestral Pueblo decorated blanket — 46

2.5. Ancestral Pueblo decorated blanket — 46

2.6. Sinagua decorated blanket — 47

2.7. Mimbres feminine and masculine figures — 48

2.8. Women's aprons — 49

2.9. Men's breechcloths — 50

2.10. Ancestral Pueblo man's kilt — 51

2.11. Ancestral Pueblo man's kilt — 52

2.12. Ancestral Pueblo male figure with full outfit — 53

2.13. Ancestral Pueblo male figure with full outfit — 54

2.14. Men's shirts — 55

2.15. Mimbres man with feather tunic — 56

2.16. Sandals — 58

2.17. Sinagua man — 62

2.18. Ancestral Pueblo female figure with blanket dress and sash — 64

2.19. Ancestral Pueblo female figure with blanket dress and sash — 65

3.1. Chaco turquoise bead necklace and pendants — 74

3.2. Copper bells — 74

3.3. Mimbres figure with jewelry — 76

3.4. Hohokam *Glycymeris* bracelets — 77

3.5. Hohokam shell-bead necklace — 78

3.6. Preclassic-period Hohokam figures with jewelry — 79

3.7. Mosaic pendants from Aztec Ruins — 83

3.8. Sinagua turquoise-inlaid armband   84
3.9. Sinagua turquoise- and shell-inlaid
      pendant   84
3.10. Sinagua turquoise- and shell-inlaid
      bracelet   85
3.11. Classic-period Hohokam man   90
3.12. Hohokam inlaid ornaments and
      shell-bead necklace   90
3.13. Bead necklaces from Paquimé   92
3.14. Casas Grandes jar with two
      standing figures   92
3.15. Composite necklace from Paquimé   93
3.16. Casas Grandes female effigy
      with composite necklace   94
3.17. Ancestral Pueblo figure with jewelry   96
3.18. Ancestral Pueblo figure with jewelry   97
4.1. Basketmaker-period hairstyles   107
4.2. Mimbres hairstyles   108
4.3. Casas Grandes male effigy with
      typical hairstyle   109
4.4. Casas Grandes female effigy vessel
      with a double macaw-headed
      diamond motif on her back   110
4.5. Ancestral Pueblo female figure
      with double side buns   111
4.6. Ancestral Pueblo female figure
      with back bun   112
4.7. Ancestral Pueblo female figures
      with long hair pulled back   113
4.8. Mimbres hair decorations   116
4.9. Casas Grandes effigy with headdress   117
4.10. Casas Grandes effigy with headdress   118
4.11. Ancestral Pueblo figure with
      headdress   119

4.12. Ancestral Pueblo male figure
      with feather in hair   120
4.13. Hair pins   122
4.14. Sinagua basket cap   123
4.15. Sinagua Magician's reconstructed
      head   124
4.16. Hohokam figures with headgear   125
4.17. Fremont feather headdress   126
5.1. Mimbres facial decorations   136
5.2. Chaco male effigy with
      facial decoration   137
5.3. Chaco facial decorations   138
5.4. Chaco and Hohokam dotted
      facial designs   138
5.5. Hohokam facial decoration   139
5.6. Hohokam facial decoration on
      possible imported effigy   139
5.7. Hohokam or Salado effigy with
      facial decoration   140
5.8. Salado effigy with facial decorations   141
5.9. Casas Grandes male effigy with
      facial decoration   141
5.10. Casas Grandes male effigy with
      facial decoration   142
5.11. Casas Grandes effigy with facial
      decoration   143
5.12. Casas Grandes male effigy with
      facial decoration   144
6.1. Map of Greater Southwest
      language families   152
6.2. Historic-period Hopi kachina
      dance   158
6.3. Hopi maidens grinding corn meal   163
6.4. Hopi woman making paper bread   164

Tables (in Appendix)

1.1. Male stature by period — 179
1.2. Female stature by period — 180
1.3. Male facial metrics by period — 180
1.4. Male facial indices by period — 181
1.5. Male femur robusticity by period — 181
1.6. Female femur robusticity by period — 182
1.7. Cranial modification in Pueblo groups — 183
1.8. Cranial modification in other cultural groups — 184
2.1. Distribution of loom-woven fabrics — 184
2.2. Distribution of applied color-decoration techniques — 185
2.3. Distribution of primary design layouts and motifs — 185
3.1. Pueblo Bonito's Burial #14 — 185
3.2. Galaz Site's most jewelry-rich burials — 186
3.3. La Ciudad's grave goods in Feature #1679 — 186
3.4. Aztec West Burial #16 — 187
3.5. Pueblo Grande's most jewelry-rich burials — 187
3.6. The Magician's burial at Ridge Ruin — 188
3.7. RB568's most jewelry-rich burials — 189
3.8. Paquimé's most jewelry-rich burials — 189
3.9. Point of Pines and Grasshopper Pueblos' most jewelry-rich burials — 190
3.10. Arroyo Hondo and Tijeras Pueblos' most jewelry-rich burials — 191
4.1. Mimbres hairstyles — 191
4.2. Casas Grandes hairstyles — 191
4.3. P-IV Ancestral Pueblo hairstyles — 192
4.4. Mimbres hair decorations — 192
4.5. Casas Grandes hair decorations — 193
4.6. P-IV Ancestral Pueblo hair decorations — 193
5.1. Mimbres facial designs — 193
5.2. Casas Grandes facial designs — 194
5.3. Other prehistoric Southwest facial designs — 195
6.1. Greater Southwest language families — 196

Preface and Acknowledgments

In this book, we consider how the prehistoric inhabitants of the North American Southwest looked and sounded and how such characteristics conveyed people's identities.

The project began with a symposium entitled "A Big View of Identity and Inter-action: Macro-Regional Cultural Variation in the U.S. Southwest," organized by Jill Neitzel for the 2009 Annual Meeting of the Society for American Archaeology in Atlanta, Georgia. The symposium was prompted by a question: how far would a traveler in the late prehistoric Southwest have to go before encountering people who were noticeably different?

At the start of the symposium, audience members were asked to imagine they had spent the previous twelve months walking to Atlanta from Vancouver, the location of the previous year's Annual Meeting. Throughout this journey, they would have continually assessed how people met along the way were both similar to and different from those in Vancouver and at points in between. They could have observed, for example, people's physiques, clothes, homes, public structures, foods, and speech. The spatial patterning of each would undoubtedly reflect the complicated relationship between culture, environment, history, interaction, and identity in Canada and the United States today.

The Atlanta symposium considered what a traveler would have seen roughly a millennium earlier in the late prehistoric Southwest.[1] Presenters described regional patterns for a series of archaeological topics and considered them in terms of identity and interaction. Some topics were the same as those that a present-day traveler might observe en route from Vancouver to Atlanta (e.g., clothes, structures). Others were specific to Southwest archaeology (e.g., ceramics, rock art). Answers to the "How far…?" question varied depending on the characteristic being considered. For some characteristics, differences would have been evident within the prehistoric traveler's home community. For others, similarities would have extended over long distances.

Our focus here is narrower than in the Atlanta symposium. We consider only those characteristics that prehistoric individuals carried on their bodies in ways that others would see and hear. We link these characteristics to the issue of identity, specifically what they conveyed about a person. The chapters include revised and expanded versions of the symposium papers on physical appearance, clothing, and language. Additional chapters consider ornaments, hairstyles, and facial decoration.

To facilitate the volume's completion, Ann Stodder (physical appearance), Laurie Webster (clothes), Hannah Mattson (ornaments), Jill Neitzel (facial decoration, hairstyles), and Jane Hill (language) met prior to the SAA's 2011 Annual Meeting in Sacramento. Kathleen Lindahl, California Senior State Archaeologist, graciously allowed us to use one of her office's conference rooms for daylong discussions. Hannah Matson subsequently withdrew from the project, and Jill Neitzel wrote a substitute chapter.

We are grateful to the original symposium participants whose papers are not included here—Scott Van Keuren (pottery), Suzanne Fish (food), Douglas Craig (residential architecture), Ruth Van Dyke (ritual and public architecture), Douglas Mitchell (burials), Polly Schaafsma (rock art), and Tim Pauketat (discussant comments). Their presentations helped inform our thinking about the links between regional patterns, identity, and interaction.

At the University of Delaware, a number of people facilitated a semester-long sabbatical for Jill Neitzel to work on this project and provided research funds to subsidize extensive illustrations—Karen Rosenberg and Peter Weil, Chair and Acting Chair of the Department of Anthropology, and Associate Deans Gretchen Bauer and Joseph Pika and Deans Mark Huddleston and George Watson of the College of Arts and Sciences. In the Anthropology Department, Sandra Wenner handled all administrative tasks efficiently and all computer crises with calm reassurance. She and Angela Holseth of the History Media Center scanned images. Independent artist Robert Schultz drafted illustrations and helped resolve image reproduction issues.

At the University of Utah Press, Reba Rauch enthusiastically encouraged a publication on personal appearance and identity and continued to offer invaluable advice and steadfast support throughout the long road to completion. Michelle Hegmon and Catherine Fowler carefully reviewed the draft manuscript for the Press, providing substantive and editorial suggestions that guided our final revisions. Copy editor Jeff Grathwohl improved our writing immensely by eliminating extra verbiage, correcting grammar, and identifying errors and inconsistencies. Production manager Jessica Booth applied her artistic and organizational talents to transform the manuscript into a beautifully designed book.

Numerous museum personnel, artists, and photographers helped locate illustrations and generously gave permission to reproduce them.[2] These individuals include: Diane Bird (Museum of Indian Arts and Culture/Laboratory of Anthropology),

Erin Bouchard (Frederick R. Weisman Art Museum), Blair Clark (Museum of Indian Arts and Culture/Laboratory of Anthropology), Chris Coleman (Natural History Museum of Los Angeles County), Roger Colten (Peabody Museum of Natural History), Scott Cutler (Centennial Museum, University of Texas–El Paso), KC DenDooven (KC Publications), Jessica Desany Ganong (Peabody Museum of Archaeology and Ethnology), Chris Downum (Northern Arizona University), David Doyel (archaeologist), Alan Fleischer (collector), Stephanie Gilmore (University of Colorado Museum of Natural History), Maureen Goldsmith (University of Pennsylvania Museum of Archaeology and Anthropology), Matthew Guebard (National Park Service), Kelley Hays-Gilpin (Museum of Northern Arizona), Erica Hoffman (Peabody Museum Press), Wesley Jernigan (author and artist), Eric Kendall (The Amerind Foundation), Erica Kinias (Telluride Historical Museum), Barry Landau (American Museum of Natural History), Steven LeBlanc (Mimbres Pottery Images Digital Data Base), Jackie Maman (Art Institute of Chicago), Darcy Marlow (Philbrook Museum of Art), Jennifer McFadden (National Geographic Society), Nicolette Meister (Logan Museum of Anthropology), Ashley Morton (National Geographic Society), Marc Muench (Muench Photography), Carolyn O'Bagy Davis (author), Lori Pendleton (American Museum of Natural History), Jessica Simpson (Museum of Peoples and Cultures), Fred Stimson (photographer), Stephanie Summerhays (Smithsonian Institution Scholarly Press), John B. Taylor (photographer), David H. Thomas (American Museum of Natural History), Meghan Vance (Northern Arizona University), Patricia Walker (Museum of Northern Arizona), Janelle Weakly (Arizona State Museum), and Viola Wentzel (widow of photographer, Volkmar Wentzel).

Finally, Jill Neitzel is deeply indebted to Ann Stodder, Laurie Webster, and Jane Hill for their ongoing contributions to this project. Their commitment never wavered, nor did their willingness to modify their papers to fit her vision of the final product. They have been ideal collaborators.

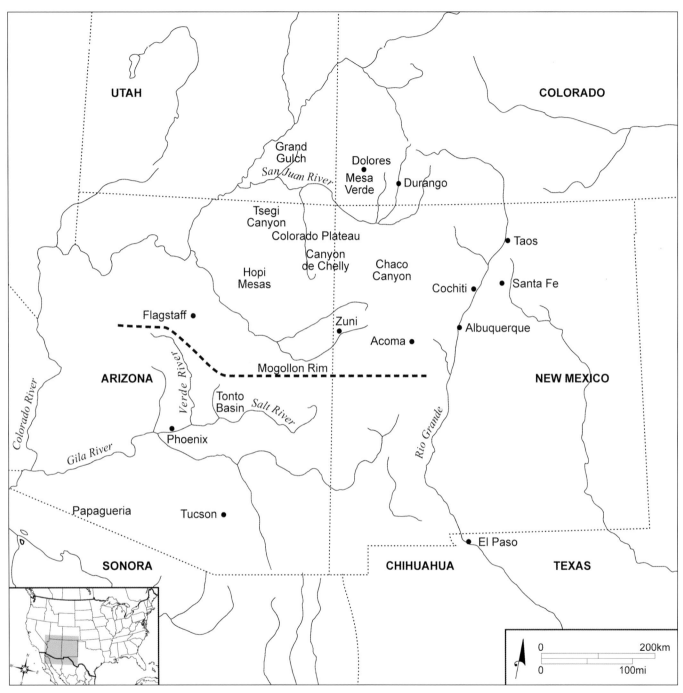

I.1. Map of the North American Southwest.

INTRODUCTION

Jill E. Neitzel

A prehistoric traveler on a journey across the North American Southwest would have encountered all sorts of people whose identities could be recognized by how they looked and talked. Each individual's appearance presented a composite of morphological and cultural attributes. The morphological would have included stature, robustness, facial features, skull shape, and skin color. Cultural attributes would have included clothes, ornaments, hairstyles, and facial decoration. Together with speech, these characteristics broadcast a variety of overlapping identity messages concerning gender, status, cultural affiliation, connections with other groups, religious beliefs, ceremonial roles, and heritage.

This book documents the appearance characteristics, speech, and associated identity messages of people who lived in different parts of the late prehistoric Southwest (Figures I.1–2). The scale of the analyses is regional, and the time period of interest extends from about AD 900 to 1450. The data are primarily archaeological, consisting of material remains that have been preserved for study. But because prehistoric Southwesterners had no written language, the chapter on speech must be based on historic-period data.

The chapters on different aspects of appearance and speech all reach similar conclusions: personal characteristics varied within and between communities; over long distances this variation created a complex mosaic of embedded and overlapping patterns; and each characteristic could convey multiple identity messages. When all characteristics are considered together, as they would have appeared on a single individual, the identity messages are expressed repeatedly.

This introduction provides background information for the chapters that follow. It begins with a brief consideration of the concept of identity and its place in Southwest archaeology and then offers thumbnail sketches of the Southwest's

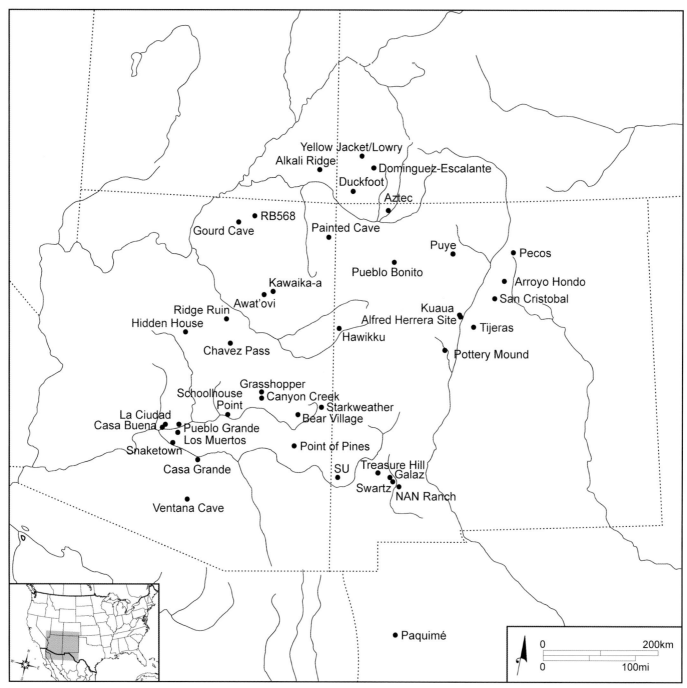

I.2. Map of site locations.

major cultural groups during three successive time periods. Finally, it previews each chapter's major findings.

IDENTITY STUDIES IN THE PREHISTORIC SOUTHWEST

The concept of identity refers to how people define themselves and how others in turn perceive them. In their considerable research on this topic among contemporary populations, cultural anthropologists have emphasized the effect that active decision-making (or agency) has on behavior.[1] They have documented how identity is an ongoing construction in which people continually reaffirm and modify who they are both as individuals and as members of groups. Since most people are associated with multiple groups of varying types and sizes, they have multiple identities, such as gender, age, status, occupation, interest groups, and cultural affiliation. These groups and their associated identities can overlap or be embedded within one another, and at any one time, some may be more important than others. Furthermore, this ranking is dynamic so that as circumstances change, so can the relative significance of a person's various identities.

The two cultural anthropological findings that are most relevant to this volume are

(1) an individual's multiple identities can be communicated to others by how she or he looks and talks;

(2) messages about the most important identities are usually the most visible and redundant.

The topic of identity has been an unrecognized presence throughout the history of Southwest archaeology. For more than half a century, researchers divided the Southwest into culture areas using broadly distributed ceramic types and architectural forms.[2] These areas, which were thought to reflect the extent of shared cultural norms, were reconceptualized in the 1970s as regional systems of interaction.[3] From both perspectives, people and their identities were at best an afterthought.

Archaeologists first began to consider prehistoric Southwesterners as people in mortuary studies that compared the skeletal remains, artifacts, and other evidence recovered from human burials. The results highlighted individuals with the richest mortuary treatment and distinguished status and gender groups.[4] Identity was implicit in these discussions, but not the focus of attention.

Recent research on immigrant enclaves has explicitly incorporated the concept of identity and the idea that it is the dynamic product of individual agency. Southwest archaeologists have long recognized these enclaves within sites and localities by

I.3. Reconstruction of a Desert Hohokam man's head, Ventana Cave, Papagueria, south-central Arizona, AD 1000–1400. Note the man's nose ornament, which adorned his mummified body along with dangling, circular shell ear pendants (not shown here).

I.4. Artist's depiction of Sedentary-period Hohokam man, south-central Arizona, AD 900–1150. Compare the man's facial designs to those illustrated in Figures 3.6a, 5.4b, his necklace to the one shown in Figure 3.6a, and his left armband to the one in Figure 3.4.

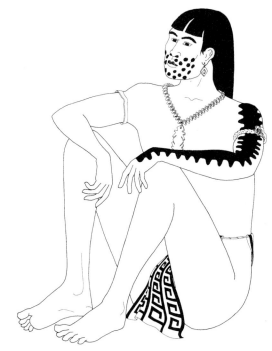

the presence of architectural forms, decorated ceramics, and types of cranial modification common to other areas.[5] Current investigations have focused on how immigrants sustained or modified their identities after settling in their adopted homes.[6]

This volume takes Southwest identity research in a new direction. Instead of focusing on how identity was conveyed by architecture and ceramics, we consider how people's appearance and speech broadcast information about who they were.[7] This is not the first attempt to recreate the appearance of prehistoric Southwesterners. To engage and educate the public, archaeology museums often include people in painted exhibit backgrounds or as modeled diorama figures. In both, their appearance is usually generic "Native American" and secondary to the depicted scene.

More detailed and empirically based illustrations have appeared occasionally in academic publications. Early examples reconstructed human heads from excavated skulls (Figure I.3; also Figure 4.15).[8] More recently in his book *Jewelry of the Prehistoric Southwest*, artist-archaeologist Wesley Jernigan included composite drawings of individuals from different prehistoric groups (Figure I.4; also Figures 2.17, 3.11).[9] We take another approach. Each chapter considers a particular personal characteristic and elucidates its associated identity messages. The concluding chapter then considers how identity messages were reiterated in a person's overall appearance.

CULTURAL AND TEMPORAL DIVISIONS

Our comparisons of personal characteristics and their associated identity messages utilize the areal divisions that were originally associated with the Southwest's major culture areas and are now viewed as regional systems of interaction. Those that get the most attention in all periods are the Ancestral Pueblo on the Colorado Plateau, the Hohokam in the Lower Sonoran desert, and the Mogollon in the central and eastern mountains (Figure I.5). We also consider the later, intermediately located Sinagua and Salado, and Casas Grandes in the Mesoamerican borderlands of northern Chihuahua (Figure I.6).

Temporally, we consider three time periods adapted from widely used regional chronologies: AD 900–1150, AD 1150–1300, and AD 1300–1450 (Figure I.7).[10] Working within limits imposed by preservation and previous research, each chapter focuses on the time periods and groups with the most plentiful data. In a few instances, the authors have adjusted the volume's temporal divisions to accommodate their data.

The AD 900–1150 period comparisons emphasize three cultural groups (Figure I.5). The Pueblo II-period Ancestral Puebloans lived on the Colorado Plateau, which spans the northern Southwest. They were distinguished by their black-on-white pottery; masonry pueblos; and circular, ceremonial structures called kivas. Best documented are the occupants of Chaco Canyon, whose spectacular vestiges

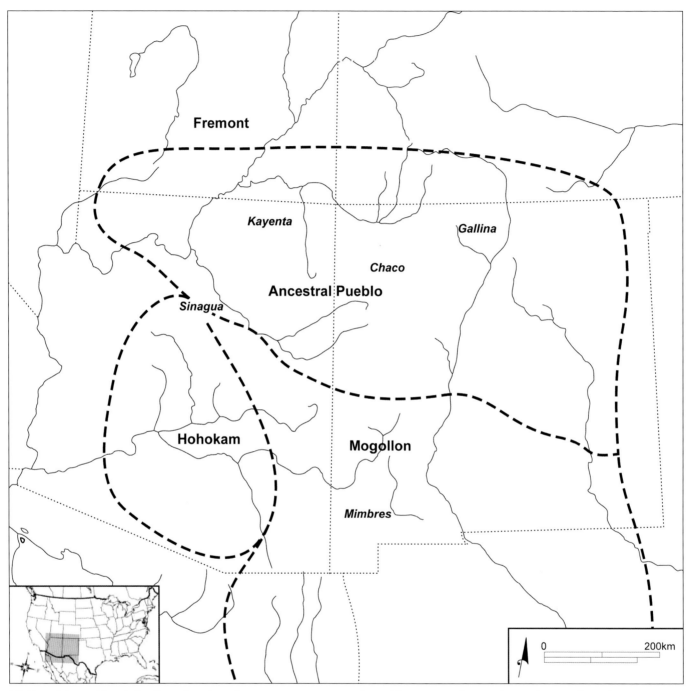

I.5. Map of the prehistoric Southwest's major culture areas, AD 900–1150. Dotted lines are used to emphasize that area boundaries were permeable, shifting, and overlapping.

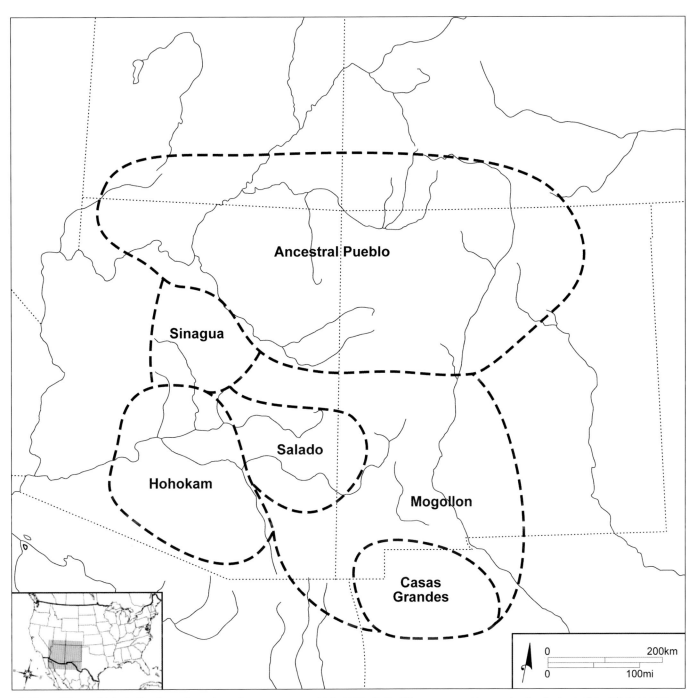

I.6. Map of the prehistoric Southwest's major culture areas, AD 1300–1450. Dotted lines are used to emphasize that area boundaries were permeable, shifting, and overlapping. The boundaries of the Salado's widely shared socioreligious belief system are not shown here.

	Hohokam	Ancestral Pueblo	Mogollon	Sinagua	Salado	Casas Grandes
1450	/\					
1400	Late	Pueblo IV	Mt Mogollon	Pueblo IV	Late	Medio
1350	Classic		Pueblo IV		Classic	Phase
1300	/\					
1250	Early	Pueblo III	Mt Mogollon	Elden	Early	
1200	Classic		Pueblo III	Phase	Classic	
1150	/\					
1100	Sedentary					
1050	or	Pueblo II	Classic			
1000	Late Pre-		Mimbres			
950	Classic					
900	/\					

*Period divisions are approximate (+/-50 years) and open to dispute. Zigzag lines are used to emphasize that the dating is imprecise and that different groups' transitions were probably not simultaneous

include multistory great houses; large, circular structures known as great kivas; roads; distinctive black-on-white pottery; and abundant turquoise jewelry.

Centered on the Lower Salt/Middle Gila River valley (a.k.a. Phoenix Basin), the Preclassic-period Hohokam occupied the desert region of south-central Arizona. They were associated with red-on-buff ceramics, shell jewelry, ball courts, and canal irrigation systems.

The Mogollon occupied the Southwest's mountainous areas where they were distinguished by red-on-brown and black-on-white pottery, pit houses, pueblos, and kivas. The Mimbres Mogollon in southwest New Mexico have received the most attention due to their exquisite black-on-white ceramic bowls.

Based on settlement characteristics and human burials, archaeologists generally agree that Chaco society was hierarchically organized, the Preclassic-period Hohokam probably were, and the Mimbres were the least differentiated.

These groups all experienced significant changes during the following AD 1150–1300 period. Among the Pueblo-III period Ancestral Puebloans, the Chacoans built a new great house complex along the San Juan River that eclipsed the power of Chaco Canyon. In contrast to their predecessors, the Classic-period Hohokam constructed platform mounds and compounds, expanded canal irrigation systems, and used red ware and polychrome ceramics. Among the Mogollon, the Mimbres faded, as the Mountain Mogollon of east-central Arizona began to thrive. A new group that emerged in the intermediate zone of north-central Arizona was the

Sinagua who were influenced by the Hohokam to the south and the Ancestral Puebloans to the north. Archaeologists think that the Chacoans, Hohokam, and Sinagua of this period were all socially stratified, but, as with the Mimbres, the Mountain Mogollon were less differentiated.

The AD 1300–1450 period was a time of environmental and social upheaval, as severe droughts compelled many to leave their homes. Entire regions were abandoned, and large settlements in better-watered locations grew with the immigrant influx. This volume compares six late period groups (Figure I.6): (1) the Pueblo IV-period Ancestral Puebloans, noted for their large pueblos on the Hopi Mesas, around Zuni, and in the Rio Grande River valley; (2) the late Classic-period Hohokam known for their platform mounds, at least two multistory "big houses," and extensive canal irrigation systems; (3) the Mountain Mogollon; (4) the Sinagua; (5) a new intermediately located group, the Tonto Basin Salado, who first emerged in the preceding period and were notable for their platform mounds and red ware and polychrome pottery; and (6) another new group in northern Chihuahua, the people of Casas Grande, whose enormous site of Paquimé evidences Mogollon, Salado, and Mesoamerican influences.

The Southwest's prehistoric period ended in AD 1540 with the arrival of Spanish conquistador Francisco Vásquez de Coronado. For indigenous peoples, the historic period has been fraught by ongoing cultural upheaval. Each of the chapters in this book concludes with a brief glimpse of a topic that deserves its own volume—how the nexus of personal appearance, speech, and identity changed after Euro-American conquest.

ORGANIZATION

The chapters here are ordered by how visible their topics would have been to an observer. Morphological characteristics are considered first, followed by the most apparent cultural characteristic—clothing. Subsequent chapters examine ornaments, hairstyles, facial decoration, and speech—the personal characteristic that an observer would have heard rather than seen. The conclusion combines this information to consider overall presence. We have minimized archaeological jargon, put data tables in the appendix, and relegated more technical discussions and all bibliographic citations to endnotes.

In chapter 1, physical anthropologist Ann Stodder considers body morphology. Paradoxically, despite extensive research on prehistoric skeletons, the topic of past people's physical appearance has until now received minimal attention. Stodder documents regional differences in stature, facial features, femur robusticity, cranial deformation, and skin color. She attributes these differences to genetics, health, technology, resources, aesthetics, and the intentional expression of individual and group identities. Focusing on identity, she considers how a person's morphology conveyed information about his or her gender, status, and cultural affiliation.

Next, textile expert Laurie Webster compares the clothes worn by the members of different groups. She applies a new, identity-based perspective to the substantial research that has been done on prehistoric Southwest textiles. Her data include preserved fragments and rare, complete garments, as well as artistic depictions on ceramics and kiva murals. Webster documents variation in raw materials, weave structures, decorative designs and colors, individual garments, and complete outfits. She finds that clothing conveyed information most strongly about a person's gender, status, and cultural affiliation and that it also broadcast messages about religion, intergroup connections, and heritage.

In chapter 3, the first of her three chapters, archaeologist Jill Neitzel compares jewelry worn in different parts of the Southwest. Drawing on substantial previous research, she focuses on ornaments from the best-documented, most jewelry-rich burials. Neitzel finds that the quantities and kinds of ornaments in these burials signaled individuals' status and the degree of social differentiation within their respective communities. But jewelry alone did not always reflect the relative prominence of different groups' richest individuals in comparison to one another. Neitzel also shows that adornments could communicate information about cultural affiliation, intergroup connections, religious beliefs, cultural heritage, and other social roles.

In her chapter on hair, Neitzel compares both styles and decorations, topics that have until now been largely unexamined. Her data include artistic depictions on ceramics and kiva murals, and preserved artifacts. Neitzel finds that gender was the primary determinant of how prehistoric Southwesterners arranged their hair and that these styles could also convey cultural affiliation. Hair decorations often signaled higher status and special ceremonial roles, but gender messages were variable depending on the cultural group. Both style and adornment could also communicate religious meanings and connections with other groups and the ancestral past.

Neitzel's chapter on facial decoration analyzes human depictions on ceramics. Building on previous research done on Casas Grandes effigy jars, she finds that facial designs were imbued with multiple layers of meaning about gender, cultural affiliation, connections with other groups, ancestral heritage, and religious beliefs. When worn on ceremonial occasions, the religious symbolism was paramount, redundantly expressing a preoccupation with water and fertility. Neitzel tracks some of these symbols over a span of 1,400 years from twentieth-century Hopi kachina masks to sixteenth-century Aztec codices and eighth-century painted murals from Teotihuacan.

In chapter 6, linguist Jane Hill uses historical data to divide the prehistoric Southwest into two language areas within which the speakers of different languages interacted, sometimes to the point of being multilingual. In the northern area, she documents a gender difference in the vocabulary associated with kachina ceremonies. Men's frequent use of loan words in rituals suggests that they traveled to distant places for ceremonies as well as trade. In contrast, women's reliance on local vocabulary for feast foods suggests that they did not travel or that this terminology reinforced community identity and hospitality in interactions with guests.

In the conclusion, Neitzel synthesizes information from the preceding chapters in two ways. First, she considers how each of a prehistoric Southwesterner's identities would have been conveyed by multiple personal characteristics. The most repeated messages concerned gender, followed in the most socially differentiated groups by status and ceremonial roles. Expressions of cultural affiliation and intergroup connections were less redundant, and repeated expressions of religious beliefs and cultural heritage were present but more subtle. Neitzel then presents composite descriptions of what the members of the best-documented groups looked like. She concludes by advocating a people-centered perspective in studies of the past.

THE JOURNEY BEGINS

Let us imagine a hypothetical traveler in the late prehistoric Southwest visiting a new community. The first question is always, "Who are these people?" While contextual information, such as architecture and ceramics, could help, our focus is on what people looked like, how they spoke, and what such characteristics revealed about people's identities. Personal appearance and speech would be the only information that a destination's residents could use to identify our visiting traveler, and the same would be true for fellow travelers encountering one another en route.

As our traveler moves across the Southwest, the patterns shift in how people look and sound, creating a kind of kaleidoscope of visual and auditory impressions. At a new location, some appearance and speech attributes may be very distinctive and others similar to or just slightly different from what was observed or heard elsewhere. The combination of all attributes would convey multiple messages about who each person was.

As you read, imagine yourself as our traveler. Although our lives today are immeasurably different from those of prehistoric Southwesterners, we all recognize others through personal appearance and speech. In appreciating this connection, we can begin to reconstruct a past that was lived by individuals and glimpse our common humanity. May you have an informative and enjoyable trip!

1

PHYSICAL VARIATION

by ANN L. W. STODDER

Throughout the Southwest, this volume's hypothetical traveler would have observed differences in people's physical characteristics. While much of this variation in stature, weight, head shape, facial features, and skin, eye, and hair color was genetic, some of it was also affected by cultural practices. These visible characteristics were part of the mosaic of features and accoutrements that conveyed information about an individual's sex, age, cultural affiliation, community location, habitual activities, status, kin group, and unique identity.

Continuing developments in the study of ancient DNA suggest that eventually we may be able to reconstruct a great deal about the appearance of prehistoric ancestors. But the current emphasis in DNA studies of archaeological skeletons is on biological relatedness and variation rather than features such as hair color or other visible differences that anyone, past or present, would note in normal interactions.[1] The bulk of our information for considering visible differences among prehistoric people consists of traditional measurements developed by early physical anthropologists.[2] Those who studied human remains from Southwest archaeological sites were interested in reconstructing the racial prehistory of humankind and of people in North and South America. When these investigators used their calipers to record skull dimensions, for example, they saw faces, which they classified in racial types with broad geographical affiliations.[3] We now know that their interpretations were often wrong; and because of its prevailingly racist tone, this early literature is generally disregarded by physical anthropologists working today.[4]

In this chapter, I revisit the long dormant interest in physical appearance and variation as part of this volume's focus on social identity. Using data from 180 Southwest archaeological sites, published by many researchers over many decades, I examine four characteristics that are commonly recorded in the analysis of adult skeletons: stature; facial features, including facial width and the shape of the eyes and nose; head shape, which prehistoric Southwesterners modified in several ways; and femur (upper leg) robusticity, which, like stature, is determined by the combination of genetics, behavior, and the environment. I also briefly consider skin color, a characteristic that can be studied through DNA but is not evident in skeletal remains.

The information used here is gleaned from dozens of published and unpublished sources and is far from perfect or comprehensive. Ancestral Puebloans are better represented, in part because there have been more studies but also because at

1.1. Male and female stature averages in major cultural groups.

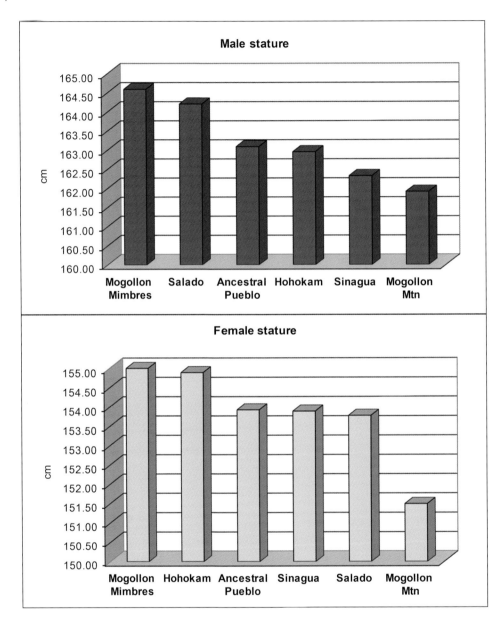

certain times some other groups—the Hohokam, Sinagua, Salado, and Zuni—practiced cremation, and there is far less morphological data available from these remains than from interments. Nevertheless, the information compiled here demonstrates the kinds of physical differences in people that this volume's traveler would have encountered during a journey throughout the Southwest. In fact, at some times and places, different-looking people would have been present within just a day's walk or even within our traveler's own home community.

STATURE

The stature attained by adults is the product of genetic potential and environmental determinants (including health and nutritional status) from before birth until the late teens. Physical anthropologists estimate this characteristic by applying different formulas to measurements of skeletal elements. The estimates reported here are all derived from complete femora or tibiae using Santiago Genovés's formula, which is most commonly used in regional publications. Vagaries of publication styles mean that while the formula is typically referenced, the number of individuals and the range of variation represented by a stature data set are not always, or even typically, reported. The data used here are based on a minimum total of 435 females and 527 males.

The major factors that affected variation in prehistoric Southwesterners' stature were sex, time, ecological context, and perhaps social status.[5] On average, males were 7.8–12.1 cm taller than females. The male group averages ranged from 157.9–167.0 cm (Appendix Table 1.1);[6] and the female group averages ranged from 150.6 to 158.9 cm (Appendix Table 1.2). Pan-regionally, average stature increased during times of population expansion, declined during periods of droughts and migrations, and then stabilized somewhat until Spanish contact.[7]

At the regional scale, there are patterns that correspond to cultural groups and their broader ecological contexts (Figure 1.1). On average, the Mountain Mogollon of both sexes were the shortest and the Classic Mimbres the tallest. Salado males and Hohokam females were the next tallest, with Ancestral Puebloans in the middle range for both males and females. While these condensed data provide the general picture of stature variation by culture, the groupings mask an underlying pattern: people living in lowland areas or in valleys along large, permanent, or managed watercourses (e.g., the Classic Mimbres, the Hohokam along canal systems, and the later Ancestral Puebloans in the northern Rio Grande River valley) were taller than people living in mountain and foothill areas (e.g., the Mountain Mogollon, Sinagua, and Salado of the Tonto Basin foothills).

1.2. Average male stature by period.

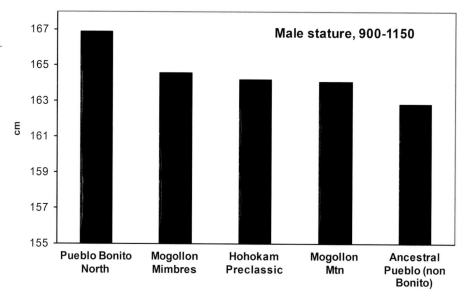

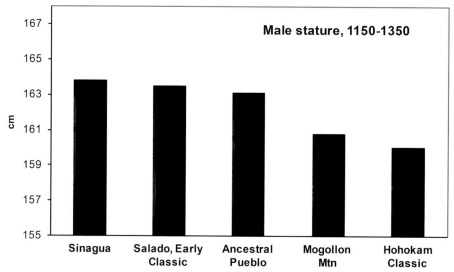

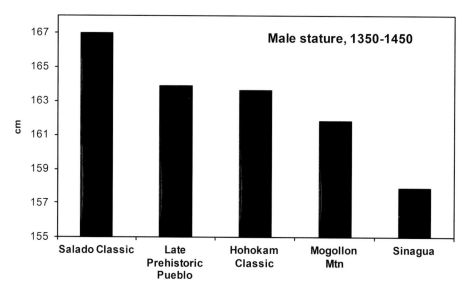

Among contemporary groups, the most striking example of height variation occurred at Chaco Canyon from AD 900–1150 (Figures 1.2–3).[8] At Pueblo Bonito, the preeminent Chaco great house, the tallest male was 173.4 cm, which was 8.7 cm taller than the average male at the canyon's small sites. At 169.3 cm, the average Pueblo Bonito male was 4.6 cm taller than his average small-site counterpart. The heights of these small-site residents were comparable to those of men elsewhere in the Southwest: they were less than 1 cm taller than the Mountain Mogollon.

Tall men were also buried at Chaco great houses located outside the canyon (e.g., Yellow Jacket, Lowry Ruin, Dominguez-Escalante Ruin). Similar to their Pueblo Bonito counterparts, they towered over the occupants of contemporary smaller sites located throughout the San Juan Basin. These tall men were probably leaders whose high status was marked at death by burial at special locations and in a few cases with lavish grave goods. While their height may have been due in part to a better diet associated with their special positions, there is surprisingly little evidence in the global archaeological record that higher status meant better health in nonstate societies. It is likely that genetics played a significant role in the height of the group(s) that comprised the Chaco elite. In any case, stature differences of 4.6 cm or more would have been evident to anybody who encountered one of these great-house men. The apparently strategic scattering of these very large individuals across the landscape suggests an intriguing aspect of the distribution and maintenance of power among the Chacoans.

From AD 1150–1350, stature declined overall (Figures 1.2–1.3). This is especially apparent for females in general and among the Hohokam. The relatively high averages of the Sinagua stand out, probably due to the combined effects of postvolcanic-eruption soil fertility and the presence of one tall individual—the so-called Magician of Ridge Ruin, whose stature is estimated at 171 cm.[9] He was interred with an assemblage of ritual materials and turquoise mosaics unparalleled outside of Chaco Canyon.

During the late AD 1300s and the 1400s, the Salado were the tallest people in the Southwest, followed by the Hohokam and the late prehistoric Puebloans in the northern Rio Grande River valley (Figures 1.2–1.3). The Mountain Mogollon and Sinagua were the shortest.

With the exception of the Chaco great-house residents, the stature differentials among most prehistoric Southwesterners were not huge; and as the case of the rather tall Magician of Ridge Ruin demonstrates, there were taller and shorter people in every community. But height is one of the most easily perceived aspects of physical appearance. In addition to whatever impression the Chacoans made, people would have been aware of the relatively shorter stature of upland residents.

1.3. Average female stature by period.

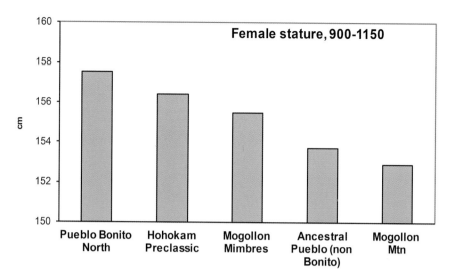

Female stature, 900-1150

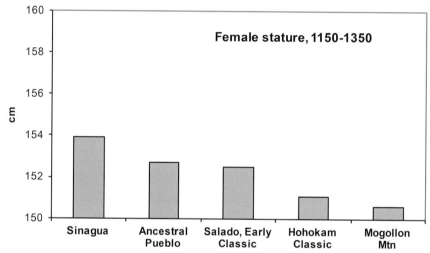

Female stature, 1150-1350

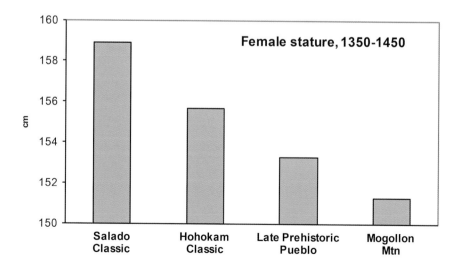

Female stature, 1350-1450

FACES

Similar to stature, variation in people's faces would have been clearly evident to our traveler. But whereas height is a single characteristic, the face is a composite of several features whose variation prehistorically was due primarily to gene flow influenced by kinship, marriage patterns, and geographic separation. The list of measurements recorded on the facial skeleton includes the maximum width of the face (bizygomatic breadth), maximum eye orbit height and width, and maximum nasal cavity breadth and height.[10] Researchers use eye and nose measurements to calculate indices that give a sense of these features' overall shapes (Figure 1.4). For the orbital index, height is divided by breadth and then multiplied by 100. An eye orbit index of 100 suggests a square or circular eye shape. Lower indices indicate eyes that are wider on the horizontal axis relative to the vertical, shaped more like horizontal ovals. For the nasal index, breadth is divided by height and multiplied by 100 with higher numbers indicating broader noses.

For the period prior to AD 900, facial data are available for Ancestral Puebloans on the Colorado Plateau (Appendix Tables 1.3–4).[11] The range of group averages for bizygomatic breadth is 5.82 mm: the Arizona (western) Basketmakers had the narrowest faces, and the widest belonged to the slightly later and farthest east Early Pueblo I-period people in the Ridges Basin near Durango, Colorado. This difference was matched by a similarity: among their contemporaries, these two groups had the most horizontally oriented eyes. In contrast, the residents of Grand Gulch in southeast Utah and nearby Canyon de Chelly in northeast Arizona had the squarest/roundest eyes. The Ridges Basin people were also distinguished by the broadest noses. These distinctions reflect the eastern (Durango area) and western (Arizona, Utah) branches of early Pueblo culture, as well as the effects of earlier genetic drift in small, local Basketmaker populations.

From AD 900–1150, facial measurements are available for the Mimbres in addition to the Ancestral Puebloans (Appendix Tables 1.3–4). The residents of Canyon de Chelly were now distinguished by the widest faces: their mean bizygomatic breadth was 5.9 mm greater than the lowest group average at the Duckfoot site in southwest Colorado. The Chaco residents of Pueblo Bonito stood out for having the highest average orbital index and the lowest average nasal index, indicating that among their contemporaries they had the most square/round eyes and the narrowest noses. In contrast, the Mimbres residents of Swarts Ruin had the lowest average orbital index and the highest average nasal index, indicating that they had the most horizontally oriented eyes and the broadest noses.

From AD 1150–1450, data are available for the first time for people from throughout the Southwest, which is a reflection of the region's increased population

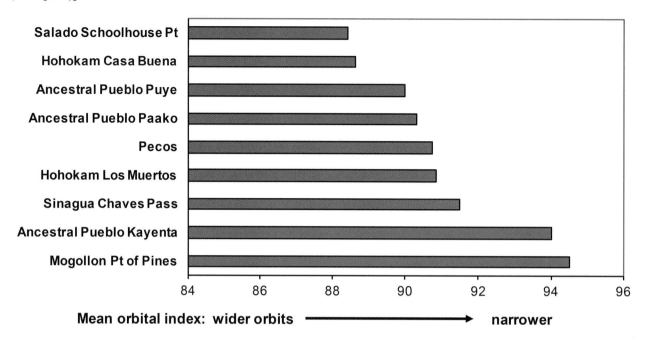

Eye orbit shape

Salado Schoolhouse Pt
Hohokam Casa Buena
Ancestral Pueblo Puye
Ancestral Pueblo Paako
Pecos
Hohokam Los Muertos
Sinagua Chaves Pass
Ancestral Pueblo Kayenta
Mogollon Pt of Pines

84 86 88 90 92 94 96

Mean orbital index: wider orbits ⟶ narrower

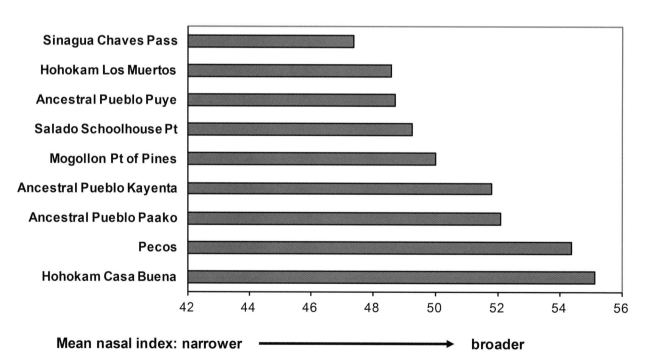

Nasal shape

Sinagua Chaves Pass
Hohokam Los Muertos
Ancestral Pueblo Puye
Salado Schoolhouse Pt
Mogollon Pt of Pines
Ancestral Pueblo Kayenta
Ancestral Pueblo Paako
Pecos
Hohokam Casa Buena

42 44 46 48 50 52 54 56

Mean nasal index: narrower ⟶ broader

(Appendix Tables 1.3–4). Considerable migration and population mixing added to the period's physical diversity. The Hohokam residents of Los Muertos in the Phoenix Basin had the widest faces, averaging 135.55 mm; and the Ancestral Puebloans at Pecos Pueblo, on the eastern margin of the Southwest, had the narrowest at 132.28 mm. The Mountain Mogollon residents of Point of Pines had the most square/round eyes, followed closely by the still-distinctive occupants of Canyon de Chelly. In contrast, the Salado residents of School House Point in the Tonto Basin had the most horizontally oriented eyes, followed closely by the Hohokam residents of Casas Buena in the Phoenix Basin. Casa Buena's residents also had the broadest noses, while the Sinagua at Chaves Pass had the narrowest.

Data from the Hohokam settlements of Casa Buena and Los Muertos in the Lower Salt River valley illustrate how facial differences could characterize settlements located less than 10 miles apart. The residents of Casa Buena had the most horizontally oriented eyes and the broadest noses, while their neighbors at Los Muertos had the widest faces and the second narrowest noses. These differences may illustrate how very small samples and simple descriptive statistics can suggest misleading patterns. Or, they may be an example of the oft-repeated caveat in population genetics about the high degree of internal variation that characterizes any human population. In this case, the data might be telling us something real: the inhabitants of these two communities may have been quite distinct from each other.

Because all of the measurements and indices presented here are averages, it is important to remember that the facial characteristics of each community's residents would have also varied. Such variation has been well documented in skeletons excavated from Pecos Pueblo on the eastern margin of the Pueblo culture area in north-central New Mexico. In the Southwest's seminal study in physical anthropology, Earnest Hooton identified the arrival of cranially distinct immigrants to the site in the early AD 1300s.[12] He also traced subsequent increases in cranial heterogeneity, which peaked around AD 1550–1600 during the era of Spanish contact. While rejecting Hooton's racial typology, Katherine Weisensee and Richard Jantz have reanalyzed his data and confirmed his conclusion that Pecos had a complicated biological history, marked by increasing biological heterogeneity due to ongoing immigration of diverse groups from other Pueblos and the Great Plains.

Hooton and his intellectual progeny are often portrayed as unscientific for their writings about the head shapes, body types, and racial affiliations of prehistoric Southwesterners. Succeeding generations of physical anthropologists conspicuously avoided this type of research, focusing instead on health and the effects of living in large communities and increased reliance on agriculture. Today the research pendulum is returning to the consideration of physical variation—this time as part of the wider movement in archaeology to explore the social lives of prehistoric people and how they constructed and communicated their identities. New kinds of data are just starting to be used. Three-dimensional scanning can capture differences in facial appearance that measurements do not, such as the shape of the brow and the chin, and forensic anthropologist Joseph Hefner and colleagues have resurrected classification systems of head and nose shape and cheekbone projection that will advance studies of physical variation.[13]

The face presents a rich and complex set of data that is filtered through an observer's personal history and degree of familiarity with "others." The salience or importance of any feature depends on how people use it (how expressive are the eyes or mouth?) and the extent to which behaviorally modulated differences are perceptually drowned out by radical differences in skin color or hair type, especially for an observer who is unfamiliar with the "racial other."

So far, this discussion has focused on facial width and orbital and nasal indices, measurable characteristics that would have been most obvious in face-to-face contact. But family members and neighbors living in close and constant proximity with one another would have become attuned to more subtle differences in specific attributes, including orbital and nasal dimensions, forehead height, and projection of the chin and ears. Familiarity would have fostered greater perceptual discrimination. Ironically, if our discussion of facial differences has been frustrating, it is because it comes too late for the generation of skull classifiers and a bit too early to take full advantage of the new methods and approaches now available for studying archaeological skeletons.

FEMUR ROBUSTICITY

Another physical characteristic that is obvious to the living but difficult for physical anthropologists to measure on skeletons is the robustness of a person's body. This characteristic can encompass the overlapping questions of whether a person was thin versus stocky and whether he or she was fat or muscular. Today there are new formulas that use measurements of a completely preserved pelvis to estimate body mass. But the preservation of Southwest skeletal remains is rarely adequate for this method, and very few studies report the data needed for such calculations. For our purposes, the best measure of robustness is the femur robusticity index, which compares the thighbone's diameter relative to its length.[14] While genetics contribute to femur robusticity, high values are also the result of routinely traversing long distances on uneven terrain. However, the visible manifestations of different robusticity indices can be subtle—certainly much less apparent than variation in stature and facial features.

Ann L. W. Stodder

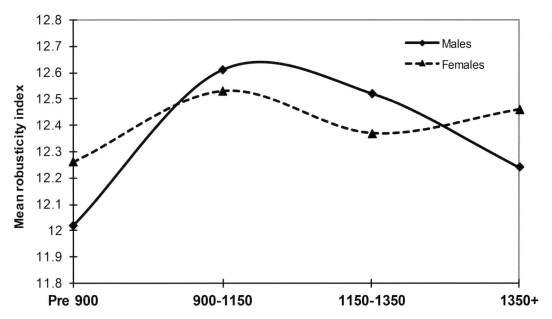

1.5. Male and female femur robusticity averages through time.

The overall temporal pattern for the prehistoric Southwest as a whole begins with an increase in femur robusticity starting in the AD 700s and continuing until approximately AD 1150 (Figure 1.5).[15] This change speaks to the hard labor of agriculture, which included travel to fields as well as to distant hunting and collecting localities. Between AD 1150–1350, in the era following migrations off the Colorado Plateau, robusticity declined somewhat. After AD 1350, the patterns diverged for the two sexes: female robusticity increased as male robusticity declined. These opposing trends offer evidence of lifestyle differences, which became more pronounced around the time of Spanish contact and into the Colonial period.

For prehistoric males, average robusticity correlates with the cultural groups' elevational ranges (Figure. 1.6, Appendix Table 1.5). The Ancestral Puebloans and the Mountain Mogollon had the highest indices as a result of regularly traversing rugged terrain. The Salado were intermediate, reflecting their use of the Tonto Basin foothills. The later prehistoric pueblos in the Rio Grande River valley and the Hohokam from the Phoenix Basin had the lowest robusticity scores.

Average robusticity shows a larger spread for females in different cultural groups, which suggests that their habitual activities varied (Figure 1.6, Appendix Table 1.6). The female averages also exhibit less congruency with topography, indicating that women's routine activities were affected by more than just walking and topographic variation. The late Pueblo I-period Ancestral Puebloans and Salado had the highest robusticity indices; the later prehistoric Puebloans were intermediate; and the Mogollon and Hohokam had the lowest scores.

1.6. Male and female femur robusticity averages in m cultural groups.

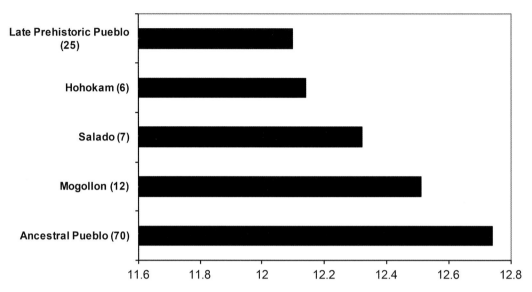

Males

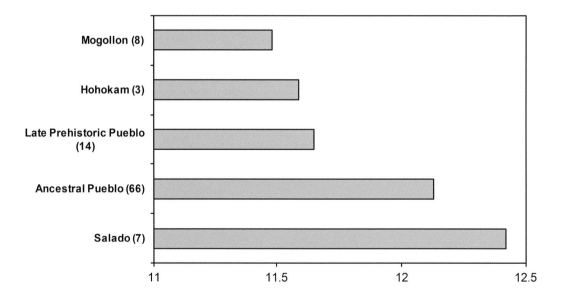

Females

Among contemporary groups, the greatest variation is in males between AD 1150–1350, and the greatest contrast during this time occurred among neighboring groups (Appendix Table 1.5). Those living on Mesa Verde had the lowest robusticity indices, whereas those living at Yellow Jacket on the sage plains below the Mesa had the highest.

Among females, the greatest variation occurred early (Appendix Table 1.6). Around AD 500–550, a Basketmaker woman living near Durango, Colorado (Tamarron Site), had the highest robusticity index; those living near today's border between central Arizona and New Mexico (SU Site) had the lowest. Around AD 900–980, women living in Pueblo I-period communities near the Dolores River had the highest indices; those living roughly 60 miles to the west at Alkali Ridge had the least.

Variation continued during the later periods, but to a lesser degree than previously. Around AD 1300–1350, Salado women had the highest robusticity index. Their counterparts in southwest Colorado (Mesa Verde) had the least, followed closely by their neighbors in northwest New Mexico (La Plata Valley). Over a century later, between AD 1425–1450, Salado women again had the highest robusticity index, and women living in the middle Rio Grande River valley (Alfred Herrera Site) and the Phoenix Basin had the lowest.

Variation in femur robusticity among members of contemporary groups and through time was the product of different combinations of factors: topography, local patterns of land use, habitual activities, and division of labor. However, it is hard to say how such variation would have affected people's appearance. The thighs of people with extremely low or high robusticity indices may have been visibly different. But for everyone else, the visible manifestations of varied robusticity scores may have been subtle.

HEAD SHAPE

Another physical characteristic for which visible variation may have been subtle, with one notable exception, is head shape. Head form is the product of genetics and any cultural activities that affect babies' skulls. A newborn's cranium consists of multiple, soft bones that gradually fuse over time. Any sustained pressure on these bones can permanently alter their orientation and shape.

In comparison to the prehistoric inhabitants of the rest of North America, ancient Southwesterners inherited noticeably broader skulls. This natural shape was often modified by the use of cradleboards.[16] While physical anthropologists have long recognized cradleboarding as the cause of prehistoric Southwest cranial modification, they have until quite recently been ambivalent about whether or not this modification was deliberate or simply the unintentional byproduct of cradleboard technology.[17] Early investigators assumed that prehistoric people would prefer symmetrical heads and thus interpreted the asymmetry of many flattened heads as evidence that it was unintentional. In our culture today it is hard to imagine that parents would be unaware of the altered shape of a child's head. But even if the creation of a particular head shape was not the main objective, the altered form may have been seen as attractive and served as a marker of cultural affiliation.

Different cradleboard technologies (harder or softer headboard, for instance) and patterns of use can modify the skull in different ways.[18] But other factors also come into play, such as traditional parenting activities and women's other responsibilities, which can affect how a child is bound into a cradleboard and for what length of time. While both social and economic factors certainly affect parenting styles, such styles may also reflect deeply held values, which would contribute to a sense of cultural identity. Even without understanding the reasons for different types of cranial modification, researchers have generally treated these forms as cultural markers and interpreted their co-occurrence within sites and localities as evidence of different cultural groups living together due to migration.

Prehistoric Southwesterners practiced three types of cranial modification.[19] One of the two most frequent was lambdoidal (more easily referred to as horizontal), in which the flattening was "applied to the upper part of the occiput [back of the head] at an angle of 50 to 60 degrees." This modification made prehistoric Southwest heads appear even broader. The other most frequent type was occipital (or vertical), in which the modification occurred at "the back of the skull quite or almost straight, at close to 90 degrees from the Frankfort plane...." The rarest type was obelionic, in which the flattening was located much higher up on the back and top of the head. While the visible contrast between horizontal and vertical modification could be subtle, obelionic modification produced a strikingly different head shape.[20]

No general temporal pattern characterized cranial modification across the Southwest: individuals with different head forms lived during each time period. Yet there are fairly clear trends among the Ancestral Puebloans (Appendix Table 1.7).[21] During the Basketmaker periods (pre–AD 700), skulls were unmodified, but sometime during the Pueblo I period (AD 700–900), horizontal (lamboidal) modification appeared. This change was not solely the result of the documented switch from soft- to hard-backed cradleboards. Rather, as Claudette Piper has described, the adoption of harder materials was in turn related to cradleboards being used in a different way as women's activities shifted. Perhaps instead of working primarily in residential areas, women were now carrying their cradleboarded babies to farm fields located away from the village and to even more distant resource procurement zones.

During the Pueblo II period, vertical (occipital) modification appeared, initiating a trend away from horizontal modification (Appendix Table 1.7). This new skull form reflects changes in cradleboard construction and use, presumably the result of social and economic changes. The earliest individuals with occipital modi-fication lived at Chaco Canyon and Mesa Verde, arguably the Colorado Plateau's most cosmopolitan locations of that time. Subsequently, the co-occurrence of both forms became the norm, with a general pattern of horizontally modified skulls pre-dominating in the east and vertically modified skulls in the west.

Also during the Pueblo II period, obelionic modification appeared among the Gallina in north-central New Mexico (Appendix Table 1.7). This starkly different head shape adds another intriguing element to the distinctive portrait of the Gallina, based on material culture and architecture. Obelionic modification was also found on a contemporary individual from Lowry Ruin in southwest Colorado and a later individual (post-AD 1150) from Mesa Verde.

After AD 1450, some Ancestral Puebloans—after more than 500 years of nearly universal modification—had unmodified skulls (Appendix Table 1.7). Modification among their Puebloan contemporaries was predominantly or exclusively vertical. As a result of continued cradleboard use, vertical modification persisted into the historic period, as seen among some 18th-century Hopi and at Taos in the 1930s.

Comparisons of Ancestral Puebloans with other groups reveal regional differ-ences as early as AD 600–800 (Appendix Table 1.8). While the Ancestral Puebloans of this time had unmodified skulls, their contemporaries at the Mountain Mogollon site of Bear Village mostly had vertical modification, with some individuals showing horizontal modification and a few with unmodified skulls.[22]

From AD 900–1150, the contrast between the Ancestral Puebloans and Sinagua was in the percentage occurrence of horizontally versus vertically modified heads (Appendix Table 1.8). Individuals with unmodified heads are reported in literature on the Preclassic-period Salado of the Tonto Basin and the Gallina.

In the period AD 1150–1450, cultural patterns diverged (Appendix Table 1.8). In contrast with the preceding pattern of co-occurring head forms, the Mimbres, Hohokam, and one Classic-period Salado group had only vertical modification. Unmodified heads continued to be present at Salado sites in the Tonto Basin, appeared for the first time at Sinagua villages, and reappeared after more than 500 years among the Mountain Mogollon at Grasshopper Pueblo.

At Grasshopper, Point of Pines, and other contemporary Mountain Mogollon sites, vertical modification was consistently the dominant form, to the extent that early researchers used it as one of the defining traits of Mogollon culture (Figure 1.7). They interpreted the presence of individuals with horizontal or no modification as evidence of ethnic co-residence, a view shared by subsequent generations of re-searchers.[23] For example, Kenneth Bennett identified the relatively large proportion of individuals with horizontally modified crania found in the middle occupation of Point of Pines as Ancestral Pueblo immigrants. More recently, Joseph Ezzo and

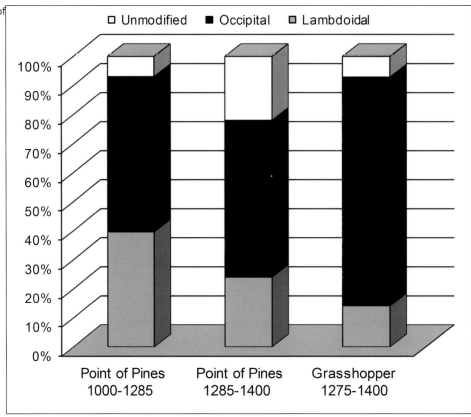

colleagues used strontium isotope analysis to confirm the immigrant status of the people with horizontal modification at Grasshopper Pueblo.

An important question about the significance of cranial modification as an identity signifier is whether it showed. While obelionic modification would have been a very visible marker of Gallina identity, the differences between horizontal and vertical modification could be subtle, especially when obscured by hair. However, people may have accentuated the shapes of their heads by adding decorations. For example, the increased broadness produced by horizontal modification would have been further enhanced by ear whorls, the traditional butterfly hairstyle with great antiquity worn by Hopi girls (Figure 6.3, and discussion in chapter 4).[24] Perhaps broad-headedness as an aesthetic was intentionally maintained and enhanced by traditional personal adornment.

Cranial modification was a kind of cultural technology that expressed the parents' (at least the mother's) identity in the form of their child's head shape. In mixed communities, head shape could be an overt signifier of ethnicity. Within an ethnic group, it could be a subtler expression of mothering styles, economic roles, and traditional aesthetics. As with facial features, familiarity through close and sustained interaction may have facilitated recognition of head-shape differences. But our traveler may have noticed only the most visibly different shapes.

SKIN COLOR

Skin color is another physical characteristic that probably varied to some degree among prehistoric Southwest groups. Although it does not show in skeletal remains, some general comments are possible. A person's skin color is determined by a combination of genetics and sun exposure. This exposure is in turn a function of the amount of time spent outdoors, where the individual lives, and the amount of coverage by clothes. People living in the desert typically have darker skin than those in forested areas. Thus, our traveler would have observed differences in skin tone while traversing the Southwest from north to south.

Historic-period data suggest that a small group of people with strikingly different skin color may have been present in the prehistoric northern Southwest. In recent history, the Hopi, Zuni, and Jémez pueblos have had a relatively high frequency of albinism, a genetic trait involving the inability to produce melanin, the substance that gives color to the skin, hair, and eyes.[25] Individuals with the most severe forms of this trait have white skin and hair and blue eyes, and they suffer from extreme sensitivity to the sun and impaired vision or blindness. The genetic founder effect may have contributed to the appearance of this rare recessive trait in the Pueblos, and the trait persisted due to the cultural practice of endogamy and the cultural selection of mates. Ancestral Puebloans with this condition were probably protected in some sense—they may have spent more time weaving than farming or hunting. The historic Puebloans' acceptance of albinism contrasts with many other societies, such as present-day Tanzania where albinos are murdered in order to sell their body parts for magic.

CONCLUSION

Within and between communities throughout the Southwest, our traveler would have noticed variation in people's physical appearance. Men were taller than women; and with the rare exception of identical twins, no faces were the same. Migrants might have had markedly different facial features, body form, and head shape. However, while moving from area to area, our traveler would have begun to see patterns in this variation, especially for the most visible characteristics and perhaps for less apparent ones as well.

Those individuals and groups who stood out the most were at the far end of the spectrum of variation for multiple characteristics. From AD 900–1150, the residents of Chaco great houses literally stood out as this period's tallest individuals. They also had the most square/round eyes, the narrowest noses, and were among the earliest groups with vertical skull modification.

In the AD1150–1450 era, the Salado of the Tonto Basin were the tallest, had the most horizontally oriented eyes, and were one of the groups with only occipital cranial modification. Their contemporary Hohokam neighbors were shorter, and their facial characteristics seem to have varied considerably from village to village.

Other individuals and groups were distinguished by being at the extremes of just one characteristic. The residents of Canyon de Chelly were at the end of the spectrum for at least one facial characteristic during each of the time periods considered here. Within specific periods, other groups that were most distinctive for single attributes included some Gallina with their obelionic skull modification from AD 900–1150; the Sinagua with at least one very tall man, the Magician, from AD 1150–1300, and with the shortest statures after AD 1350; and the residents of Point of Pines with the most square/round eyes, and those of Pecos Pueblo with the broadest noses from AD 1150–1450.

But having internalized their own groups' standards of "normal" appearance, people were probably also attuned to modest variation in physical attributes. For example, as they traveled to higher elevations, they would have noticed that people were shorter, stockier, and perhaps had somewhat lighter skins. At home, among the people with whom they interacted on a daily basis, they certainly would have been aware of even the most subtle differences in appearance, differences that have been masked in this paper by the reliance on average measurements and indices.

One interesting way to think about how (and how frequently) prehistoric people might have perceived physical differences is to ask the question: how far would a prehistoric Southwesterner have to go to see someone who looked obviously different? At some times and places, not very far at all. If you lived at Bear Village in the Mogollon Mountains from AD 600–800, you would need only look at your neighbors in a nearby pithouse. Or if you lived in the same area a few centuries later at Point of Pines or Grasshopper Pueblos, or at Pecos Pueblo at the edge of the northern Southwest and the Great Plains, different-looking people lived in the next room block. Others would see distinctive-looking people if they walked just a short distance. In Chaco Canyon from AD 900–1150, they lived a stone's throw away in the great houses on the other side of Chaco Wash. If you were a Classic-period Hohokam, you might see them in settlements located on the other side of the Lower Salt River.

A few days' walk would bring more encounters with people who looked different. Around AD 1350, a Hohokam traveler going about 80 miles up the Salt River to the Tonto Basin would have met the tallest people in the Southwest at this time, perhaps reflecting better nutrition than those who lived in the densely settled Hohokam heartland, or an admixture of local people with taller immigrants. Similarly, a resident of the Tonto Basin could travel just 40 miles north up Tonto Creek and then over the Mogollon Rim to meet some of the Southwest's shortest people.

Researchers have generally associated distinctive physical appearance with particular cultural groups. Consequently, they have interpreted the co-occurrence of different-looking people within individual settlements or between neighboring ones as indicating the co-residence of different cultural groups due to migration. The most notable exception of this standard practice has been at Chaco Canyon where disparate appearances seem to have marked distinctive kin groups, or at least groups with varying status.

Archaeologists have traced migrations and co-residence using both architectural and ceramic styles, and early historic records mention natives who traveled for trade and employment. For example, members of the Oñate expedition passing through the Lower Rio Grande River valley met "migrant laborers" who had been working in Zuni cotton fields.[26] In addition to the evidence for co-resident groups presented in this chapter, physical anthropologists have also documented population movement using the distribution of coccidioidomycosis, sometimes called valley fever, a fungal infection localized to lowland desert areas. Human skeletons with this pathogen have been identified well outside its range at late Ancestral Pueblo sites in Zuni and Taos. These individuals must have been in the low desert at some point during their lives. Given that Hawikku is an ancestral Zuni site whose elevation is some 6,100 ft, one wonders if the infected people there were migrant workers from desert lowlands, similar to those observed by the Oñate expedition.

While various skeletal measurements help us picture what prehistoric people living in different parts of the Southwest looked like during different periods of time and to document migration episodes, they do not reveal the meanings that people assigned to what they saw when they encountered one another. Perception and how it shapes social and political behavior is the complex product of the context of the encounter, a viewer's personal and group history, and the history of previous interactions. Based on studies of contemporary groups, we know that the relative importance of particular facial features varies across cultures,[27] but we cannot say which features were more or less important to prehistoric Southwesterners and what meanings they assigned to them. Did they have specific associations with broad noses or oval eyes? Similarly, was stature significant in the "us versus them" sense? We just can't say. But if present-day North American culture is representative, then distinctive facial features and body forms may have held many layers of social and emotional meaning that affected prehistoric people's perceptions of each other and their interactions.

CLOTHING

2

by LAURIE D. WEBSTER

A traveler in the prehistoric Southwest would have learned a lot about people met along the way just by looking at their clothing. As the most visible, technically complex, and expressive form of adornment, clothing can convey a myriad of identity messages, including the wearer's gender, age, social status, religion, cultural affiliation, and connections with other cultural groups.[1] These messages are encoded in the materials, weave, form, and decoration of individual garments; the way in which garments are worn; and how they are combined in complete outfits.

For our traveler, clothes would have reinforced messages about gender that were evident in an individual's physical characteristics. By AD 1200, everywhere in the Southwest, a typical woman's outfit consisted of an apron and blanket, sometimes with a sash belt and sandals. Men had more options that included breechcloths, kilts, shirts, ponchos, shoulder blankets, sashes, and sandals. Variation in these gender-specific outfits occurred in the combinations of fibers, weaving techniques, and decorations that were preferred in different parts of the Southwest.

In this chapter, I compare these regional clothing styles and their associated identity messages. I begin with an overview of prehistoric Southwest fabrics, then consider individual garments, and finally reconstruct everyday- and special-occasion outfits that were worn after AD 1100. The results reveal a stark contrast in the clothes of the most geographically distant cultural groups—the Ancestral Puebloans of the Colorado Plateau and the Hohokam of the southern Arizona desert.[2] The clothing of the geographically intermediate Sinagua, Salado, and Mogollon was less distinctive, due to its blending of Ancestral Pueblo and Hohokam weaving techniques and styles.

FABRICS

The primary evidence for the raw materials and weaving techniques used to make prehistoric Southwest clothing consists of thousands of preserved fabric fragments. These remains are disproportionately Ancestral Pueblo due to the intensive use of alcoves on the Colorado Plateau.[3] Sinagua, Salado, and Mogollon assemblages are less prevalent, and Hohokam assemblages are the rarest and most poorly preserved. Evidence for clothing styles and fabric decorations comes from larger preserved fragments, complete garments, and artistic depictions of clothing on Mimbres and Casas Grandes ceramics and Ancestral Pueblo kiva murals.[4]

Raw Materials

Most prehistoric Southwest clothing was made from wild plant or domesticated cotton fiber. Yucca predominated during the early periods in all areas.[5] Regional clothing patterns became more pronounced after cotton was introduced to the southern Southwest from Mexico and as it was adopted for loom weaving in different areas.

Mesoamerican cotton first appeared about 300 BC in the southern Southwest, but it was not widely grown there until the mid-sixth century.[6] By AD 700, cotton dominated textile production in that region's river valleys. Several hundred years after the plant's introduction in the south, northern farmers adapted it to the Colorado Plateau's higher elevations and shorter growing seasons.[7] Prior to AD 900, evidence of cotton production in the north is limited to a few Pueblo I-period sites in northeast Arizona, and for at least another century, much of the cotton that was used in the north was probably imported from the south.

Cotton did not dominate the production and use of textiles on the Colorado Plateau until the eleventh or twelfth century. Most of this cotton production occurred in the well-watered canyons of southeast Utah and northeast Arizona, which offered the best growing conditions. During the late Pueblo II and Pueblo III periods, these areas appear to have specialized in both cotton cultivation and weaving, and they probably exported raw fiber and finished textiles to neighboring areas with less favorable growing conditions, such as Mesa Verde and the San Juan Basin.

Even after cotton became the dominant fiber for loom weaving, yucca continued to be used for finger-woven fabrics throughout the Southwest and for loom weaving in the south. Observers who were familiar with the two materials would have been able to distinguish them and gain information about the people who wore them. The wearing of cotton cloth probably signified an individual's social and trading connections, as well as social status and economic resources. Cotton may have also had symbolic significance during that time, as it does among many historic-period Southwest groups who associate the fiber with clouds and rain.[8]

Animals were another, less frequently used source of weaving materials. On the Colorado Plateau, such materials included the hair of people, dogs, and rabbits in woven items, and rabbit fur and domesticated turkey feathers in twined blankets.[9] The Mogollon made use of many of the same raw materials as their northern neighbors. The Hohokam and southern Sinagua used rabbit fur, but rarely turkey feathers, in their twined blankets.[10] Although the use of animal fibers declined after the adoption of cotton, the Ancestral Puebloans and Sinagua continued to use human hair for leggings, and the Salado used the hair of bighorn sheep in woven fabrics.

In addition to these plant and animal fibers, the Hohokam, Mogollon, and Ancestral Puebloans made minor use of asbestos, alone or mixed with other fibers, in woven fabrics.[11] Because these diverse plant, animal, and mineral materials were so visually distinctive, and their usage varied by region, clothing made from them would have conveyed information about cultural affiliation and intergroup connections.

Weaving Techniques

Prior to the introduction of the loom, and to a lesser extent afterwards, prehistoric Southwesterners transformed raw materials into fabrics using a variety of finger weaving techniques—twining, looping, oblique interlacing (braiding), plain weaving, and tapestry weaving.[12] Weavers in both the north and south made twined yucca bags and rabbit-fur blankets, and Ancestral Pueblo and Mogollon weavers also made twined blankets of turkey feathers. Weavers in both the north and south made looped yucca bags, and Ancestral Pueblo and Mogollon weavers looped human hair into leggings and braided animal hair into sashes.

In the south, by AD 1000, cotton was being braided into bands, and as it became more available in the north, it was also braided into sashes and bands there. Initially, an over-two, under-two (2/2) braiding rhythm was used in both regions (Figure 2.1), but later an over-three, under-three (3/3) rhythm also became popular in the south. Sometime during the Pueblo IV period, this 3/3 rhythm spread north, eventually reaching the Zuni and Hopi areas. The Hopi still use this 3/3-weave structure for their cotton-braided sashes.

The introduction of the loom revolutionized cotton fabric production by mechanizing the weaving process and facilitating the production of new fabric structures.[13] Fabrics made on different loom types varied in size, density, and warp or weft dominance. The backstrap loom entered the southern Southwest from Mexico by AD 700 and spread north of the Mogollon Rim by AD 900. After employing the same loom technology for at least a century, weavers in the two regions diverged in supplementing the backstrap loom with new loom forms. In the south, the horizontal staked-down loom was probably adopted from Mexico by AD 1000. On the Colorado Plateau, the upright loom became dominant after AD 1100, especially in southeast Utah and northeast Arizona, where residents specialized in cotton growing and weaving. After AD 1300, the upright loom spread east to the Rio Grande River valley.[14]

Approximately 85 percent of the prehistoric Southwest's loom-woven fabrics were simple over-one, under-one plain weaves (Figure 2.2a).[15] Both cotton and yucca were used to make loom-woven plain-weave cloth in the south, but only cotton was used for loom weaving on the Colorado Plateau until about AD 1300, when some loom-woven yucca plain-weave fabrics appear. The latter have been recovered primarily in the Zuni area, where southern migrants probably introduced the practice.[16]

The remaining 15 percent of loom-made archaeological textiles reveal pronounced regional patterns (Appendix Table 2.1). While the Ancestral Puebloans emphasized twill weaves (Figures 2.2b–c), southern groups produced a greater variety of weave structures, including plain weave with supplementary weft (Figure 2.2d), gauze (Figure 2.2e), weft-wrap openwork (Figure 2.2f), and warp-faced belting—all of which were introduced from Mexico.[17] Sinagua assemblages exhibit the most diverse array of loom-woven fabric structures, including two not reported elsewhere—gauze weave with supplementary weft, and plain-weave tapestry. The Hohokam probably produced equally diverse assemblages, but little evidence has survived because of poor preservation.

The different weave structures used in the Southwest would have conveyed messages about cultural affiliation and interaction with other cultural groups (Appendix Table 2.1). These patterns divide the Southwest into two main interaction zones north and south of the Mogollon Rim. Ancestral Puebloans would have been recognizable by their twilled garments, southern groups by their openwork and supplementary-weft weaves. The textile traditions of the Sinagua show the most connections with other cultural groups, sharing twilled and tapestry weaves with the Ancestral Puebloans and rag weft, supplementary weft, gauze, weft-wrap openwork, and warp-faced belting with other southern groups.

The most labor intensive and visually unique fabric structures would have conveyed information about the wearer's special status. The presence of three Meso-american weave structures in the southern Southwest—weft-wrap openwork, gauze, and interlinking—raises the possibility that some fabric structures were adopted because of their embedded religious meanings.[18] The small, grid-like pattern produced by openwork weaves resembles the symbols for serpent skin and maize that Mesoamerican people associated with fertility and used to decorate both ritual and high-status fabrics. The tie-dye motif, discussed below, had a similar symbolic connotation.

Decoration

Although the vast majority of their cotton fabrics were solid white, prehistoric Southwesterners also decorated fabrics in ways that communicated a variety of visual messages.[19] Unlike raw material and weave structure, which are a fabric's critical components, decoration is optional and often more visible. In the prehistoric Southwest, colors and designs signaled a person's cultural identity and relationships with other groups. Fabrics with more unique colors and designs, especially ones requiring more labor-intensive application techniques, broadcast the wearer's special religious or social status.

Decoration was added in a variety of ways. Some weavers used yarns dyed in two or more colors to create patterns, such as stripes or plaids. Other weave structures, such as diamond-twill and openwork weaves, created visually distinctive textures that were decorative even without the addition of color. When executed in different colored yarns, twill and supplementary-weft patterns became even more pronounced.

Color was also added after fabrics had been woven (Appendix Table 2.2). Cloth could be submerged in dye to produce a solid color or a resist-dyed design. Resist-dye methods included tie-dyeing, which is known to have been practiced by the Ancestral Puebloans, Sinagua, and Salado, and a technique similar to batik that was apparently practiced by the Hohokam.[20] Some woven fabrics were painted, a technique most widely used by the Ancestral Puebloans, to create intricate negative designs. Only the Salado are known to have used stamped designs.

The same basic colors were used throughout the Southwest—natural white or tan supplemented with red, black, and brown—but different color combinations

2.2. Weave structures: (*a*) plain weave; (*b*) diagonal twill; (*c*) twill tapestry; (*d*) plain weave with supplementary weft; (*e*) gauze weave; (*f*) weft-wrap openwork.

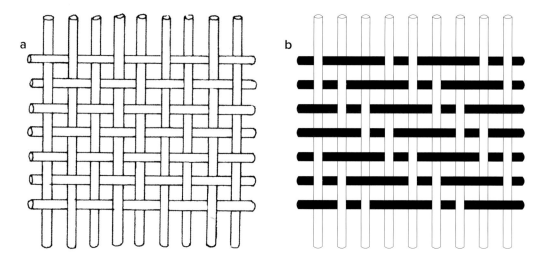

a

b

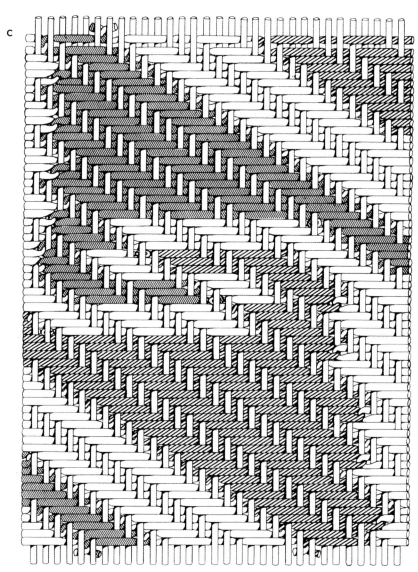

c

d

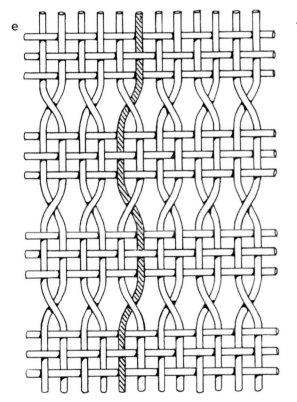

e

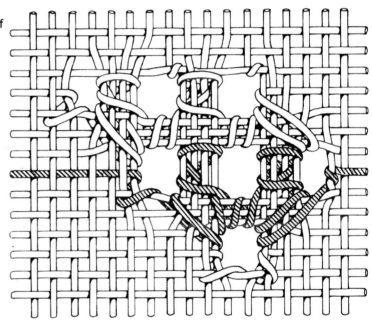

f

were preferred in different regions.[21] Ancestral Puebloans primarily used white, red, black, and brown in their loom-woven fabrics, a palette that perpetuated Basketmaker preferences. For their tie-dyed, plain- and twill-tapestry, and negative-painted fabrics, they favored a bichrome palette of dark and light hues. For other painted fabrics, they favored red, followed by brown, black, yellow, white, and green.

After AD 1200, southern groups made increasing use of blue and blue-green, colors produced from dyes that probably contained indigo.[22] The Sinagua and Salado executed many of their tapestry and supplementary-weft designs in polychrome patterns of black and blue, or brown and blue, on a white background. The Hohokam presumably used similar color combinations.

Using their preferred colors, fiber structures, and decorative techniques, weavers in different areas created distinctive designs (Appendix Table 2.3).[23] During the late Pueblo II and Pueblo III periods, Ancestral Puebloans emphasized horizontally banded patterns executed in diagonal, diamond, and herringbone twills worked in red, black, and brown (Figure 2.3). They also produced centered designs with terraced (stair-stepped) motifs that were most often woven in plain and twill tapestry or sometimes added by painting and tie-dyeing (Figures 2.4–5). This emphasis on terraced motifs perpetuated earlier Basketmaker textile patterns. During the Pueblo III and Pueblo IV periods, some Ancestral Pueblo designs were arranged in an offset-quartered layout (Figure 2.5), a concept probably introduced from the south.[24] The most common motif for tie-dyed fabrics was the dot-in-square (Figure 2.4), which was also painted on plain-weave cloth in imitation of tie-dye.[25]

The designs used by southern groups contrasted with the Ancestral Puebloans' in two ways. First, instead of centered motifs, southern designs were uncentered, with allover patterns of steeply pitched triangles, hooked scrolls, and finite designs of serrated diamonds (Figure 2.6). This design system spread into the southern Southwest from Mexico. Second, instead of horizontal stripes and bands, the Sinagua, Salado, and Hohokam created bichrome and multicolored checks and plaids.

Northern and southern weavers shared certain designs. Two motifs—the hooked triangle and the triangle with the hypotenuse parallel to the weft—were used by the Ancestral Puebloans, Sinagua, and Salado. Based on the presence of the hooked triangle on Classic-period Hohokam pottery and shell jewelry, this motif was probably also used to decorate Hohokam textiles, although no examples have survived.

Some colors and designs probably had sacred meanings and expressed the wearer's religious beliefs. Blue-green was undoubtedly a sacred color, as evidenced by its use in ceremonial contexts and regalia by both prehistoric- and historic-period groups.[26] Among the historic Pueblos, the color signifies sky, rain, and directionality—all relating in some way to fertility. Similar to weft-wrap and gauze openwork patterns, the dot-in-square motif on tie-dyed and painted fabrics may have symbolized serpent skin, corn, and fertility in the Southwest, just as it did on Mesoamerican ritual and high-status fabrics.[27] The stepped triangle and the hooked triangle may have referenced the fertility symbols of clouds and rain, as they do among the historic Pueblos.[28]

GARMENTS

Although prehistoric Southwesterners of the same sex generally wore similar kinds of garments, the appearance of such articles varied by region in terms of construction and how they were worn. With all of this potential diversity, any one item of clothing could potentially convey multiple identity messages, such as cultural affiliation, connections with other groups, and social status.

Unisex Garments

One body garment worn by both men and women throughout the prehistoric Southwest was the cotton blanket (Figures 2.3–6; also Figures 2.17, 6.3). The large cotton blankets worn by the Ancestral Puebloans, Sinagua, Salado, and Mogollon were usually square to rectangular. Probably, they were often used as a shoulder robe,

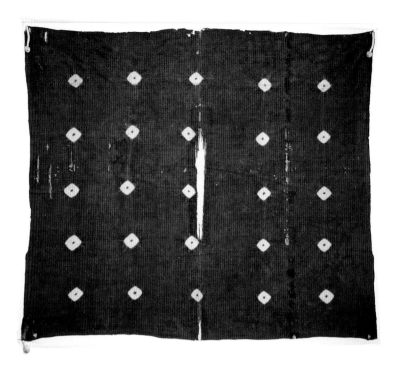

2.4. Ancestral Pueblo brown cotton plain-weave blanket with tie-dye pattern, southeast Utah.

2.5. Artist's reconstruction of Ancestral Pueblo cotton plain-weave blanket with painted red, green, yellow, and black polychrome design, Painted Cave, northeast Arizona.

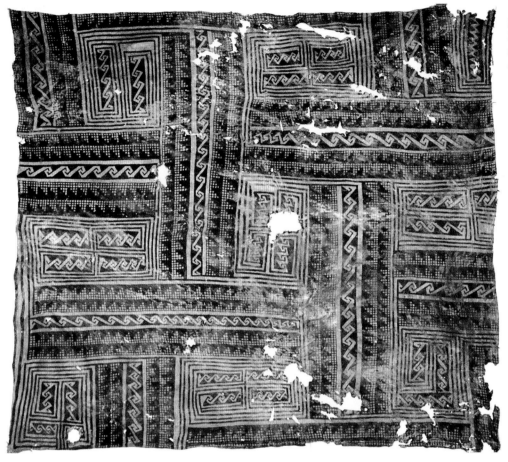

2.6. Sinagua cotton plain-weave blanket with black-and-white design, Hidden House, north-central Arizona.

similar to the blanket worn by modern Hopi brides.[29] Some Hohokam blankets were long and rectangular, made by sewing together two narrow pieces of cloth.[30] Most cotton blankets were white, but some were dyed solid red, brown, or black, and others were decorated with woven-in or applied designs.

Among the Ancestral Puebloans, some cotton blankets were decorated with horizontal, twill-woven bands worked in red, brown, and white stripes (Figure 2.3). More rare blankets, decorated by painting, tie-dye, or diamond-twill tapestry, were probably reserved for ceremonial occasions or individuals of a special status (Figures 2.4–5).

In contrast with the Ancestral Puebloans' preference for horizontal stripes, the Sinagua, Salado, and Hohokam decorated some of their cotton blankets with checks and plaids. These southern groups may also have decorated blankets using complex weave structures such as weft-wrap openwork, gauze weave, interlinking, or supplementary weft, although no definite blankets worked in these techniques

2.7. Mimbres ceramic depiction of the Hero Twins showing feminine figure wearing an apron (*left*) and masculine figure wearing a sash (*right*), Treasure Hill, southwest New Mexico. Also note figures' headbands and facial decorations, the left figure's necklace and leggings, and the right figure's armbands (probable *Glycymeris* bracelets, as in Figure 3.4).

have survived. Southern groups also made burlap-like blankets from yucca fiber and rag-weft blankets from recycled cotton and yucca cloth strips, some of which could have been used as clothing.[31]

When the weather was cold, Ancestral Puebloans and the Mogollon wore an outer blanket twined from turkey feathers or sometimes rabbit fur. The most elaborate turkey-feather blankets are reported from the Mesa Verde, Aztec Ruin, and Grand Gulch areas, where geometric designs were created using dark and light shades of turkey down.[32] The Hohokam also wore blankets twined from rabbit fur, but not turkey feathers to any extent. Only one rabbit-fur blanket is known from the southern Sinagua region,[33] and no examples of rabbit-fur or turkey-feather blankets have been documented for the Salado.

Women's Garments

Women wore a finger-woven string apron as a breech covering (Figures 2.7 [left], 2.8; also Figures 4.2a, 5.1a).[34] Ancestral Pueblo and some Sinagua and Salado aprons were made of cotton or yucca with a narrow waistband and a pendent fringe. Some

Laurie D. Webster

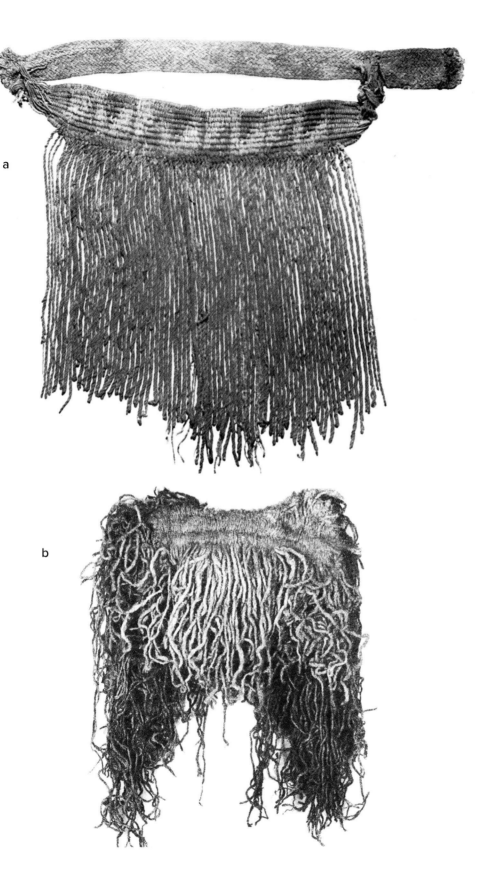

2.8. Women's aprons: (*a*) Ancestral Pueblo cotton with decorated tapestry-woven front panel, pendent fringe, and 2/2 braided cotton back belt, northeast Arizona; (*b*) Salado coarse yucca or agave with center pad and string fringe, Canyon Creek Pueblo, east-central Arizona.

2.9. Men's breechcloths: (*a*) Ancestral Pueblo decorated cotton with reverse twill panel, Gourd Cave, northeast Arizona; (*b*) Salado decorated cotton with loom-joined, twill-tapestry double-front panel and tapered tail, Tonto Ruins, east-central Arizona.

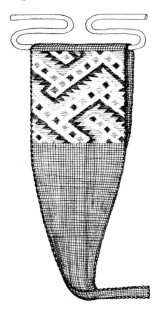

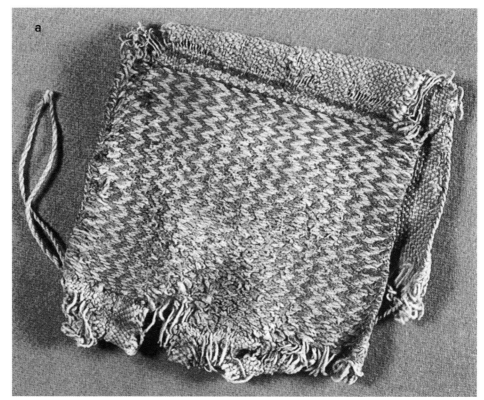

Ancestral Pueblo aprons from the Kayenta region were decorated with tapestry-woven designs, continuing a Basketmaker decorative tradition (Figure 2.8a). Sinagua, Salado, and Hohokam women also wore crude yucca or agave aprons with a center pad and string fringe (Figure 2.8b). Similar to the historic-period O'odham, some Hohokam women may have worn skirts made of free-hanging bark or long, rectangular cotton blankets wrapped around the waist.[35]

At some point, Ancestral Pueblo and perhaps also Sinagua and Salado women started wearing large, cotton blankets as wrap-around dresses.[36] Pueblo IV-period kiva murals show women wearing large blankets in this manner, tying the blanket over one shoulder and securing it with a sash belt in the manner of historic Pueblo women (Figures 4.5 and 6.4).

Men's Garments

Most Southwest men's everyday clothing consisted of a loom-woven cotton breechcloth (Figure 2.9).[37] These garments were composed of a narrow rectangular panel fastened to a belt in front, while the longer, woven or fringed end passed between the legs and was attached to the belt in back. The Ancestral Puebloans' breechcloths

2.10. Ancestral Pueblo mural depiction of a man's kilt with decorative border suggestive of painting, supplementary weft, or embroidery, Awat'ovi, northeast Arizona. Also note the sash.

were short and fringed, and their fancier examples had elaborate twill-woven front panels (Figure 2.9a).

Except for one example from the Tonto Basin, all known breechcloths from south of the Rim were undecorated, possibly because they were worn beneath kilts. Some Sinagua and Salado breechcloths had a loom-joined front panel and a long, woven tapered tail (Figure 2.9b). In the Verde River valley, other Sinagua breechcloths were long, unshaped rectangles that may have been similar to those worn by the Hohokam. The only definite Mogollon man's breech covering consists of a simple hank of cordage suspended from a waist cord found in the Upper Gila region.[38] Depictions on Mimbres bowls suggest that some men in that region may have worn a sash with the ends tied over the abdomen in lieu of a formal breech covering (Figure 2.7 [right]).

Kilts were a late addition to men's apparel (Figures 2.10–13; also Figures 2.17, 3.11, 4.11–12, 6.2).[39] Loom-woven of cotton, they consisted of long, rectangular fabrics wrapped around the hips and secured with a sash. Probably introduced from Mexico, they were widely worn in the southern Southwest by the AD 1200s and eventually spread north to the Ancestral Puebloans. Kiva murals show kilts as

2.11. Ancestral Pueblo mural depiction of a man's kilt, with decoration suggestive of painting or twill tapestry, and sash, Pottery Mound, north-central New Mexico. Also note the figure's sash, armbands, and legbands.

2.12. Ancestral Pueblo mural depiction of a male figure wearing a tie-dye or negative-painted short shoulder blanket, decorated kilt, sash, and garters or leggings, Awat'ovi, northeast Arizona. Also note the figure's hair decoration and elaborate sash fringe.

2.13. Ancestral Pueblo mural depiction of a male figure wearing a resist-dyed or negative-painted kilt, white sash with elaborate fringe, and white shirt or body paint, Pottery Mound, north-central New Mexico. Also note the figure's hairstyle, feather headdress, and bracelets.

a

b

2.14. Men's shirts: (*a*) artist's reconstruction of Ancestral Pueblo cotton plain-weave sleeveless shirt with painted design, Painted Cave, northeast Arizona; (*b*) Salado cotton openwork shirt, vicinity of Tonto Ruins, east-central Arizona.

an important component of Ancestral Pueblo ceremonial dress no later than the AD 1400s. Although no definite kilts have been identified in pre–AD 1300 Ancestral Pueblo assemblages, this does not negate the possibility that men wore folded blankets around their hips before actual kilts were made.

Kilts varied in their appearance. The four preserved Sinagua and Salado examples include two that were plain woven and undecorated, another made from a white, plain-weave fabric with tapestry insets, and one made with a gauze weave. A ceramic depiction from the site of Paquimé shows a flying man wearing a decorated kilt. Ancestral Pueblo kiva murals depict kilts that suggest decoration by tie-dyeing, painting, tapestry weave, supplementary weft, or embroidery (Figure 2.10–11; also Figure 4.11). A few appear to be made from fur or hide.

In addition to breechcloths and kilts, some men also wore cotton shirts or longer versions known as tunics (Figure 2.14). The Ancestral Puebloans constructed most of these garments from plain-weave cloth and decorated some in a variety of

2.15. Mimbres ceramic depiction of a male figure wearing a probable feather tunic, Swarts Ruin, southwest New Mexico. Also note the figure's facial decoration and leggings.

ways. Two tunics from Mesa Verde are undecorated and sleeveless, and two decorated shirts from the Kayenta region are seamed at the shoulders and left open along the sides. One is sleeveless and painted with a positive geometric design (Figure 2.14a); the other has long, unseamed sleeves and a negative-painted or resist design.[40] The Ancestral Puebloans' only preserved openwork shirt, made from intricate 2/2 braiding, was recovered from Canyon de Chelly.[41] A tailored buckskin shirt recovered from Mesa Verde documents the occasional use of materials other than cotton. Pueblo IV-period murals illustrate shirts and tunics that appear to be decorated by negative-painting, tie-dye, and openwork.[42]

South of the Mogollon Rim, the fanciest shirts were lace-like affairs, produced primarily by interlinking or weft-wrap openwork. The best-known, complete example is a sleeveless interlinked shirt from the Tonto Basin (Figure 2.14b).[43] Additional openwork shirts may be represented by a fragmentary interlinked specimen from the Upper Gila and a braided openwork fragment from a Salado site. The construction of the braided specimen is similar to that of the Canyon de Chelly shirt. A Mimbres bowl depiction suggests the use of feather tunics in the southern Mogollon region (Figure 2.15; also Figures 3.3, 5.1a–b for other Mimbres tunics).

Belts and Sashes

Both men and women secured garments around their waists with tied belts or long, fringed sashes (Figures 2.1, 2.7 [right], 2.10–13; also Figures 2.18–19, 3.11, 4.7–8, 4.11, 5.2). During the Basketmaker and Pueblo I periods on the Colorado Plateau and in the Mogollon highlands, long, flat sashes were finger-braided in a 2/2 rhythm using animal fibers, such as dog, rabbit, and human hair. Eventually these raw materials were replaced by cotton, first in the south and then in the north. Weavers in both regions continued to use the 2/2 braiding rhythm (Figure 2.1), but after AD 1100, a 3/3 braiding rhythm also became popular in the south. Some southern sashes had ornamental fiber rings on their fringes, similar to those found on modern Hopi braided sashes.

While southern groups were adopting these new techniques, Ancestral Puebloans continued to rely primarily on the 2/2 braiding rhythm until AD 1300, when southern influences became more pronounced and widespread on the Colorado Plateau. In the Little Colorado River area, some Pueblo IV-period sashes were braided with the 3/3 rhythm. Kiva murals from both the Hopi and Rio Grande areas illustrate numerous examples of wide white sashes with long pendent fringes (Figures 2.11–13; also Figures 2.18–19, 4.7, 4.11). Presumably, most were braided using cotton, but one preserved 2/2 braided sash from the site of Awat'ovi was made from asbestos.[44] Not all finger-woven belts were braided. An unusual preserved band from Aztec Ruin that may have been used as a belt was finger-woven in weft-faced, plain-weave yucca and decorated with feather pile.[45]

After AD 1100, belts were also loom-woven in warp-faced plain weave. Later, warp-float belts were made by floating warps over wefts to produce geometric designs. Both warp-dominant weaves were introduced into the Southwest from Mexico. Ancestral Hopi kiva murals suggest an increase in the use of loom-woven warp-faced belts on the Colorado Plateau after AD 1400.

Footgear and Leg Coverings

Sandals made from yucca were the primary footgear for men and women until about AD 1400, when they were almost completely replaced by hide moccasins in all but the southernmost deserts (Figure 2.16). Sandals differed depending on where they were made and probably their intended use for practical or special occasions.[46]

Coarsely woven, yucca plain-weave sandals, sometimes referred to as wicker-work sandals, first appeared in the Southwest during the late Archaic or early Basketmaker II period and became widely used throughout the region. Most early Colorado Plateau examples had 4–6 warps. A later Ancestral Pueblo variation continued this warp structure but added a rounded or pointed toe. Mogollon coarse plain-weave

2.16. Sandals: (*a*) Salado coarsely woven 1/2 twill-plaited yucca with elements folded up at heel, Canyon Creek, east-central Arizona; (*b*) Ancestral Pueblo finely woven 2/2 twill-plaited yucca with toe jog, Aztec Ruins, northwest New Mexico; (*c*) Ancestral Pueblo finely woven twined yucca with geometric designs on upper surface, raised design on underside, and toe jog, Aztec Ruins, northwest New Mexico; (*d*) Hohokam braid-like sandal, Winchester Cave, southeast Arizona; (*e*) Sinagua finely woven yucca 2/2 plaited sandal with flat braided, H-shaped strap, Rarick Canyon, north-central Arizona. (Not to scale.)

a

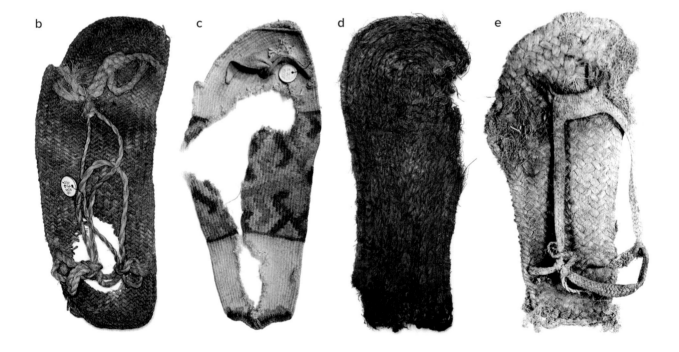

b   c   d   e

sandals usually had 2–4 warps, and Hohokam examples had two. Around AD 1100, a variation of the Hohokam and Mogollon 2-warp style, woven in a figure-8 weave, appeared on the Colorado Plateau. After AD 1200, some Ancestral Pueblo and Sinagua people wore a 4-warp plain-weave style with a square toe and an extended heel that covered the back of the foot.

While the Hohokam continued to wear coarse 2-warp plain-weave sandals for everyday use throughout their history, the Ancestral Puebloans, Mogollon, and later the Sinagua and Salado eventually adopted diagonally plaited (braided) sandals as their dominant form. South of the Rim, these sandals were coarsely woven from wide-leaf elements (usually yucca, but sometimes agave) in a 1/1, 1/2, or 2/2 pattern (Figure 2.16a). This southern footgear typically had a square or rounded toe and a square heel composed of folded-up elements.[47] It was usually joined to the foot by running a heel tie of narrow yucca strips over the instep to a toe loop. Among the Ancestral Puebloans, the most distinctive diagonally plaited sandals were woven from fine- to medium-leaf elements in a 2/2 twill and had a double toe loop, a rounded toe with a jog along the outer edge, and a slightly cupped heel (Figure 2.16b).

In addition to these plain-woven and diagonally plaited sandals, which were worn throughout most of the Southwest, three highly distinctive styles were limited to specific regions. Their more labor-intensive technology suggests that they had a specialized purpose. The Ancestral Pueblo style was twined with finely spun yucca cordage warps and wefts and was decorated with colored designs on the upper face and raised geometric designs on the sole (Figure 2.16c).[48] This northern style developed during the Basketmaker II period, reached its greatest elaboration during the late Basketmaker III period, and continued to be popular into the early AD 1200s. Pueblo II- and Pueblo III-period examples were simpler than their predecessors and had a raised geometric tread on the underside and sometimes a colored geometric design on the upper surface. By AD 1100, most also had a double toe loop and a toe jog at the outer edge.

A second distinctive sandal style, worn by the Hohokam, resembles a flat-coiled braid (Figure 2.16d).[49] This style first appeared during the late Colonial or early Sedentary period (AD 750–900) and continued into the Classic period. The third distinctive style, worn after AD 1300 in the Salado, Sinagua, and Mogollon regions, was finely woven in a 2/2 twill weave of yucca cordage and had a distinctive braided strap that was flat and H-shaped (Figure 2.16e).[50]

Ancestral Puebloans also wore looped leggings and sock-like foot coverings (Figures 2.7 [left], 2.15, and 3.3 show Mimbres examples).[51] The rare examples recovered from prehistoric burials were interred with either males or individuals whose sex is indeterminate. During historic times, these accessories were associated primarily, but not exclusively, with men. From Basketmaker through late Pueblo times, human hair was the preferred raw material for leggings. A popular sock style during the Pueblo III period was a yucca- or cotton-looped sock with a pile of turkey quills or strips of animal fur. Sometimes the looped upper was attached to a twill-plaited yucca sandal sole to create a "shoe-sock." The only definite example of legwear from south of the Rim is a pair of looped, human-hair leggings that had been modified into bags and interred in a thirteenth-century Sinagua burial. A small fragment of looped human hair from the Mogollon region may be the remains of another example.

COMPLETE OUTFITS

While an unusual or flashy garment might catch the attention of our traveler and provide some information about the person wearing it, a full assessment could be gained only by considering his or her entire outfit. The complete ensemble would convey all of the messages embedded in the individual garments plus any additional information associated with how the garments were worn. The entire outfit would also signify the nature of the occasion and whether it was an ordinary or special day. Here, I reconstruct the types of outfits that were probably worn for everyday and special occasions after AD 1100. The information is much more complete for the northern Southwest because of the better preservation of textile remains and the availability of artistic representations on kiva murals.

Everyday Outfits

In Ancestral Pueblo communities after AD 1100, women's everyday attire typically consisted of a fringed apron, probably a blanket worn over the shoulders, and some-times sandals. The apron was made of cotton or a combination of cotton and yucca, and its fringe was short and suspended from a waist cord that was sometimes deco-rated in plain-weave tapestry. The white or colored cotton blanket was wide and undecorated, and in cold weather, it was replaced or augmented by a turkey-feather robe. By this time, some women may have worn their blankets as wrap-around dresses, tied around the waist with a cotton sash, although we lack direct evidence of this practice until after AD 1300. Sandals were plain woven, twined, or twill plaited. It is unknown whether certain sandal styles were more closely associated with men or women.

The man's typical outfit consisted of a breechcloth together with a shoulder blanket and sandals probably similar to those described for women. The breechcloth was made of cotton, and its front panel was sometimes decorated in a light-and-dark color palette of twill-tapestry or reverse twill. As with women, the wide blanket was made of white or dyed cotton, supplemented by a turkey-feather robe in cold weather. It is possible that some men wore sleeved shirts or sleeveless, open-sided tunics for everyday wear, or covered their lower limbs with looped leggings, looped socks, or looped shoe-socks made of human and animal hair, turkey feathers, or cotton. Or perhaps these items were reserved for special occasions.

Like their northern neighbors, Sinagua and Salado women typically wore an apron, a large blanket, and sometimes sandals. Some of their aprons were made of fine cotton or yucca cordage with a narrow waistband and pendent fringe like those worn in the north. It is possible, though unproven, that their large cotton blankets were worn as wrap-around dresses that were secured with a sash. Farther south, some Desert Hohokam women may have worn wrap-around skirts made from long, rectangular, cotton blankets.

Some women's everyday garments worn south of the Mogollon Rim were made from rougher raw materials that gave them a much cruder appearance. Aprons were woven from coarsely processed yucca or agave and had a center pad and a short string fringe. Loom-woven blankets made from rag-weft or yucca fiber might also have been worn as clothing. While the Mogollon wore turkey-feather and rabbit-fur blankets, and the Hohokam and southern Sinagua used rabbit-fur ones, there is no evidence that the Salado wore cold weather blankets made from these materials.

Sinagua and Salado men's everyday outfits also consisted of the same basic garments as those worn in the north—a breechcloth, shoulder blanket, and sandals. As with the Ancestral Puebloans, the breechcloths were made of cotton, and at least one Salado man wore a loom-shaped breechcloth that was embellished with the popular northern technique of twill tapestry. But the forms of most Sinagua and Salado breechcloths were different from those worn in the north, and most lacked decoration. One popular style had a loom-joined front panel and a tapered tail, and another had a hemmed front panel and a rectangular tail. After AD 1200, some Sinagua and Salado men added a new garment—a wrap-around kilt secured with a sash.

The Sinagua, Salado, and Mogollon used coarse yucca leaves for their everyday sandals. By AD 1100, most of this southern footwear was diagonally plaited rather than plain woven and had elements folded over at the heel to make a heel pad. Some Sinagua shared the Ancestral Pueblo style of a coarse, plain-weave sandal with an extended heel covering the back of the foot. While some Hohokam wore distinctive sandals shaped like a coiled braid, and a few may have worn diagonally plaited ones, many retained the coarse, 2-warp plain-weave sandal style for everyday wear.

Differences in everyday garments, especially when combined in complete outfits, would have conveyed information about the wearer's gender, cultural affiliation,

2.17. Artist's depiction of a Sinagua ceremonial leader (AD 1200), based on the Magician's burial, Ridge Ruin, north-central Arizona. The drawing accurately shows the Magician's beaded cap, nose plug (also illustrated in Figure 4.15), shell earrings, turquoise-bead bracelet, and knee loops of shell tinklers that he wore in his grave. Along both of his legs, the Magician had lines of shell tinklers, which unlike the drawing, the excavator, John McGregor, thought had been attached to leggings. The carved stick and inlaid bird bracelet (also illustrated in Figure 3.10) were among his grave goods. No blanket, kilt, sash, or sandals were found with the Magician. While he probably wore these types of garments, the decorative details shown here are the artist's.

and connections with other cultural groups. Women and men were distinguished by their use of aprons or breechcloths. Ancestral Pueblo and southern groups could be distinguished by the raw materials they used for blankets and aprons and by their breechcloth and apron styles. Clothing similarities would have evidenced the close connections between particular groups and their neighbors. Within each of these groups, variants of everyday dress, such wrap-around dresses or kilts, probably signaled additional identity messages about the wearer's locality, community, status, or other social roles.

Special-Occasion Outfits

Outfits that combined the most finely made or highly decorated garments were probably worn on special occasions or by high-status individuals (Figure 2.17). Given the frequency of ceremonies among native Southwest groups during the historic period, and the evidence for social differentiation during the prehistoric period, a traveler who lingered in any community probably would have observed fancy outfits before too long. Apparently worn mostly by men, these ensembles were more complexly made and more highly decorated versions of everyday attire.

Northern Special-Occasion Outfits, AD 1100–1300

Evidence for Ancestral Pueblo special-occasion outfits during this period comes primarily from large, well-preserved textile fragments, a few complete garments, and inferences from ceremonial depictions on later Pueblo IV-period kiva murals. For men, these outfits probably consisted of a highly decorated cotton breechcloth and shirt or blanket along with finely made accessories—a sash, sandals, and sometimes leggings. The breechcloth's front panel could be decorated in a variety of twill patterns. Most decorated shirts were painted or resist-dyed, but at least one shirt was intricately braided and had an openwork appearance, probably inspired by openwork shirts worn south of the Rim. A solid white tunic and a tailored hide shirt from Mesa Verde may also have been part of special attire.

The fancier cotton blankets were large and typically decorated with bands of red, white, and brown twill. More eye-catching examples decorated in tie-dye, painted in an offset-quartered layout, or woven in allover diamond-twill tapestry were probably worn by persons of a particular social or religious status or used in certain ceremonies. At Aztec Ruin, Mesa Verde, and in southeast Utah, fancy turkey-feather blankets were decorated with brown and white feathers arranged in geometric patterns.[52] Although burial data suggest that the more highly decorated cotton blankets were often used by men, two beautifully painted blankets and some decorated feather blankets were associated with women and children.[53]

Special-occasion accessories included sashes, human hair leggings, and finely woven sandals. White cotton sashes were woven with a 2/2 braiding rhythm. In the Chaco Canyon and Aztec Ruins areas, a sash and several probable headbands incorporated the feathers of northern flickers or other wild birds. The fanciest sandals were twined with raised designs on the underside of the sole, or they were finely twill-plaited. Both styles had a jog at the toe, a feature not seen elsewhere in the Southwest.

Northern Special-Occasion Outfits, AD 1300–1630

Kiva murals document a tremendously rich and diverse array of ceremonial outfits during the post-AD 1300 period (Figures 2.10–13, 2.18–19; also Figures 3.17–18, 4.11–12).[54] These paintings have been recorded at the Ancestral Hopi site of Awat'ovi and the Ancestral Keresan site of Kawaika'a, both located near the Hopi Mesas, and two Ancestral Tiwa sites, Pottery Mound and the later site of Kuaua, located in the Rio Grande River valley.[55] The diverse costumes depicted at each village probably represent a range of ceremonial and leadership roles. They also highlight the incompleteness of the archaeological textile record used to reconstruct special-occasion clothing during the preceding period.

The depictions are mostly of men, whose outfits typically include a kilt accessorized with a sash, and sometimes also a shirt, tunic, blanket, footwear, or legwear (Figures 2.11–13). Men from different areas of the Colorado Plateau wore different ceremonial styles. Ancestral Hopi shirts and tunics were either solid white with openwork designs, or black with negative-painted or resist-dyed designs. At Pottery Mound, Ancestral Tiwa shirts were decorated either with solid colors (white, red, yellow, and others) or by painting, openwork, tapestry weave, or stripes. In contrast, virtually all Ancestral Tiwa shirts from Kuaua were solid black. The exception is a depiction of a flared, long-sleeved tunic, probably intended to represent hide.[56]

Kilts were similarly varied.[57] Ancestral Hopi kilts were either solid white or decorated with designs suggestive of tapestry weave, twill weave, painting, supplementary weft, or embroidery (Figure 2.10, 2.12). One kilt from Kawaika'a had an offset-quartered design reminiscent of large Pueblo III-period painted blankets from the Kayenta area. Another suggests manufacture from hide. In contrast, Ancestral Tiwa kilts were typically either solid black or black with asymmetrical negative-painted or resist-dye designs (Figure 2.13). A few kilts from Pottery Mound appear to be painted, striped, woven in tapestry weave, or covered in feathers (Figure 2.11). As at Kawaika'a, one kilt from Pottery Mound appears to be made of hide. At all of these sites, men's kilts were typically secured with a white-fringed sash that was sometimes ornamented with tassels and usually tied on the wearer's right side.

2.18. Ancestral Pueblo mural depiction of a female figure wearing a black wrap-around garment and white sash with long fringe and probable fiber rings, Awat'ovi, northeast Arizona. The garment border suggests painting, supplementary weft, or embroidery. Also note the figure's hairstyle, necklace, and armbands.

2.19. Ancestral Pueblo mural depiction of a female figure wearing a resist-dyed or negative-painted blanket dress and white sash with short fringe, Pottery Mound, north-central New Mexico. Also note the figure's hairstyle, feather headdress, and bracelets.

Men's ceremonial outfits also included legwear and footwear, either alone or in combination.[58] The leggings depicted in the murals appear to be made of hide or woven fabric and were secured around the ankles and calves with ties or woven bands that sometimes had attached rattles (Figure 2.11). One vaguely defined form of male footwear depicted in kiva murals may represent hide moccasins.

Interestingly, the kiva murals depict no one wearing a large blanket over the shoulders. Instead, Ancestral Hopi men at Awat'ovi and a possible woman at Pottery Mound wear short, cape-like shoulder blankets that are solid black or black with negative painting or resist-dyeing (Figure 2.12).

In the mural depictions of women, their ceremonial attire usually consists of a wrap-around blanket worn as a dress (Figures 2.18–19). Ancestral Hopi women and probably dual-gendered personages are shown with the blanket wrapped around the torso and under both arms (Figure 2.18). In contrast, Ancestral Tiwa women tied the blanket over the right shoulder and draped it under the left arm, in the manner of modern Pueblo women (Figure 2.19, 6.4). Both styles were customarily secured with a white cotton sash tied on the wearer's left side, the opposite of men's sashes.

The wrapped blanket dress was often solid black or elaborately decorated with resist-dyed or negative-painted designs. The Ancestral Hopi decorated ceremonial blanket dresses with asymmetrical tie-dye designs or white openwork patterns. For the Ancestral Tiwa, the designs were asymmetrical, composed of diagonal lines, hook-like elements, or white circles (Figure 2.19). The kiva murals show several large, eye-catching blankets hanging from racks on kiva walls and decorated with probable resist-dyed and painted designs arranged in an offset-quartered layout. The resist-dye blankets resemble those worn as wrap-around dresses by female personages in the murals.

Southern Special-Occasion Outfits

In contrast to the rich archaeological textile and painted mural record of the Colorado Plateau, most of the evidence for special-occasion outfits worn by southern groups consists of small numbers of preserved fragments and extremely rare complete garments that are scattered among Sinagua, Salado, Mogollon, and Hohokam assemblages. Although such fragments confirm that these people used intricately decorated fabrics, they are rarely sufficiently complete to determine the original garment form.

Some Mimbres and Casas Grandes ceramics depict styles of clothing that were probably used for special occasions, but these images lack the richness and diversity of the Ancestral Pueblo kiva murals. Consequently, reconstructions of southern special-occasion outfits are generalized, composite images derived from evidence for different groups. We may assume that similar to the regional differences in ceremonial styles noted in Ancestral Hopi, Keresan, and Tiwa kiva murals, special-occasion outfits worn by people living south of the Mogollon Rim varied within culture areas as well.

Southern men probably combined the same garments in their special-occasion outfits as their Ancestral Pueblo counterparts: a decorated cotton breechcloth or kilt, shirt, and blanket, accessorized by a finely made sash and sandals. Decorated breechcloths were probably replaced by kilts in most areas by the AD 1200s. A preserved Sinagua kilt was embellished with intricate tapestry insets, and kilt depictions on Casas Grandes pottery from northern Mexico suggest the use of other kinds of decoration, such as painting and resist-dye. The most eye-catching shirts were made from exquisite openwork fabrics, and some breechcloths and kilts may also have been decorated in openwork. Supplementary weft, painting, and resist-dye were probably used to decorate shirts, blankets, and other fancy garments.

Southern men probably secured some of their kilts with white cotton sashes that were braided in a 2/2 or 3/3 rhythm. One braided Mogollon example was adorned with wrapped-fiber rings similar to those found on modern Hopi braided sashes. The Sinagua, Salado, and Hohokam also used loom-woven cotton or yucca warp-faced belts. A late Salado example was made with the warp-float technique. Fancy sandals also varied. For the Hohokam, their distinctive coiled-braid sandal that appeared after AD 900 may have been part of special-occasion attire. After AD 1300, some Mogollon, Sinagua, and Salado adopted a finely woven 2/2 twill-plaited cordage sandal with a highly distinctive H-shaped strap, a style shared with northern Chihuahua, Mexico.

The paucity of evidence for southern special-occasion outfits severely limits comparisons with the north, although some basic observations can be made. During the AD 1100–1300 period, someone wearing a cotton blanket decorated with twill-woven stripes and fine-twined or twill-plaited sandals was most likely an Ancestral Puebloan from the Colorado Plateau. In contrast, someone wearing a cotton blanket with plaid decoration, an openwork shirt, and coiled-braided sandals was probably Hohokam. The Sinagua and Salado would have been recognized by their blend of Ancestral Pueblo and Hohokam clothing characteristics.

By the Pueblo IV period, certain decorative practices, such as resist-dye and openwork, were used to decorate special-occasion clothing on a pan-Southwest scale. This more prevalent use of design styles probably signified broadly shared ideas about marking status, ritual roles, and leadership and was tied to the proliferation of religious symbolism associated with certain designs and colors.

CONCLUSION

In the absence of any conversation, a traveler could have learned the most about people met along the way from their clothing. Arriving in a new community, our traveler probably could have discerned immediately whether it was an ordinary day or a special occasion based on the kinds of clothes residents were wearing. Multiple identity messages were embedded in what everyone wore, with the most important messages expressed most visibly. Less-obvious clothing characteristics reinforced these messages and conveyed additional meanings.

Everywhere, women and men were easily distinguished, not just by their physical characteristics but also by clearly visible differences in their garment forms and outfits. Individuals who were fulfilling special leadership or ceremonial roles could often be identified by their resplendent attire: shirts, blankets, kilts, wrap-around dresses, or sandals that were finely made with fancy weaves or decorated with elaborate designs. Broad-scale cultural affiliation was signaled by the materials, weaves, colors, and designs of people's garments, but an observant traveler would also have noticed more subtle variation in the clothing worn by people of different localities within a particular region.

Our traveler would have noted the most visible differences in Ancestral Pueblo and Hohokam clothing. These groups were separated by the greatest geographical distance and had the least direct interaction with each other. The geographically intermediate Sinagua and Salado wore clothing that was strongly influenced by Ancestral Pueblo and Hohokam styles, and the Mogollon shared a number of clothing traditions with the Ancestral Puebloans, Hohokam, and people of northern Chihuahua, Mexico. Many of these regional clothing distinctions broke down during the late Pueblo III and Pueblo IV periods, as Ancestral Pueblo groups from the Kayenta region migrated into southern Arizona and as southern groups migrated north and east to the Colorado Plateau—all bringing their clothing styles and ceremonies.

The clothing worn north and south of the Mogollon Rim was inspired by different cultural influences. The Ancestral Puebloans wore striped twill blankets, braided sashes, twined sandals, and other garments that expressed continuity with their Basketmaker past. In contrast, much of Hohokam clothing was inspired by Mesoamerica. The most distinctive aspects of the Hohokam textile tradition—gauze weave, weft-wrap openwork, supplementary weft, and warp-faced belting—spread into the southern Southwest from Mexico.

Most textile and clothing traditions that were widely shared throughout the Southwest originated in Mesoamerica, spreading initially to the Hohokam and then farther and farther north.[59] These introductions began with cotton and the loom, followed by textile techniques and designs intended mostly for high-status or ceremonial use. Two-dimensional patterning, offset-quartered layouts, openwork, and tie-dye were all adopted from Mexico. The proliferation of these elaborate techniques and designs throughout the Southwest was not just the product of occasional trade or some other kind of limited interaction. Rather, it was tied to the spread of new religious and political ideas and practices. The sacred and ideologically charged meanings embedded in the colors and designs of these special garments reflect the adoption of Mesoamerican religious symbolism. The use of this clothing by political and religious leaders and ritual societies signifies shared beliefs about appropriate ways for marking their special positions, all of which seem to reference the powerful theocratic states of Mesoamerica.

Just as Ancestral Puebloans drew on their Basketmaker heritage for their clothing choices, contemporary Pueblo people continue to draw on their ancestral past.[60] In the centuries following European contact, many native Southwesterners relinquished traditional weaving techniques and garments and adopted Western dress, which became the norm by the early 1900s. On ceremonial occasions, however, Pueblo people continue to wear textiles and garments rooted in prehistoric traditions (Figure 6.2). Women still wear their manta dresses over the right shoulder, under the left arm, and tied on the left side with a woven sash.[61] For men, the kilt is still the most prominent ritual garment, and they continue to wear breechcloths, fancy shirts, blankets, belts, and leggings. Cotton maintains its symbolic importance even though most of the fiber now comes from far away, and new materials and techniques have been adopted.

Different styles of contemporary ritual regalia convey information about the wearer's gender, marital status, religious and political position, and sodality, moiety, or clan membership, as well as tribal group and pan-Pueblo connections. Given these multiple connotations, we must assume that prehistoric clothing was also imbued with many more meanings than those touched upon in this chapter.

By signaling cultural identity, continuity, and heritage in a conscious and visible way, contemporary ritual apparel plays a vital role in keeping Pueblo cultures distinctive and alive in the midst of strong, outside pressures to assimilate into mainstream American society. This clothing integrates the old with the new, often interpreting ancient visual symbols and garment styles with modern materials and processes. By maintaining ancestral traditions and the demand for Pueblo-made textiles, contemporary Pueblo people perpetuate the forces of continuity and change that have shaped Southwest clothing for millennia.

ORNAMENTS

3

by JILL E. NEITZEL

At most destinations across the prehistoric Southwest, a traveler would have noticed people wearing ornaments on various parts of their bodies. Made primarily of marine shell, turquoise, and black and red stone, this jewelry came in a variety of forms: necklaces, bracelets, anklets, earrings, brooches, rings, and nose and lip plugs.[1] These accessories broadcast the wearer's status, gender, cultural affiliation, intergroup connections, religious beliefs, and heritage—messages that reinforced those of the individual's clothes.[2]

Unlike preserved textiles, which are rare in the Southwest and predominantly Ancestral Pueblo, recovered ornaments conservatively number in the hundreds of thousands and represent all cultural groups. Jewelry from burials is especially significant for this volume's interest in personal identity, because it is associated with particular individuals.[3] Researchers can use this association to assess an interred person's status relative to other group members. Generally, social prominence in the prehistoric Southwest was correlated with increased quantities of adornments and more intricate forms. Only those with greater political and ceremonial power and greater access to resources could obtain more lavish jewelry.

This chapter considers how ornaments broadcast the preeminence of the prehistoric Southwest's highest status individuals. I compare different groups' best-documented, most jewelry-rich burials for three time periods: AD 900–1150, AD 1150–1300, and AD 1300–1450.[4] The results show that adornments reiterated a person's prominence through their numbers, forms, raw materials, and religious symbolism. Tremendous variation in the richest burials' quantities of ornaments indicates that some groups were much more stratified than others. But jewelry alone reveals just one dimension of the prehistoric Southwest's remarkable organizational diversity. A fuller, more nuanced picture emerges when each group's number of rich burials and settlement patterns are also considered.

AD 900–1150

The three groups with the best documented, most jewelry-rich burials dating to AD 900–1150 are the Chacoans, Mimbres, and Hohokam. For the Chacoans and Mimbres, adornments worn at the time of interment can be distinguished from those that were added grave goods. This separation is not possible for the Hohokam due to their practice of cremation.

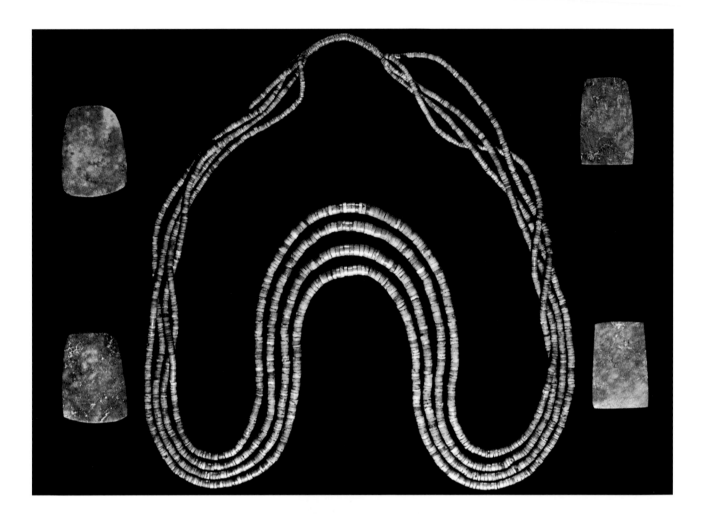

3.1. Pueblo II-period Ancestral Pueblo turquoise-bead necklace and pendants, Pueblo Bonito, Chaco Canyon, northwest New Mexico. When hung from the neck, the length of the necklace is 14 inches. This was the most lavish, intact jewelry recovered during the Pueblo Bonito excavations.

3.2. Copper bells from northwest Mexico collected in north-central Arizona, probably from a Sinagua or Hohokam northern periphery site. The bells are each approximately one-half inch in diameter.

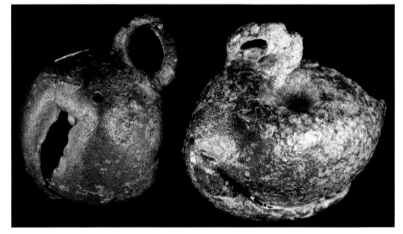

Quantities

The richest Chaco burial (#14) belonged to a 40–45-year-old man interred in the sacred precinct of Pueblo Bonito, Chaco Canyon's largest great house (Appendix Table 3.1).[5] When he was placed in his grave, he wore more than 6,000 pieces of turquoise. On his chest, was a brooch made of almost 2,000 beads; on each of his wrists were bracelets, strung respectively with more than 750 and 2,500 beads and pendants; and on each of his legs were anklets, one with more than 300 beads and pendants and the other with almost 450. The bracelets and one anklet also included a few shell beads and pendants, and black stone beads.

If, when alive, this man wore even a fraction of the jewelry that adorned him at death, it would have clearly conveyed his preeminent status to his fellow Chacoans. In his grave, he wore more than twice as many ornaments as Pueblo Bonito's second richest individual (#13). At the other end of the social spectrum, roughly half of Chaco Canyon's small-site burials contained no ornaments, and the rest had only a few beads or pendants made of turquoise, shell, bone, nuts, or reeds.

The contrast between the man in Burial #14 and other Chacoans would have been amplified if he also wore some of the numerous loose beads and pendants that were deposited in his grave. On his abdomen were 2,642 turquoise beads and 172 turquoise pendants, along with roughly 10 pieces of turquoise and jet inlay. By his right knee, were 26 complete and 15 fragmentary *Glycymeris* bracelets and a turquoise-inlaid cylinder basket filled with 2,150 turquoise beads, 174 turquoise pendants, and almost 3,500 shell beads and pendants. In stark contrast, fewer than 600 turquoise beads and pendants were added to Pueblo Bonito's second richest burial (#13).

While the mortuary jewelry in Burial #14 was incredibly lavish, it did not include the full assortment of Chaco ornaments.[6] Absent were turquoise-bead necklaces, such as the multistrand example shown in Figure 3.1, as well as necklaces strung with shell and jet beads and whole *Olivella* shells.[7] Other notable Chaco ornaments not found in Burial #14 were jet plaques inlaid with turquoise and shell; shell plaques carved into zoomorphic forms; round pendants made from *Haliotis* shell and jet; and copper bells, similar to the examples from north-central Arizona shown in Figure 3.2.[8]

At the Mimbres site of Galaz Ruin, a 100-room pueblo located along the Mimbres River, four adults of unknown sex and one infant were interred with significantly more ornaments than anyone else (Appendix Table 3.2).[9] One adult (#2-267) was adorned with a necklace made of an approximately eight-foot-long strand of black beads interspersed with 173 turquoise beads and pendants, three *Glycymeris* shell bracelets, an anklet of more than 500 shell beads, and another anklet

3.3. Mimbres ceramic depiction of figure with multistrand necklace and four bracelets on upper left arm, southwest New Mexico. Also note the figure's cap, facial decoration, tunic, and leggings.

of more than 150 red shell and stone beads and pendants. Figure 3.3 illustrates how the Mimbres wrapped long bead strands multiple times around the neck to create loosely hanging necklaces (also Figure 2.7 [left]; Figure 5.1a shows another necklace type). Adorning this individual's left arm are four bands, most likely *Glycymeris* bracelets, which in this case should more accurately be called armbands (also Figure 2.7 [right], and examples from a Hohokam site in Figure 3.4).

Another of Galaz Ruin's richest adults (#15-235) wore an almost 11-foot-long shell bead necklace interspersed with 29 turquoise beads and pendants. A third adult (#2-256) wore a pair of turquoise-inlaid shell earrings and two necklaces, one with more than 1,100 black and red stone beads, and the other with more than 230 shell beads. The fourth adult's (#2-200) grave contained more than 1,100 black stone and

Jill E. Neitzel

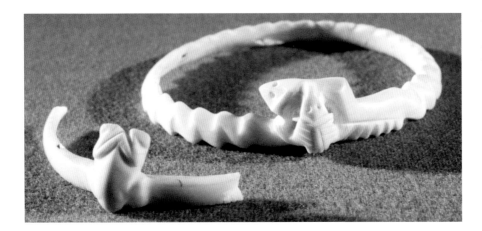

3.4. Preclassic-period Hohokam carved *Glycymeris* bracelets: front left, fragment with carved frog; back right with carved snake and bird, Snaketown, south-central Arizona.

200 *Olivella* beads, all of which were added grave goods. The rich infant (#15-305) also had only added grave goods, which included a nine-foot-long strand of shell beads, six *Glycymeris* bracelets, two shell pendants, and one stone palette. Missing from these rich burials was the Mimbres' full range of zoomorphic pendant types and extremely rare copper bells (Figure 3.2).[10] Nevertheless, if, when alive, the individuals in burials #15-235 and #2-256 ever wore a fraction of the jewelry that adorned them at death, they would have stood out among the site's other residents, 90 percent of whom were interred with no jewelry.[11]

Using quantities of ornaments to study status messages among the Preclassic-period Hohokam is problematic. Their best-documented, most jewelry-rich burial (Feature #1679) was excavated from the periphery of La Ciudad, a large site in the Lower Salt River valley (Appendix Table 3.3). This subadult's cremation contained just 66 shell beads and 20 *Glycymeris* bracelets. Examples of decorated *Glycymeris* bracelets can be seen in Figure 3.4 (also Figure I.4).

With its relatively small assemblage, La Ciudad's Feature #1679 lacked the full range of Preclassic-period Hohokam ornament types. Missing were the whole shells and diverse shell-bead and pendant forms that the Hohokam frequently strung to be worn on various parts of the body. Figure 3.5 illustrates a necklace with two shell-bead types, and Figure 3.6 shows Hohokam human effigies wearing necklaces that were most probably made of shell beads (also Figure 4.16). Hanging from the necklace in Figure 3.6a is a lizard-shaped pendant (also illustrated in Figure I.4). In Figure 3.6b, the individual's right wrist is adorned with multiple bracelets that could be carved *Glycymeris* shells or strings of beads, probably made of shell. Also absent from La Ciudad's Feature #1679 were turquoise and other stone beads and pendants; earrings; rings; and ear, nose, and lip plugs made of shell, stone, and clay

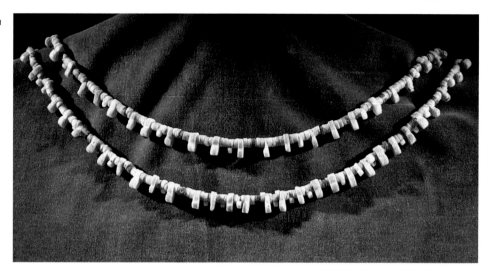

3.5. Preclassic-period Hohokam necklace of pink, purple, and white shell beads, Snaketown, south-central Arizona.

(Figure 3.6b; also Figures I.3–4); and the rarest Hohokam ornaments—copper bells (Figure 3.2) and turquoise-inlaid shell.

Given that almost 90 percent of La Ciudad's documented cremations contained no ornaments, wearing some fraction of Burial #1679's jewelry could have signaled modest status differences within the community. But richer, Preclassic Hohokam cremations have been reported, and the individuals associated with them undoubtedly had higher status than the subadult in La Ciudad's Feature #1679.[12]

Raw Materials

Much of jewelry's role as a status marker was a function of the raw materials from which it was made. Obtaining turquoise and shell could be costly, and the distant sources and intermediate connections that were part of the procurement process added to the raw materials' status messages. These messages were further enhanced by the costs of crafting raw materials into finished ornaments, especially when done in large quantities or for more intricate forms.

The Chacoans were the Southwest's greatest consumers of turquoise (Figure 3.1), which they obtained from the Cerrillos Hills near Santa Fe and from more distant deposits in southern New Mexico, Arizona, Colorado, and Nevada.[13] Much of this turquoise was transformed into ornaments by craftsmen in Chaco Canyon. The mines that supplied turquoise for Mimbres ornaments have not been identified, but the Chacoans may have served as intermediaries for both raw materials and finished items. The sources of Hohokam turquoise included the Cerrillos Hills, as well as a mine near Halloron Springs, California. The absence of turquoise jewelry

Jill E. Neitzel

workshops indicates that the Hohokam mostly imported finished ornaments rather than the raw material.

The Hohokam were the Southwest's major consumer of marine shell (Figures 3.4–5), most of which was native to the Gulf of California.[14] During the Preclassic period, groups in the western Papagueria collected raw shell, crafted it into ornaments, and traded these products and some unmodified shell to the Phoenix Basin. The Hohokam in turn traded shell jewelry to the Mimbres and the early Sinagua, both of whom may have been the Chacoans' suppliers. The Pacific Coast was a secondary source of shell for the Hohokam and Sinagua; and the Sinagua may have been intermediaries in supplying it to the Chacoans and perhaps the Hohokam. The sources of the Mimbres' black stone are unknown, but may have been local.

Different groups' raw material preferences may have marked their cultural affiliation: turquoise for the Chacoans; shell, and especially *Glycymeris* bracelets,

3.6. Ceramic depictions of Preclassic-period Hohokam figures with jewelry, south-central Arizona: (*a*) ceramic human effigy jar with zigzag line depicting a necklace that has a dangling composite pendant with lizard form, Snaketown. Also note the figure's facial decoration; (*b*) clay figurine with multistrand necklace, bracelets, and ear plugs, Van Liere site. Also note the figure's hairstyle.

for the Hohokam; and perhaps black stone for the Mimbres.[15] If true, then secondary ornament raw materials may have broadcast a person's connections not just with distant sources but also with particular intermediate groups. A Hohokam or Mimbres individual wearing turquoise jewelry may have signaled ties with the Chacoans. Similarly, the *Glycymeris* bracelets and shell beads interred with Pueblo Bonito's Burial #14 and the rich Galaz Ruin burials may have signaled ties with the Hohokam. More distant, Mesoamerican contacts were conveyed by rare copper bells, imported from northwest Mexico, and by the Southwest's turquoise inlaid ornaments, which may have emulated even more intricate and elaborate examples from the powerful Toltec empire in highland Mexico's central valley.[16]

Religious Symbolism

Jewelry was also imbued with sacred meanings that added a supernatural dimension to its status messages, especially when large numbers of ornaments were worn. Evidence for this symbolic content comes from ritual deposits in both ceremonial structures and burials.[17] The inclusion of unmodified turquoise and shell, production debris, and broken beads and pendants in these deposits suggests that the raw materials had religious significance. Further evidence from burials is the association of finished ornaments and raw turquoise and shell with ritual objects. In addition to his ornament caches, Pueblo Bonito's Burial #14 had offerings of turquoise matrix, four whole *Haliotis* shells, a bivalve shell, a shell trumpet, and turquoise- and shell-inlaid basketry. At Galaz Ruin, the rich infant burial (#15-305) contained a ritual palette, and the nine-foot strand of shell beads was probably also a ritual offering. At La Ciudad, Feature #1679's offerings included three unmodified shells, a ritual palette, an obsidian projectile point, and a piece of hematite.

Colors and raw materials were also sacred, which may be why raw turquoise and shell, production debris, and broken ornaments were used as ritual offerings. According to Steve Plog, Chaco turquoise carried the same sacred meanings that historic Puebloans associated with the color blue-green: the sky, rain, and the west/southwest direction, all of which related to an overriding concern with fertility.[18] The color white had its own set of meanings that also related to fertility.

Certain forms and designs were also symbolic. Similar to the historic-period Puebloans, Chaco frog and tadpole-shaped pendants probably represented rain and fertility, meanings that were reinforced by the blue-green color of the turquoise from which they were made. The carved snakes and snake-derived motifs that decorated Hohokam *Glycymeris* bracelets (Figure 3.4) probably reflected the influence of Basin of Mexico empires whose serpent motifs signified fertility. Hohokam jewelry that depicted lizards, frogs, and birds probably had similar symbolic content (Figures 3.4, 3.6a; also Figure I.4). Finally, the religious meanings of some ornaments may have been auditory as well as visual—most notably the sounds made by copper bells (Figure 3.2) and *Conus*-shell tinklers when the wearer walked or danced (Figure 2.17 shows a later Sinagua example).

Messages about ancestral heritage may have added to jewelry's sacred meanings. In the northern Southwest, including finished and unfinished shell ornaments as well as production debris in ritual deposits dates to the late Basketmaker period; and the practice of adding shell beads and pendants to child burials is even older, dating to the late Archaic period.[19] Among the Hohokam, *Glycymeris* bracelets were present in the Tucson Basin during the Early Ceramic Period. This longevity suggests that ancestral heritage and its religious associations may have been an important part of defining Hohokam identity. The same may be true for the Chacoans and their turquoise jewelry.

Organizational Variation

When visiting Pueblo Bonito, Galaz Ruin, and perhaps La Ciudad, our traveler could have identified the highest status residents by how many and what kinds of ornaments they wore. However, the traveler could not have relied on jewelry alone to assess the relative prominence of these individuals in comparison to one another. For example, all accounts of rich Hohokam cremations pale in comparison to Pueblo Bonito's Burial #14. At first glance, this difference would seem to suggest that the Chacoans were more stratified than the Hohokam and that their most prominent member was wealthier and more powerful than any of his Hohokam counterparts. However, research by Richard Blanton and colleagues suggests that jewelry could be used to assess which groups were more or less stratified only if the same leadership strategies were being employed.[20]

This was clearly not the case for the Chacoans and the Hohokam. The lavish adornments in Pueblo Bonito's Burial #14 are consistent with a leadership strategy that is individually focused and invests resources in public displays of the leader's power. The centralization of authority is also evident in Pueblo Bonito's enormous size and central location both in Chaco Canyon and the surrounding San Juan Basin.[21] In contrast, among the Hohokam, the relatively modest contents of their most jewelry-rich cremations and their tremendous investment in constructing extensive irrigation systems are consistent with a leadership strategy in which power is shared and directed to benefiting the group as a whole.[22] Rather than one enormous site, the Hohokam had several large sites, which indicates that their sociopolitical organization was decentralized, consisting of multiple polities.[23]

The Mimbres add to this picture of organizational diversity.[24] Galaz Ruin was just one of several large Mimbres sites, and it had five jewelry-rich burials. Their total quantities of ornaments far surpassed those reported for any Hohokam cremations.

Differences in data recording (bead numbers vs. bead strand length) constrain comparisons between Mimbres and Chaco for adornments worn by individuals in their graves, but quantities of added grave goods differ greatly. While Pueblo Bonito's Burial #14 had more than 8,500, the greatest quantities added to a Mimbres adult grave were approximately 1,300, with the other rich adult burials having only 0–2. Finally, the scale of Mimbres construction was much less than Chaco great houses and miniscule in comparison to the investment in Hohokam irrigation canals. In contrast with the hierarchical Chacoans, Mimbres organization may have been more horizontally differentiated around kinship or sodality groups.[25]

AD 1150–1300

The best documented, most jewelry-rich burials dating to AD 1150–1300 represent once again the Chacoans and Hohokam, as well as two new groups, the Sinagua and Kayenta. For the Chacoans and Sinagua, the numbers of ornaments worn at the time of interment can be distinguished from those that were added grave goods. This separation was not recorded for the richest Kayenta and Hohokam burials.

Quantities

The most jewelry-rich, undisturbed Pueblo III-period Chaco burial belonged to an adult of unknown sex (part of Burial #16) from Aztec Ruins, the new preeminent Chaco center located along the San Juan River.[26] In his grave, this individual wore an *Olivella* shell anklet and was "completely covered from throat to thighs with beads, abalone shell, and mosaic pendants" (Appendix Table 3.4).[27] Figure 3.7 illustrates two mosaic pendants recovered from Aztec Ruins. In the corner of the room near his and an adjacent individual's feet were 31,000 very small black disc beads in a ceramic duck effigy, 400 *Olivella* beads strung into a necklace, three *Conus* beads, and two partially inlaid shell discs, which are probably the remains of pendants, similar to Figure 3.7. This burial lacked one rare ornament form found elsewhere at the site: copper bells (Figure 3.2).

Among the early Classic-period Hohokam, the best documented, most jewelry-rich burial belonged to a 30-year-old male (#184) interred at Pueblo Grande, one of the three largest platform mound sites in the Lower Salt River valley.[28] The man's 1,251 ornaments consisted almost entirely of disc-shaped beads made primarily from slate, argillite, and other unidentified stone (Appendix Table 3.5). The remaining adornments included 50 turquoise beads, one piece of turquoise mosaic, and 40 shell beads.

Similar to the previous period, Pueblo Grande's Burial #184 may not have been the richest at this or other Hohokam sites.[29] However, more prolific burials have

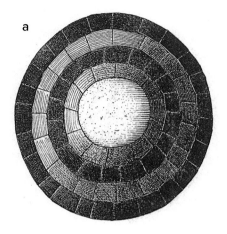
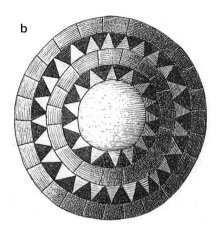

3.7. Pueblo III-period Ancestral Pueblo mosaic pendants inlaid on shell disks, Aztec Ruins, northwest New Mexico. The pendants were suspended from the neck by a cord: (*a*) red stone circle surrounded by alternating rings of turquoise and black stone; (*b*) red stone circle surrounded by alternating rings of solid turquoise and black stone/mirror-like galena triangles.

either been destroyed by pothunters or lack recorded grave-good tallies. Typical ornaments that were not interred with Burial #184 include *Glycymeris* bracelets, which in contrast to those in Figure 3.4 were mostly plain during this period; *Conus*-shell necklaces; and pendants that were typically shell but sometimes turquoise or other stone. Also absent were rare turquoise-inlaid shell and copper bells (Figure 3.2).

The richest Sinagua was interred at the site of Ridge Ruin, a small pueblo with 20 ground-floor rooms, located near Flagstaff, Arizona (Appendix Table 3.6). Archaeologists have named this 35-year-old man "the Magician" due to his unusual assortment of ritual artifacts.[30] When he was interred, the Magician wore a red argillite nose plug with circular turquoise inlays, turquoise pendant earrings with inlaid shell, and a bracelet on each wrist—one with 73 turquoise beads, and the other with two turquoise grasshopper heads (Figures 2.17, 4.15). He also wore *Conus*-shell tinklers in loops around his knees and in strings along his legs (Figure 2.17). On his head was a cap made of 3,600 extremely small, black stone beads and several hundred shell beads (Figures 2.17, 4.15).

Ornaments that were added to the Magician's grave included a basketry armband covered with 1,500 pieces of turquoise inlaid with orange, red, and black decoration (Figure 3.8); turquoise-inlaid pendants in the shapes of a circle (Figure 3.9), a bird, and an ear;[31] a *Glycymeris*-shell bracelet decorated with a turquoise-inlaid bird-in-flight (Figure 3.10; also Figure 2.17); three shell pendants, one of which was lizard-shaped; four painted stone pendants; and a necklace made from mountain-lion claws and teeth.

The Magician's diverse adornments did not include the full range of typical Sinagua forms. Missing were red stone lip plugs, beads made from *Olivella* and

3.8. Artist's depiction of Sinagua Magician's possible basketry armband inlaid with turquoise, orange rodent teeth, red argillite, and black stone, Ridge Ruin, north-central Arizona. The armband is 4.7 inches tall with a diameter of 3.4 inches.

3.9. Artist's depiction of Sinagua Magician's circular pendant with turquoise and shell inlaid on molded lac, Ridge Ruin, north-central Arizona. The pendant's diameter is 2.1 inches.

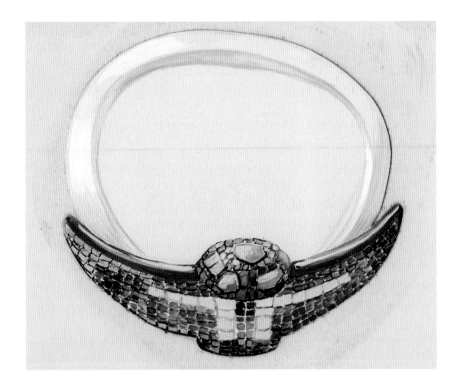

3.10. Artist's depiction of Sinagua Magician's *Glycymeris*-shell bracelet with bird-shaped ornament inlaid with turquoise, shell, and iron pyrite on molded lac, Ridge Ruin, north-central Arizona. The bird's width is 2.8 inches.

other shell species, and zoomorphic pendant forms and silhouettes. The Sinagua also wore brightly painted armbands made from bark, wood, or woven material that occasionally incorporated other ornaments, such as turquoise pendants.[32] The Magician's turquoise-inlaid armband may have been a fancier version of this form. He also lacked copper bells, such as those in Figure 3.2, which may have been recovered from a Sinagua site.

The two richest Kayenta burials were excavated at the site of RB568, a pueblo with over 100 rooms in northeast Arizona (Appendix Table 3.7). The richest, a 30–35-year-old woman (#50), was interred with more than 50,000 extremely small, black-and-red stone disc beads that had once been strung into a necklace.[33] She also had two matching turquoise pendants, a wooden pendant inlaid with 17 pieces of turquoise, and a wooden bracelet painted black and green. The second richest, a 20–25-year-old man (#26), was interred with an armband woven from approximately 39,000 black and red stone beads and a few turquoise disks. He also had a necklace consisting of 80–90 turquoise beads and pendants.

If, when alive, the individuals in this period's richest burials wore even a fraction of the ornaments in their graves, their social prominence would have been evident to their fellow group members. At all four sites, the vast majority of burials contained no jewelry at all, and those that did generally had only a few pieces.[34] The quantities that accompanied the second- and third-richest were consistently much lower than the richest.

Raw Materials

As in the previous period, the status messages conveyed by wearing greater quantities of ornaments were reinforced by the costs of procuring the raw materials, crafting them into finished forms, and engaging in trade when production occurred elsewhere. The distant connections signified by shell and turquoise further enhanced their associated status messages.

Turquoise sources are not well documented for this period but probably continued to include the Cerrillos mines and others throughout the Southwest and beyond. However, while most shell was still collected from the Gulf of California, ornament production had shifted from sites in the western Papagueria to large platform-mound settlements in the Phoenix and Tucson Basins, presumably under the control of their elite residents.[35] The sources of RB568's black stone are unknown.

Crafting raw materials into large quantities of adornments would have been a significant time and labor investment. According to Helen Crotty, just drilling the holes in the estimated 90,000 beads interred with RB568's two richest burials would have taken five years of daily full-time work.[36] The production of fancier items, such as the Magician's intricate turquoise mosaics, would have required highly skilled craftsmen.

Unlike the previous period, raw material preferences were no longer a consistently reliable indicator of cultural affiliation. While shell was still the Hohokam's most frequently used raw material and their ubiquitous *Glycymeris* bracelets probably continued to signal cultural identity, black stone had increased so much in popularity that it predominated in Pueblo Grande's richest burial. Both the Sinagua and Kayenta emphasized black and red stone, which makes the Magician's burial with its prevalence of turquoise and shell an anomaly, probably due to his special status. Among the Chacoans, the popularity of shell and black stone seems to have increased at the expense of turquoise.

Despite this blurring of preferences, raw materials and the finished ornaments made from them may have continued to signal intergroup connections: turquoise with the Chacoans, shell with the Hohokam, and turquoise-inlaid shell among different groups' high status leaders. James Bayman thinks that Hohokam leaders wore inlaid frog and bird pendants as symbols or badges of their special positions (Figure 3.12 shows late Classic-period examples).[37] The Sinagua Magician had similar bird-shaped inlays, one of which was attached to a *Glycymeris* bracelet, emphasizing ties with the Hohokam (Figure 3.10). The Magician's Chaco connections can be seen in the resemblance between his inlaid circular brooch and the pendants from Aztec Ruins (Figures 3.7, 3.9). Through emulation, Southwest turquoise mosaics may have also expressed more distant contacts with more powerful Basin of Mexico empires. Obtained through trade, copper bells broadcast more direct relationships with northwest Mexico.

Religious Symbolism

As in the past, religious symbolism added to jewelry's status messages. Evidence for this sacred content is the same as previous examples: ritual offerings in ceremonial structures and burials, the association with ritual objects in burials, and ornament forms and colors.

The Chacoans at Aztec Ruins used raw turquoise and shell, production debris, and whole and broken beads and pendants as ritual deposits in both kivas and burials. In addition to the blanket of beads that covered the site's richest individual, and the more than 30,000 beads by his feet, additional deposits were made in this room's other corners that lacked burials. These ornaments included 8,500 very small, pink disc beads; a necklace strung with roughly 400 *Olivella* beads; an anklet of 70 *Olivella* beads; 6 abalone-shell pendants; 172 large disc-shaped beads; several hundred unsorted beads; several hundred mosaic fragments made of turquoise and other stone; and many bird-bone tube beads. The inclusion of whole shells in these deposits bolsters the claim that the raw material itself was sacred. Ritual objects were also associated with this jewelry. Galena crystals, which historic-period Puebloans used for ceremonial purposes, were added to the bead-filled ceramic duck effigy by the man's feet. Deposits in the room's other corners included a cache of 200 projectile points and a painted stick.

The Sinagua Magician's burial displays a clear association of jewelry with a rich assemblage of ritual objects: ceremonial sticks whose turquoise inlay, shell decoration, and deer foot and human-hand carvings added to their sacred symbolism; a turquoise-inlaid bone awl; whole and fragmentary shell, whose presence provides further evidence that ornament raw materials were sacred; a mass of specular iron crystals on shell fragments; a scattered mass of copper ore; and paint contained in reeds, skin sacks, and a gourd. Hundreds of miniature wooden bows and reed shafts with 420 projectile points were placed on the top of his grave.

Given the Magician's ceremonial role, the jewelry that he wore in his grave may have been part of his regalia. If so, it must have been imbued with religious meanings. While the bird, grasshopper, and lizard-shaped ornaments may seem most obviously symbolic to us, other adornments may have had their own sacred content. For example, the armband's resemblance to the inlaid basket interred at least 130 years earlier with Pueblo Bonito's Burial #14 suggests religious and heritage ties with the earlier, more powerful Chacoans.

Hohokam jewelry continued to depict frogs, birds, and lizards, which according to Doug Mitchell, represented sacred concerns with water and fertility.[38] *Conus*-shell tinklers seem to have been part of ceremonial regalia, evidenced by their recovery on and near platform mounds.[39] Further evidence that raw materials were sacred comes from the practice of including whole shell and production debris in burials.

Ornament colors added another layer of religious symbolism. The Pueblo III-period Chacoans must have shared the sacred meanings that their Pueblo II-period predecessors and historic-period descendants attributed to blue-green and white. Other evidence comes from the ceremonial staffs that the Sinagua painted blue and green and from Pueblo Grande's color-stained skeletons, which were probably the remains of body paint applied as part of mortuary rites.[40]

Organizational Variation

As in the previous period, our traveler could have identified the highest status individuals at Aztec Ruins, Pueblo Grande, Ridge Ruin, and RB568 based on quantity and kinds of ornaments. But again, jewelry alone would not have been a reliable measure of the relative prominence of these individuals when compared to one another. The reason is the same as before: the groups relied on different leadership strategies.

Comparing quantities of jewelry for the richest Chaco and Hohokam burials presents difficulties. Given the widespread disturbance at Aztec Ruins and its many multiple burials, other individuals may have been interred with as many or even more ornaments as the man considered here from Burial #16. Furthermore, since his only worn jewelry was a shell anklet, it is reasonable to ask whether the tens of thousands of beads that covered his body and were deposited by his feet are an accurate reflection of what he wore when alive. The problem with including the Pueblo Grande's Burial #184 in intergroup comparisons is that richer Hohokam burials may have been destroyed or undocumented.

Given the problems with Chaco and Hohokam mortuary data, information on leadership strategies must come from the groups' settlement patterns.[41] Similar to its Chaco Canyon predecessor, the Aztec Ruins complex was clearly the Pueblo III-period Chacoans' dominant center. Aztec West, which was just one of the several great houses in this complex, may have had as many as 400 rooms arranged in three stories. Pueblo Grande's size is difficult to quantity due to its platform-mound construction and uncertain boundaries, but this site was not the Hohokam's singular center as Aztec Ruins was for the Chacoans. Instead, several major platform-mound sites of roughly equal size and importance were present in the Lower Salt and Middle Gila River valleys. The settlement pattern data indicate that leadership was more centralized among the Chacoans and decentralized among the Hohokam.[42] If true, then we might expect that the highest status Chacoans may have broadcast their preeminence with much more lavish displays of jewelry than their Hohokam counterparts.

Further organizational variation is evident among the Kayenta and Sinagua.[43] The richest Kayenta (#50) from RB568 had almost ten times more ornaments than the Sinagua Magician. But the Magician had a diverse assemblage of ritual artifacts, while RB568's two richest burials had none. Settlement pattern comparisons reveal more differences. Just one fourth the size of Aztec West, RB568 was one of several equally large Kayenta sites. Ridge Ruin in turn was roughly one-fifth the size of RB568, and was smaller than several other Sinagua sites.

AD 1300–1450

The best-documented, most jewelry-rich burials dating to AD 1300–1450 again represent the Hohokam as well as the Casas Grandians, Mountain Mogollon, and Ancestral Puebloans of the Rio Grande River valley. Comparisons are done using all recorded jewelry, because published grave-good tallies do not distinguish worn from added adornments.

Quantities

The late Classic-period Hohokam have two candidates for the best-documented, most jewelry-rich burials, both from the site of Pueblo Grande. The richest was a seven-year-old child (#1428) interred with 1,634 ornaments that were predominantly "other stone" disk beads and were accompanied by a very small number of turquoise and shell beads, pendants, and tesserae. The second richest was a 27-year-old male (#2319) with 1,447 ornaments that were almost entirely shell disk beads along with one *Glycymeris* bracelet, three turquoise pendants, one turquoise bead, and one bone ornament.

The man depicted in Figure 3.11 illustrates some late Classic-period ornaments that were not found in Pueblo Grande's two rich burials: an inlaid hairpin; pendant earrings; necklaces strung with whole shell beads, disk beads, and shell pendants; a disk-bead bracelet; and an anklet strung with small *Olivella* shells.[44] An example of a late Classic period necklace strung with shell disk beads can be seen in Figure 3.12. Also missing from the Pueblo Grande burials and not depicted in Figure 3.11 are rings made of shell or stone and the extremely rare copper bells and turquoise

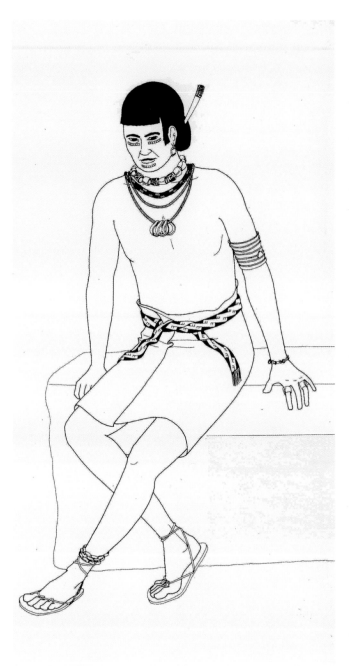

3.11. Artist's depiction of Classic-period Hohokam (AD 1300–1450) man wearing jewelry, south-central Arizona. Note the figure's hairpin, facial decoration, kilt, sash, and sandals.

3.12. Classic-period Hohokam turquoise-and-shell mosaics and shell-bead necklace, Casa Grande, south-central Arizona. The ornaments were recovered along with a pair of shell pendants from a room-floor cache. The stylized frog (*top*) is 4.25 inches in diameter, and the larger bird's width is 4.5 inches. The necklace consists of 980 beads.

and shell mosaics (Figure 3.12).[45] The frog-shaped example on the top of Figure 3.12 is virtually identical to ones found elsewhere in the Southwest at this time, and the birds resemble the Magician's, which date to the previous period (Figure 3.10).[46] According to James Bayman, the Hohokam inlaid pendants continued to be symbols of leadership.

At the Casas Grandes center of Paquimé in northwest Chihuahua, several burials were distinguished by their quantities of ornaments (Appendix Table 3.8). Most prolific was a pair of six-to-seven-month-old infants (#384/385) interred together with 4,179 ornaments, predominantly disk beads made mostly of shell along with slate, turquoise, a variety of other stone materials, and two copper tinklers. The next richest burials were single interments with roughly the same numbers of shell beads: a 36–50-year-old male (#314) had 1,246, and an 18–35-year-old male (#157) had 1,122.

The contents in these burials do not represent the full range of ornaments worn at Paquimé. Absent were diverse shell-bead and pendant forms; turquoise and other stone pendants; and turquoise and shell mosaics. The Casas Grandians strung beads and pendants for necklaces and bracelets in arrangements that could be relatively simple (Figures 3.13–14) or elaborate composites that incorporated mosaic effigies (Figures 3.15–16). Also missing from Paquimé's were *Glycymeris* bracelets; finger rings made of stone, shell, and copper; bells, armbands, earrings, and plaques made of copper; and bone nose skewers that were 8–23 cm long and often decorated with multicolored pseudo-cloisonné.

The best-documented, most jewelry-rich Mountain Mogollon burials belong to two subadults from Point of Pines Ruin in east-central Arizona (Appendix Table 3.9). An infant (#271) was interred with 723 ornaments that included 564 disk beads of unknown stone and 159 whole shell beads; and an adolescent (#128) was interred with 556 disk beads, whose stone material is also unknown. The richest adult (#148) was a woman with 43 whole-shell beads.[47]

The burial of a 40–45-year-old man (#140) from nearby Grasshopper Pueblo provides stronger evidence for status differences in the form of a rich assemblage of ritual artifacts and ceramics (Appendix Table 3.9). But his jewelry consisted of only 10 ornaments: eight *Glycymeris* bracelets and a pair of turquoise earrings. Missing from the Point of Pines and Grasshopper burials were small, stone animal pendants and the Mountain Mogollon's rare, turquoise-inlaid shell pendants.

Among the Pueblo IV-period Ancestral Puebloans, those burials with jewelry contained very little of it (Appendix Table 3.10). At the site of Arroyo Hondo in the Middle Rio Grande River valley, the most jewelry-rich burial belonged to a 7.5–8-month-old infant with 183 beads, 177 made from juniper seed and the

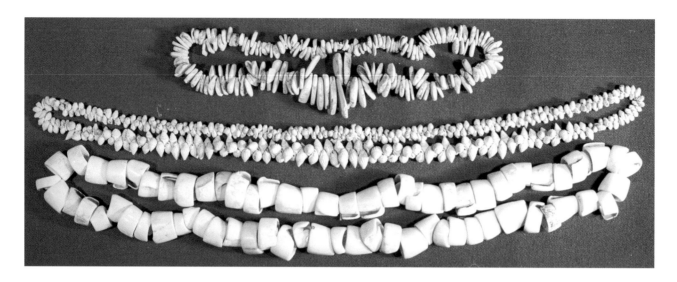

3.13. Casas Grandes strings of turquoise bead pendants (*top*); *Nassarious* shell beads (*middle*); and *Conus* shell beads (*bottom*); Paquimé, northern Chihuahua.

3.14. Jar with two standing human figures wearing feathers at elbows and hands, and figures of birds, Casas Grandes, Ramos polychrome, AD 1280–1450, 18.7 × 22.5 cm. (7⅜ × 8⅞ in.).

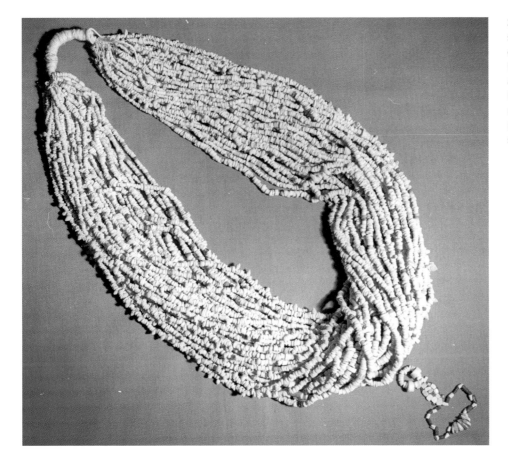

3.15. Casas Grandes multistrand shell-bead necklace with dangling composite-bead loop and turquoise inlaid copper turtle effigy pendant and larger bead-and-pendant loop, Paquimé, northern Chihuahua. This necklace also includes some beads made of turquoise, copper, other stone, and ceramics.

remainder from jet and turquoise, along with one whole- and one fragmentary-shell pendant. The site's richest adult had only a single turquoise bead. At nearby Tijeras Pueblo, the most jewelry-rich individual was a male 30 years or older with only one shell pendant and one stone bead.

If when they were alive, the individuals in this period's richest Hohokam, Casas Grandes, and Mountain Mogollon adult burials wore some portion of the ornaments with which they were interred, they would have contrasted with the vast majority of individuals from their respective settlements whose burials contained no jewelry. However, this contrast would have been only modest among the Hohokam and Casas Grandians and minimal among the Mountain Mogollon.

Other evidence indicates that some individuals from these three groups may have conveyed their high status more emphatically. Among the Casas Grandians, composite necklaces, decorated nose skewers, and copper plaques would have dramatically broadcast the high status of their wearers. Among the Hohokam, mosaics

3.16. Casas Grandes ceramic female effigy wearing multistrand necklace with dangling composite pendant, Paquimé, northern Chihuahua. Also note the figure's facial decoration and compare to Figure 5.9.

and other fancy adornments would have effectively conveyed the high status of the few individuals who wore them. The same would have been true for the Mountain Mogollon's rare turquoise-inlaid shell pendants.

That only one or two ornaments were found in the Ancestral Puebloans' richest adult burials suggests either that there were no status differences to broadcast or that such differences were not signified in visibly obvious ways. Evidence of the latter comes from the burial of a 22–24-year-old male from Arroyo Hondo who was interred with an assortment of ritual items but no ornaments.[48] This paucity of mortuary jewelry is a stark contrast with the necklaces, pendants, bracelets, and earrings depicted in Ancestral Pueblo kiva murals (Figures 3.17–18, also Figures 2.11–13, 2.18–19, 4.6, 4.12).[49] As part of ritual regalia, these adornments distinguished people with different ceremonial roles from each other and from their audience. The individuals who wore this jewelry were apparently not buried with it, perhaps because it was not a personal possession but rather belonged to their lineages or religious societies.

Raw Materials

Whatever their numbers, turquoise and shell ornaments conveyed the wearer's ability to procure valuable raw materials from great distances. The Cerrillos mines probably continued to be important during this period, along with other turquoise sources within the Southwest and beyond. Shell exchange networks were now dominated by two major centers: the Hohokam, and the site of Paquimé, which may have also become an intermediate supplier of copper bells.

The Hohokam continued to craft shell ornaments, as indicated by production debris at platform-mound sites, and to trade these products, evidenced by the *Glycymeris* bracelets in Grasshopper Pueblo's Burial #140. The contents of two storage rooms at Paquimé show the scale of its participation in the shell trade: over three million whole-shell beads, 33,000 shell-disc beads, and 21,000 shell tinklers that altogether represented over 70 Gulf of California species.[50] The presence of some *Glycymeris* bracelets and the absence of raw *Glycymeris* shell suggest that Paquimé's residents traded at least minimally with the Hohokam.

As in the previous period, raw material preferences no longer consistently signaled a person's cultural identity. Shell was most popular among the Casas Grandians, but their most reliable cultural markers were nose skewers, which seem to have been absent from the rest of the Southwest. The Hohokam continued to wear shell frequently, and *Glycymeris* bracelets—now mostly undecorated—probably continued to mark their cultural identity. However, the popularity of "other"

3.17. Ancestral Pueblo mural depiction of figure wearing a multistrand necklace with shell pendant and possible bead bracelets, Pottery Mound, north-central New Mexico. Also note the figure's headdress, hairstyle, and red strip hair decoration.

3.18. Ancestral Pueblo mural depiction of figure wearing multistrand necklace with front loop and ear pendant, Pottery Mound, north-central New Mexico. Also note the figure's headdress and hairstyle.

stone, usually black, had increased even more. "Other" stone was also the Mountain Mogollon's most frequently used raw material. The jewelry depicted in Ancestral Pueblo kiva murals seems to have been made mostly of shell (Figures 3.17–18, also Figures 2.12, 4.6).

For all groups, turquoise was at best the second- or third-choice material, but when inlaid on large shell pendants, it continued to broadcast the preeminence of high-status leaders and connections among them and with their predecessors. More distant connections strengthened the status messages of turquoise-inlaid ornaments and Paquimé's nose skewers, which emulated the adornments and ritual objects of rulers, priests, and warriors in the much more powerful Basin of Mexico empires.

Religious Symbolism

The sacred meanings associated with turquoise and shell jewelry persisted after AD 1300. The evidence of this religious content is similar to previous periods, but with one significant addition: the widespread presence of jewelry-rich, subadult burials. Raw turquoise and shell, unfinished and broken ornaments, and production debris were added to Hohokam, Casas Grandes, Mountain Mogollon, and occasional Ancestral Pueblo burials and to ritual deposits in Ancestral Pueblo kivas. Ritual deposits in Paquimé's various architectural features included shell, stone, and turquoise beads. Michael Whalen thinks that the site's two jewelry-filled storage rooms were ritual caches imbued with supernatural power.[51] Ornaments were also part of two of the site's most remarkable ritual objects: a human mandible inlaid with turquoise, and a human skull with turquoise ear pendants.

Jewelry also continued to be interred with ritual objects. At Paquimé, a prayer stick and pigments were associated with the ornaments in the two rich infant burials (#384/385). At Grasshopper Pueblo, Burial #140's assemblage of ritual artifacts included 74 projectile points, a bone wand, a bone rasp, a turquoise-and-shell-inlaid bone awl, and pigments, which together suggest that the interred man had a special ceremonial role.[52] If his *Glycymeris* bracelets and earrings were part of his ritual regalia, then they would have had been imbued with sacred meanings, similar to the jewelry depicted in Ancestral Pueblo kiva murals (Figures 3.17–18; also Figures 2.12–13, 2.18–19, 4.6).

Ornament colors continued to be symbolic, evidenced by the inclusion of ceremonial pigments in Paquimé's richest infant burials and Grasshopper Pueblo's Burial #140, as well as the discovery of pigment color stains on human bones and ritual artifacts at Pueblo Grande and Arroyo Hondo.[53] Hohokam zoomorphic forms probably also continued to represent core religious beliefs. Given that the turquoise-inlaid shell ornaments worn by the Hohokam, Mountain Mogollon, and Salado were turtle, frog, and bird effigies, they must have been imbued with multiple layers of symbolic meaning associated with their combinations of raw materials, forms, and colors.

Organizational Variation

The AD 1300–1450 period was characterized by a new range of organizational variability that would have affected a traveler's ability to identify high-status individuals by their jewelry. Such individuals would have been clearly visible among the Hohokam and Casas Grandians, less apparent among the Mountain Mogollon, and on everyday occasions absent among the Ancestral Puebloans. These differences reflect an overall decline in the degree of stratification throughout the prehistoric Southwest. The Ancestral Puebloans were now ostensibly egalitarian, and the ornament quantities in the richest Hohokam and Casas Grandes burials were less than five percent of those of their richest predecessors at Pueblo Bonito and RB568. Furthermore, in contrast with previous periods, no post–AD 1300 group had a single, most jewelry-rich burial, which suggests that decentralized leadership was now the norm.

The significance of the widespread appearance of rich subadult burials is unclear. At least a few infants, children, and adolescents were buried with 1,000 or more ornaments in previous periods.[54] But they are more obvious after AD 1300 due to the disappearance of very rich adult burials. Their visibility during this later period could also reflect a pan-Southwestern shift either in the quantities of ritual offerings added to infant and child graves or in how surviving family members expressed their own status when burying a son or daughter.

The picture of post–AD 1300 organizational variation becomes more complicated when settlement pattern data are considered.[55] Pueblo Grande was just one of three major platform-mound centers in the Lower Salt River valley, which, similar to the mortuary data, suggests group-oriented, decentralized leadership.[56] In contrast, Paquimé, with its platforms, effigy mounds, and ballcourts, was the Casas Grandians' primary center. So while their mortuary data indicate power-sharing, their settlement patterns suggest centralization.

The Mountain Mogollon and Ancestral Puebloans were much more egalitarian than their southern neighbors. Although both Point of Pines and Arroyo Hondo were very large pueblos, they seem to have been relatively independent and lacked the monumental structures of Pueblo Grande and Paquimé. Mortuary jewelry indicates modest status differences at best at Point of Pines, and minimal differences at Arroyo Hondo. However, this does not mean that every person of the same age and sex at Arroyo Hondo had equal status. The man interred with ritual paraphernalia clearly had a special ceremonial role, but any higher status that was associated with this role was not broadcast by adornments of any kind.

CONCLUSION

Upon arriving at most prehistoric Southwestern communities, our traveler could have identified the highest status residents by their greater quantities and kinds of ornaments. Limited only by access to the necessary resources, cultural norms, and body size, jewelry was additive. This gave it tremendous potential for emphasizing and reiterating a person's prominence. Necklace strands could be strung with more beads and pendants, a shell brooch or bracelet could be decorated with intricate turquoise mosaic, and multiple forms and arrangements could be worn on different parts of the body simultaneously. The status messages conveyed by wearing more jewelry were further reinforced by information about distant connections, religious beliefs, and heritage encoded in the adornments' raw materials, forms, decorations, and colors.

Moving from one group to another, our traveler could not have relied on jewelry alone to assess which was more stratified. Additional information would be needed. Did just one or several individuals wear more jewelry than everyone else? Was there only one very large site or several? What kinds of nonresidential architecture were present? Were there any other large-scale construction projects? After making such comparisons, a traveler would undoubtedly conclude that the late prehistoric Southwest was characterized by tremendous organizational variation for which jewelry revealed just one dimension.

From our contemporary perspective, we can see something in the most-prominent individuals' jewelry that our traveler could not: evidence of change.[57] For the Ancestral Puebloans, the change is dramatic. It begins with the highly stratified and centralized Pueblo II-period Chacoans whose leaders were adorned with lavish ornaments and ends with their ostensible egalitarian Pueblo IV-period descendants whose most prominent individuals wore minimal jewelry at most. Throughout the Southwest, the maximum quantities of mortuary jewelry declined after AD 1300; multiple burials containing more jewelry became the norm; the most jewelry-rich burials included subadults; and ornament markers of cultural affiliation were blurred. These changes were undoubtedly related to the social upheavals that accompanied late-period droughts, widespread migrations, and their associated organizational and ideological transformations.

In the northern Southwest today, Native peoples continue to craft and wear jewelry made of turquoise and silver, a historic-period introduction. Sold primarily to non-Indians in the United States and abroad, these adornments are highly visible examples of Native Americans' integration in the global capitalist economy. This jewelry also conveys messages similar to those seen prehistorically. Since both silver and the work of the best-known artists are expensive, an exquisitely crafted necklace or bracelet can broadcast a person's economic status. For contemporary Puebloans and Navajos, jewelry can also signal tribal affiliation or more often a generalized Southwest Native American cultural identity. Turquoise and designs that duplicate prehistoric religious symbols reference an ancestral heritage with deep historical roots. Wearing reminders of this heritage helps Native Southwesterners maintain their distinctive cultural identities in the face of tremendous outside pressure to assimilate into mainstream American society.

4

HAIR

by JILL E. NEITZEL

Throughout the prehistoric Southwest, a traveler would have observed people wearing a variety of hairstyles and hair decorations. Virtually everyone's hair was black, thick, and straight until middle age when its color gradually turned gray. But within this overall uniformity, hair was arranged and decorated according to cultural norms and personal preferences. As a result, it could communicate a lot about a person, including gender, social status, ceremonial roles, cultural affiliation, intergroup ties, ancestral heritage, and religious beliefs.[1] These messages further increased the redundancy of information broadcast by the individual's physical appearance, clothing, and ornaments.

Because intact human hair is rarely preserved in archaeological sites, most information about prehistoric hairstyles comes from depictions by Mimbres, Casas Grandes, and Ancestral Pueblo artists. Hair decorations are also illustrated and can be studied for these and other groups using excavated hairpins, caps, and headdresses.

I begin with a brief review of historic-period hairstyles and their associated identity messages.[2] Then, for the prehistoric period, I describe Mimbres, Casas Grandes, and Ancestral Pueblo coiffures and what they signaled about the people who wore them. This is followed by a consideration of hair decoration, which communicated a greater variety of messages. The most important messages also differed. While a person's hairstyle primarily conveyed gender, adornments mostly broadcast information about status and ceremonial roles.

HISTORIC-PERIOD HAIRSTYLES

According to historic-period accounts, indigenous Southwesterners took pride in their hair's appearance. They kept it clean, combed it using brushes made of grass or maguey fibers, and arranged it in a variety of styles. Long hair could hang freely or be tied, braided, or rolled. Tied hair and braids could be folded and wrapped with textile bands, and hair rolls could be wound over the top of the head. Cut hair ranged from shoulder length to very short, sometimes with bangs. One eye-catching style was ear whorls formed with the aid of a helper using a special wooden bow. Hair decorations included mud, paint, bone pins, turbans, and ceremonial headdresses.

Within any historic-period group, adult men and women typically arranged their hair differently, as did young and adult women. For example, at Taos pueblo, men wrapped braids behind each ear, and women twisted their hair at the back of the neck "chignon style." At the Hopi pueblos, young women who were past puberty but unmarried wore ear whorls (Figure 6.3);[3] married women wore two long ponytails with tied ends (Figure 6.4); and adult men wrapped a figure-eight bun at the back of the neck.

The styles worn by groups at the Southwest's western and southern margins also varied. Mohave women let their shoulder-length hair hang loose, while men rolled their long hair into 20–30 rope-like strands that hung down the back. Among the Yavapai, both genders wore bangs, but the women's style was loose and shoulder length, similar to the Mohave, and the men's was "often long and tied back." Among the Northern Tepehuan, adult men wore a pageboy cut, while women and girls wore braids. Seri styles included letting long hair hang loose, securing it in one or two braids, twisting it about the temples, and tying it over the head.[4]

In addition to their gender messages, historic-period styles often signified connections with neighboring groups. One interaction zone encompassed the Colorado Plateau where young women from many pueblos had ear whorls and clown kachinas wore anomalous arrangements—ear whorls at Isleta, topknots at Isleta and Cochiti, and horns made with cornhusks and mud at Santa Domingo and San Ildefonso.

A second interaction zone encompassed the south-central and western desert. Mohave, Quechan, Cocopa, and Maricopa men all wore hair rolls either down the back or twisted around the head. These groups also applied mud, sometimes combined with mesquite sap, to their hair. Quechan and Cocopa men used the mixture to keep their rolls in place and as decoration; the Mohave and Pima to keep their hair clean; and the Pima to kill lice and darken the color. Some Pima covered their hair with mud and then twisted it into a "helmet-like form" before drying, a practice that may have been for cleaning or for creating a distinctive coiffure.[5] The Gila River Pima and Colorado River Quechan also wore turbans made by wrapping woven bands around the head. This practice gave the illusion of increased hair bulk, which the Pima also achieved by adding braided horsetail hair to their own.

Some hairstyles were shared by members of disparate groups: allowing long hair to hang loose; braiding it in single or double strands; gathering, folding, and then wrapping it either on the side of the face or on the back of the neck; wearing bangs; and cutting hair very short as a sign of mourning. This sharing could have been the result of broad-scale interaction or deep historical connections.

Because group members typically wore a variety of styles, historic-period coiffures did not signal cultural affiliation. One possible exception comes from the Greater Southwest's outermost margins. The Spanish recorded shaved heads in northeast Mexico and called one group the Pelones, which means bald. The Pelones plucked out bands of hair from the front hairline to the top of the head and then decorated the exposed skin with painted and tattooed lines that continued across the forehead to the bridge of the nose.

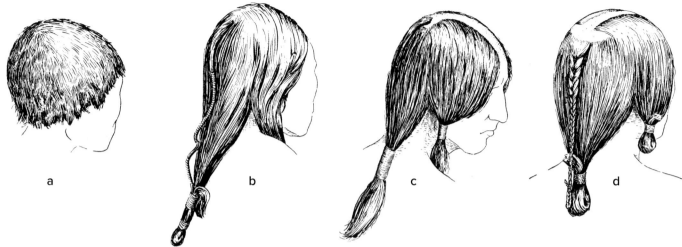

4.1. Basketmaker-period hairstyles, northeast Arizona.

PREHISTORIC HAIRSTYLES

Southwest archaeologists have published descriptions of only six preserved hairstyles that were recovered from prehistoric burials. Four date to the Basketmaker period, roughly 1,000 years earlier than this volume's time frame (Figure 4.1). The one woman had a short, ragged bowl-cut (Figure 4.1a). The Basketmaker men had longer hair, which was divided into segments and often folded before being wrapped at the ends (Figures 4.1b–d). This style was embellished with a thin, wrapped strip; a braid; or a shaved area on the top of the scalp. One of the two preserved hairstyles dating to the time period covered in this volume belonged to a Sinagua man (AD 1100–1250) whose long hair was gathered in back, possibly knotted, and then wrapped.[6] The other was a human-hair wig with multiple tufted braids found among a Desert Hohokam man's (AD 1000–1400) grave goods.[7]

Hairstyle Depictions

Depictions of people by prehistoric artists illustrate a much wider variety of hairstyles for this volume's timespan.[8] Mimbres bowls dating to AD 1000–1150 show most women with a pair of side buns and men with a folded and wrapped back bun or long hair loose in back (Figure 4.2; Appendix Table 4.1). Occasionally, women pulled long hair back and tied the end with an ornament, and men wore side ponytails or arranged a fringe on the top and back of the head.

Casas Grandes ceramic effigy vessels (AD 1200–1450) portray virtually everyone with their hair cut straight across the forehead and nape (Figures 4.3–4; Appendix Table 4.2).[9] However, men generally wore this style behind the ears, and women

4.2. Mimbres ceramic depictions of hairstyles, southwest New Mexico: (*a*) female figure with double side buns, Baca Site. Also note the figure's headband/cap and apron; (*b*) male figure with single back bun. Also note the figure's headband.

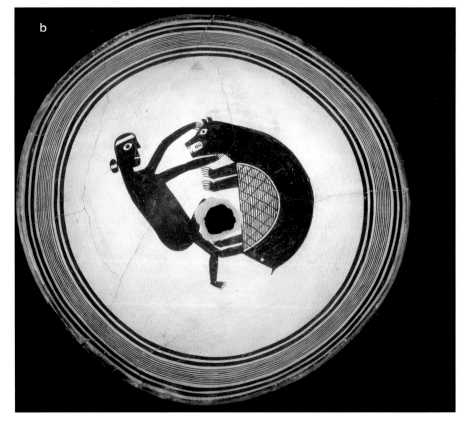

4.3. Casas Grandes ceramic male effigy with typical short, behind-the-ears hairstyle, northern Chihuahua. Also note the figure's headband and facial decoration.

in front.[10] A rare arrangement worn by one man and several gender-indeterminate individuals consisted of a large spit curl on each cheek.

Finally, both women and men wear the most popular Ancestral Pueblo hairstyles depicted in Pueblo IV-period kiva murals (AD 1300–1600): long hair loose and the uneven side cut (Figures 2.12–13, 3.17–18, 4.11–12; Appendix Table 4.3).[11] Only women wore ear whorls (Figures 2.19, 6.3) and two arrangements that may be poofed-out or unraveled ear whorls (Figure 4.5).[12] Among the less frequent styles, women also wore the side bob ("page boy") and the back bun (Figure 4.6); men wore medium-length hair loose; and both women and men wore long hair in back with an end wrap (Figure 4.7).

Some of these styles may have been restricted to certain pueblos. The bob and hair long in back with wrapped ends are seen only at the Ancestral Hopi site of Awat'ovi, and the single back bun, sideways M, and side comma only at the Ancestral Tiwa sites of Pottery Mound and Kuaua.

4.4. Female effigy vessel with a double macaw-headed diamond motif on her back. Also note the figure's hairstyle, headband, and facial decoration. Casas Grandes, Ramos Polychrome, AD 1280–1450, 30.5 × 20.6 × 23.9 cm (12 × 8⅛ × 9⅜ in).

4.5. Ancestral Pueblo mural depiction of female figure with double side buns, Pottery Mound, north-central New Mexico. This hairstyle was worn by young, unmarried women.

4.6. Ancestral Pueblo mural depiction of female figure with back bun, Pottery Mound, north-central New Mexico. This hairstyle was worn by married women. Also note the figure's necklace, earrings, and the strings of beads hanging on the kiva wall.

4.7. Ancestral Pueblo mural depiction of female figures with long hair pulled back and folded at ends, Awat'ovi, northeast Arizona. Also note the figures' feather hair decorations, wrapped blanket dresses, and sashes.

Hairstyle Identity Messages

The identity message that these hairstyles conveyed most consistently was gender. Mimbres men and women wore different coiffures; Casas Grandes men and women were distinguished by variants of the same style; and Ancestral Pueblo men and women were differentiated by less frequent arrangements. Laurie Webster has suggested that the Ancestral Puebloans' uneven side cut may have been associated with dual-gender individuals.[13]

Prehistoric coiffures may have also signaled cultural affiliation. The roughly contemporaneous Casas Grandes and Pueblo IV-period Ancestral Pueblo styles were completely different. Casas Grandians would have been easily identified by their short, sharp cuts and cheek curls, and the Ancestral Puebloans' by their ear whorls and uneven side cuts.

Some styles show historical connections. The pulled back, folded, and wrapped bun worn by Mimbres men resembles the preserved Sinagua coiffure. Given the roughly 50-year overlap between the Mimbres Classic period (AD 1000–1150) and the Sinagua specimen's dates (AD 1100–1250), this resemblance may be the result of either Mimbres-Sinagua interaction or historical ties. Either way, the style persisted among the Pueblo IV-period Ancestral Puebloans and historic-period Hopi.

The resemblance between Mimbres women's side buns and Pueblo IV-period Ancestral Pueblo ear whorls suggests historical connections between the two groups, but the style has a much longer history.[14] In northeast Arizona and northwest New Mexico, it is depicted on ceramics dating to AD 675–900; and in Canyon de Chelly in northeast Arizona, it was portrayed on a pictograph dating to AD 250. Pueblo women continued to wear the style during the historic period and still do today on special occasions. This continuity suggests that one of the identity messages conveyed by young women's side buns/ear whorls was their cultural heritage.

Perhaps even more important were this style's redundant messages about fertility.[15] For the historic-period Hopi, ear whorls signaled that the wearer was a young, unmarried female past puberty and able to produce children. The labels for this style—butterfly and squash-blossom whorls—also suggest deeper symbolic associations. In traditional Pueblo religions, butterflies and squash blossoms represent virginity, rain, abundant crops, and fertility.

HAIR DECORATION DEPICTIONS

While virtually all prehistoric Southwesterners had hair that needed to be tended, adding decorations was optional. Mimbres, Casas Grandes, and Ancestral Pueblo artists depicted a variety of adornments that broadcast more diverse identity messages than hairstyles.

Both Mimbres women and men used textile bands to secure side and back buns (Figure 4.2).[16] Other decorations that were worn predominantly, but not exclusively, by one gender were headbands and hats—mostly by women—and single and double feathers—mostly by men (Figures 4.2, 4.8a; also Figures 2.7, 3.3, 5.1b; Appendix Table 4.4). The association of women with headbands and hats was even stronger for those with patterned designs. Men wore the only gender-exclusive adornment—rare headdresses that included antlers, animal heads, rings of triangles and half circles, arrays of feathers, and a conical hat (Figures 4.8b–d).

Among the Casas Grandians, both women and men wore the most popular decorations: headbands and coverings that could be either headbands or hats (Figures 4.3–4; also Figures 5.10, 5.12; Appendix Table 4.5).[17] For both genders, these adornments shared the same color combinations, the most frequent design of a hollow square with a dot in the middle, and the rarer checkerboard pattern. However, only women had running zigzags, angular scrolls, and dotted triangles; and only men had solid bands, repeated solid steps, and hatched triangles or diamonds. Both genders wore stepped crowns (Figures 4.9–10), but only men wore snake headdresses and crowns with a large circle inside a square (Figure 4.9).[18]

Among the Pueblo IV-period Ancestral Puebloans, nearly all hair decorations were worn primarily, but not exclusively, by men (Appendix Table 4.6).[19] Most popular was a single stripe, usually red, extending down just one side of loose hair of varying lengths, including the uneven side cut (Figure 4.11; also 3.17). This decoration, which may have been painted or a woven fiber extension, could be combined with others.

Next most frequent decorations were elaborate headdresses of which almost three-fourths were complex arrays of feathers (Figure 4.11; also Figures 2.13, 2.19 and 3.18). The others took a diversity of forms, including flowers with multiple feather extensions, a flowering plant, a rainbow with extending branches, and elaborate branches with extending curlicues (Figure 3.17).

Slightly less popular were more modest feather combinations, consisting of sets of two to four plumes or a distinctive array of two long feathers with three to five associated short ones (Figure 4.7). The rarest feather decoration illustrated in kiva murals was a single plume, which was generally worn by women (Figure 4.12).

Similar to hairstyles, some Ancestral Pueblo decorations may have been restricted to certain groups.[20] Only kiva murals from the Ancestral Hopi site of Awat'ovi depict the two long-feather/three-to-five short-feather combinations. Only kiva murals from the Ancestral Tiwa sites of Pottery Mound and Kuaua depict elaborate headdresses and single feathers.

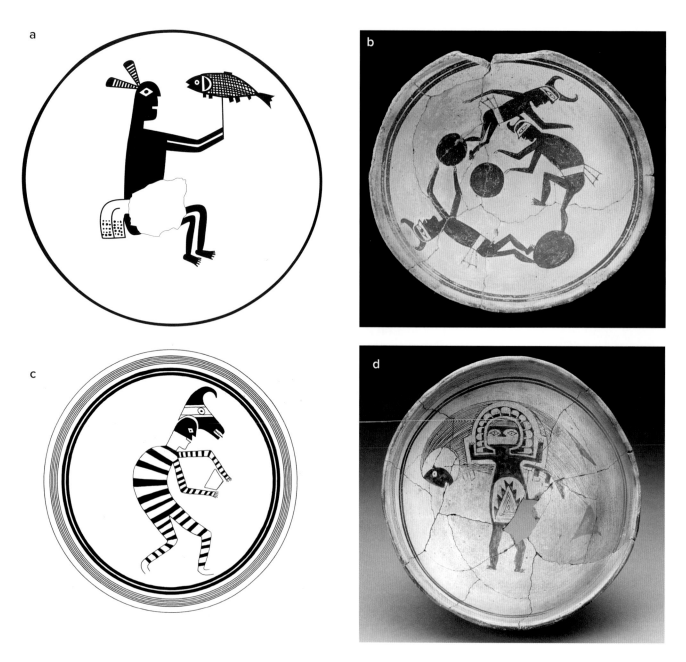

4.8. Mimbres ceramic depictions of hair decorations, southwest New Mexico: (*a*) male figure with double-feather adornment (also note his sash); (*b*) male figures with animal antlers (also note the figures' sashes); (*c*) figure with animal-head adornment. (Also note that the figure's encircling black-and-white bands resemble those of Pueblo clown kachinas as in Figure 6.2); (*d*) figure with feather headdress, Mimbres culture (southwest New Mexico, Galaz Site), classic black-on-white bowl (style III, ca. AD1000–1150), earthenware with slip and pigments, 5¼ × 9½ in.

4.9. Casas Grandes ceramic effigy with stepped headdress with circle, Casas Grandes, northern Chihuahua. Also note the figure's facial decoration. Ramos polychrome, ca. 1200–1450.

Identity Messages of Depicted Hair Decorations

The redundancy of gender messages conveyed by hairstyles and their decorations varied depending on the group. Only Mimbres women and men were distinguished by both their coiffures and adornments. Casas Grandes women and men wore variants of the same hairstyle, and both wore the popular headbands/hats and rare, stepped crowns. Their adornments differed only in some headband/hat designs and the exclusive association of snake headdresses and the circle-in-square crowns with men. Pueblo IV-period Ancestral Pueblo women and men both wore the most popular hairstyles. Most adornments were associated primarily with men, with only the single feather being worn more frequently by women.

While most people needed to arrange their hair on a regular basis, headdresses were impractical for everyday life and probably reserved for ceremonial occasions (Figures 4.8b–d, 4.11; also Figures 2.13, 3.17–18). Kiva murals depict them being worn in religious scenes (Figure 6.2 shows a painting by a present-day artist). These

4.10. Casas Grandes ceramic effigy with stepped headdress with checkerboard pattern, near Casas Grandes, northern Chihuahua. Also note the figure's facial decoration. Polychrome jar, ca. 1200–1400.

4.11. Ancestral Pueblo mural depiction of a "butterfly maiden" with wood and feather *tablita* headdress, Pottery Mound, north-central New Mexico. Also note the figure's hairstyle, red stripe hair decoration, decorated kilt, and fringed sash.

4.12. Ancestral Pueblo mural depiction of a male figure with single-feather adornment holding two parrots, Pottery Mound, north-central New Mexico. Also note the figure's hairstyle, kilt, and possible bracelet.

ritual activities seem to have been the domain of men, always for the Mimbres and usually for the Casas Grandians and Ancestral Puebloans. All aspects of ceremonial headdresses were probably imbued with religious symbolism—feathers and their colors, zoomorphic forms such as snakes and antlers, and geometric patterns—with the most elaborate adornments having the greatest symbolic content. This addition of meanings through embellishment was not possible for hairstyles alone.

Decorations also reinforced messages about cultural affiliation and heritage. The somewhat contemporary Casas Grandians and Pueblo IV-period Ancestral Puebloans could be distinguished by their adornments as well as their coiffures. Similarly, historical connections between the Mimbres and Pueblo IV-period Ancestral Puebloans are evident in both their decorations and hairstyles. Most striking are the two groups' elaborate feather headdresses, as shown in Figures 4.8d and 2.19. Both also adorned their hair with single feathers, although for the Mimbres this was done mostly by men, and among the Ancestral Puebloans mostly by women.

PRESERVED PREHISTORIC HAIR DECORATIONS

Hair decorations can also be studied using preserved specimens that include numerous bone hairpins and extremely rare caps and headdresses recovered from throughout the Southwest. These remains allow broader scale comparisons of the Mimbres, Casas Grandians, and Pueblo IV-period Ancestral Puebloans with other contemporary groups.

Pre–AD 1150

The Southwest's earliest hairpins date to the Basketmaker II period in northeast Arizona. Made from bone and wood, these 5–10-inch-long pins were topped with feathers and bound together in groups of three to six. Pictographs depict Basketmakers adorning their hair with one or two of these comb-like ornaments.

Later pins were generally a single piece of polished bone, often with carved or incised decorations (Figure 4.13a). The large number recovered from Mimbres sites indicates that they were used routinely to secure and decorate hair.[21] The tops of Mimbres pins were typically decorated with carved mountain sheep heads or horns. Less frequent were simple, painted or incised geometric designs; stepped carvings; and perforations for attaching feathers.

Among contemporaries of the Mimbres, only the Preclassic-period Hohokam had carved and incised snakes encircling pin shafts (Figure 4.13a).[22] The Hohokam also decorated pin tops with carved mountain sheep and probably inspired other groups, such as the Mimbres, to use the same embellishment. The Chacoans' most frequent decoration was carved geometric shapes, but similar to the Mimbres, they

4.13. Hairpins: (*a*) early bone pins; (*b*) late bone-and-wood pins.

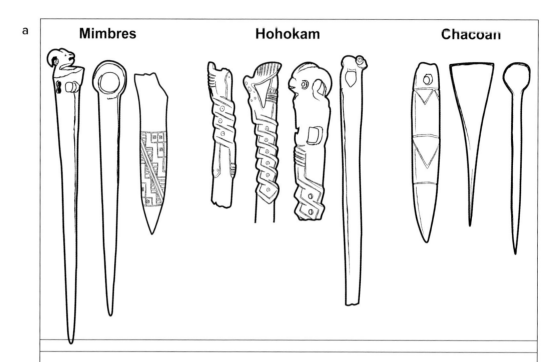

a

Mimbres   **Hohokam**   **Chacoan**

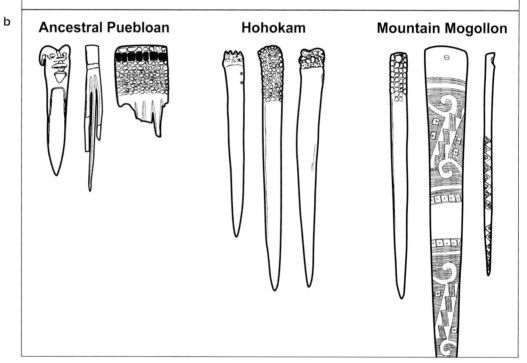

b

Ancestral Puebloan   **Hohokam**   **Mountain Mogollon**

sometimes perforated pin tops for feather dangles and incised simple geometric lines along pin shafts. The early Sinagua had the most diverse pins, embellished primarily with carved forms: geometric shapes that they shared with the Chacoans, mountain sheep that they shared with the Hohokam and Mimbres, and steps or notches and incised and painted designs that they shared with the Mimbres. Similar to the Mimbres and Chacoans, the Sinagua also perforated pin tops to attach feather dangles.

In stark contrast with hairpins, preserved head-coverings are extremely rare. All date to the late prehistoric period. During the AD 900–1150 period, a few Chacoans wore clay-covered basket caps that were sometimes decorated with painted designs.[23] The Sinagua later adopted this type of headgear (Figure 4.14). In addition to having two possible basket caps included among his grave goods, the Sinagua Magician wore a cap woven from approximately 4,000 extremely small, dark stone and white shell beads (Figure 4.15; also Figure 2.17).[24] Another Sinagua man, the one with the preserved coiffure, had a turban woven from white, tan, and red-brown cotton yarn.[25] The Hohokam also wore other kinds of headgear, as depicted on a set of late Preclassic-period Hohokam figurines (Figure 4.16).

4.15. Sinagua Magician's reconstructed head, Ridge Ruin, north-central Arizona. Note the figure's beaded cap and turquoise-inlaid red argillite nose plug. The beaded cap was made of 3,600 extremely small, black stone beads arranged in an alternating pattern with several hundred white shell beads. In McGregor's published illustration (1943:293), the bust has dangling circular ear pendants made of turquoise with inlaid shell, as shown in Figure 2.17.

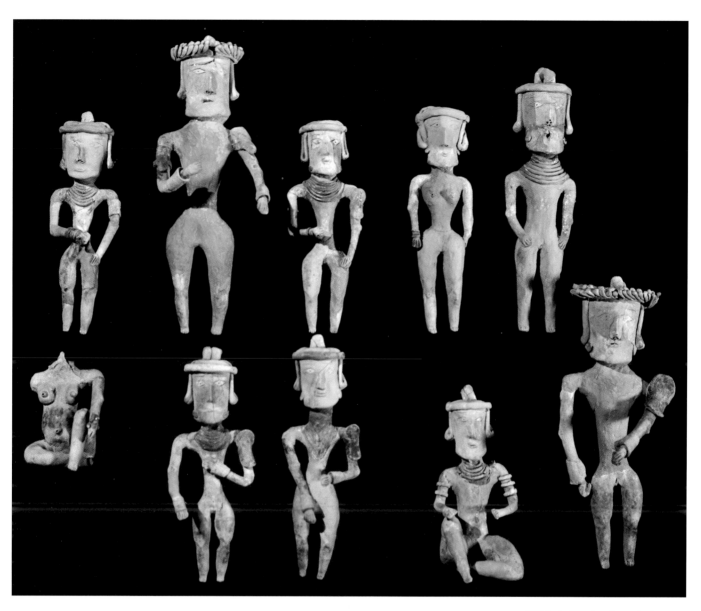

4.16. Late Preclassic-period Hohokam ceramic effigies with headgear, south-central Arizona. Also note the figures' hairstyles, necklaces, and bracelets. The arm and shoulder pads resemble those worn by Mesoamerican ballplayers.

4.17. Fremont feather headdress, Mantle's Cave, northwest Colorado.

The most spectacular preserved head-covering is a Fremont ceremonial head-dress composed of 370 colorful woodpecker tails on a fur base (Figure 4.17). Located mostly in Utah, the Fremont are often considered part of the Southwest because of their Pueblo characteristics. Their artists frequently depicted this kind of elaborate regalia in rock art.[26] The recovered specimen offers a tantalizing glimpse of the kinds of hair decorations that have not been preserved and of the colors that Mimbres artists were unable to show in their black-on-white headdress depictions (Figure 4.8d).

Post–AD 1150

The hairpins worn by post–AD 1150 groups varied in size, shape, embellishment, and material (Figure 4.13b).[27] At Paquimé, over three-quarters of the excavated bone hairpins were decorated, mostly with incised, linear designs on the top and occasionally along the shaft as well.[28] Rarer decorations included carved shapes, turquoise mosaic, pseudo-cloisonné, and painted designs.

In contrast, Pueblo IV-period Ancestral Pueblo bone hairpins mostly had carved tops depicting geometric shapes, steps, and animals such as mountain sheep (Figure 4.13b). The Ancestral Zuni site of Hawikuh was unusual in its preponderance of bone pins with simple, incised geometric designs; fork-like pins carved from single pieces of wood; and the addition of crude turquoise and jet inlay on some bone and/or wood pins.

The Classic-period Hohokam, Mountain Mogollon, and later Sinagua all perforated pin tops for feather dangles. Similar to the Zuni, the Classic-period

Hohokam and the Mountain Mogollon occasionally decorated bone pins with crude turquoise and occasional shell inlay (Figure 3.11). Some Mountain Mogollon pins are also notable for their incised designs. In addition to their bone pins, the Tonto Basin Salado sometimes wore wood pins embellished with carved zoomorphic figures.

Preserved head-coverings continue to be extremely rare after AD 1150. The Mesa Verde area is notable for two leather caps dating to the Pueblo III period and a child's looped cap with feathered yucca cordage that may date to either the Pueblo II or Pueblo III periods.[29] Another Pueblo-period looped cap that lacks precise dates has been recorded from northeast Arizona. To the south, preserved painted basket caps, similar to those worn by the Chacoans and Sinagua, have been reported for the Hohokam and Salado.[30]

Identity Messages of Preserved Hair Decorations

The primary messages conveyed by preserved hair decorations concerned social roles. Randy McGuire believes that Hohokam pins were worn by the leaders of courtyard groups; and Jeff Reid and Stephanie Whittlesey think that they signaled membership in Mountain Mogollon and Tonto Basin Salado sodalities.[31] The rare pseudo-cloisonné and painted pins of the Casas Grandians, as well as the inlaid pins of the Casas Grandians, Ancestral Puebloans, Classic Period Hohokam, and Highland Mogollon, may all have been markers of high status. Among the Sinagua, the Magician's beaded cap may have signified his high status or his role as a ceremonial leader. Nancy Odegaard and Kelley Hays-Gilpin have offered a similar interpretation for Chaco, Sinagua, Classic-period Hohokam, and Salado painted basket caps. The Fremont feather headdress clearly broadcast a ceremonial role.

With the exception of the snake designs on Hohokam pins, preserved hair decorations generally did not signal cultural affiliation. Instead, they evidenced intergroup connections for which the Sinagua had the most diverse array. The trading of pins may have contributed to their intergroup similarities. However, the extent to which local craftsmen imitated pin embellishments and finished pins were traded is unclear. Turquoise for mosaics was usually imported, but the final product may have been locally made to evoke widely shared views about marking high status.

Some later decorations also evidence connections with earlier groups and the continuing importance of heritage in defining identity. The zoomorphic forms carved on some Pueblo IV-period Ancestral Pueblo hairpins resemble earlier Mimbres and Sinagua decorations. Perforating pins for feather attachments was done first by the Mimbres and Chacoans, then the Sinagua, and finally the Classic-period Hohokam. Late turquoise-inlaid hairpins may have emulated earlier Chaco mosaics, and as such, enabled their wearers to legitimize and enhance their higher status, visibly referencing a much more powerful past.

Painted basket caps also show ancestral connections. Worn initially by the Chacoans, they were subsequently adopted by the Sinagua and later by the Classic-period Hohokam and Salado. This continuity may reflect ongoing, shared beliefs about marking high status or appropriate ritual regalia. It could also reflect the enduring influence of the earlier, more powerful Chacoans.

The Fremont feather headdress reinforces the continuity that is evident in Mimbres and Pueblo IV-period Ancestral Pueblo headdress depictions. The feathers and their colors were probably imbued with religious symbolism that would have also applied to feather pin dangles. Similarly, the colors and designs on painted basket caps and the color of turquoise on inlaid pins most likely had deeper meanings as well.

CONCLUSION

Our traveler could have discerned many aspects of people's identities from how they arranged and decorated their hair. To varying degrees, the messages conveyed by coiffures and their adornments reinforced one another as well as those broadcast by physical appearance, clothing, and jewelry. However, because of their potential for elaboration, decorations could communicate more information than hairstyles. Furthermore, their most important messages differed. The way people arranged their hair primarily signaled their gender, and how they decorated it highlighted their status and ceremonial roles.

The association of styles and decorations with other messages varied. Both could convey cultural affiliation, but hair decorations also broadcast connections with other groups. Some later coiffures and adornments referenced ancestral heritage, and both could be imbued with religious symbolism. However, decorations could further convey sacred meanings through materials, colors, arrangements, and designs.

The diversity that characterized prehistoric and early historic-period hairstyles gradually disappeared among indigenous Southwesterners after the Spanish arrived, followed by Euro-Americans. The most dramatic decline occurred with the establishment of Indian boarding schools in the late nineteenth century. In an effort to eliminate all practices that conveyed tribal identity and Indian-ness in general, these schools cut their students' hair.[32] Similar to the U.S. military in its treatment of new recruits, the intent was to visibly transform student identity.

Most twenty-first century indigenous Southwesterners arrange their hair in ways that may convey a generalized Native American identity. But traditional coiffures and decorations retain meaning and connection in special-occasion regalia. During religious and community ceremonies and in performances for outsiders, some young Pueblo women wear ear whorls and some women and men don headdresses. These practices honor their ancestral heritage and reassert their cultural distinctiveness within contemporary American culture.

5

FACIAL
DECORATION

by JILL E. NEITZEL

At some destinations, this volume's traveler would have observed people with painted or tattooed designs on their faces. Among the diverse personal characteristics that convey information about identity, the face is special and is the only one with a central role in developing social relationships and marking identity from infancy. Babies are drawn to faces and soon learn to distinguish those of their caregivers.[1] For adults, an unadorned face broadcasts a person's age, gender, and ethnicity. Added decoration can reinforce these messages and signal others regarding social roles, intergroup connections, heritage, and religious beliefs, to name a few.

Evidence of prehistoric Southwest facial designs comes from artistic representations of people on ceramics, kiva murals, rock art, and clay figurines.[2] Ceramics provide the most information for multiple groups—large samples for the Mimbres and Casas Grandians and very small samples for the Chacoans, Hohokam, and Salado. Yet for each of these groups, facial decoration reiterated the identity messages conveyed by other aspects of appearance.

To get a sense of the range of variation that may have characterized prehistoric facial decoration and its associated identity messages, I begin with a brief review of historic-period practices, and then proceed to the designs used prehistorically by the Mimbres, Chacoans, Hohokam, Salado, and Casas Grandians. I also consider the designs' symbolic meanings through comparisons with the historic-period Puebloans and the Aztecs and their predecessors in the Basin of Mexico.

I find that prehistoric Southwest groups decorated their faces with different design repertoires that conveyed cultural affiliation. The few shared designs were the product of shifting interaction patterns and suggest that heritage was an important part of cultural identity. The designs' sacred meanings generally related to water and fertility, concerns that were central to a pan-Southwestern/Mesoamerican cosmology.

HISTORIC-PERIOD FACIAL DECORATIONS

Historic-period groups throughout the Southwest painted designs on their faces. Those located along the Colorado River, its adjacent areas, and in northwest Mexico also applied facial tattoos.[3] The two modes of decoration were not mutually exclusive, for the majority of groups with tattoos also painted their faces.

Virtually all tattoos were applied using cactus spines or mesquite thorns to prick or cut a design onto the skin. The wound was then rubbed with charcoal dust, which upon healing left a permanent, black imprint. The notable exception to this standard practice was Tarahumara men who burned marks onto their faces.

Tattooed designs generally consisted of simple lines and dots whose meanings varied. For example, during puberty rituals, groups living along the Colorado River tattooed multiple vertical lines on young women's chins as a visual symbol of adulthood. Among the Seri, a single line on a woman's chin indicated that she was a captive. Along the Colorado River and in adjacent areas, tattoos also signaled intergroup connections and distinguished these groups from those in other parts of the Southwest.

Unlike tattoos, face paint was temporary and could be done in a variety of colors: black, white, red, and sometimes yellow or blue. The pigments were obtained from readily accessible charcoal and tree leaves or from clays and minerals, whose sources could be distant. The Seri stored dry pigments in a shell; ground them with a hard stone on a flat, circular palette made of granite; added water; and applied designs with a feather while viewing their reflections in a bowl of water.

Painted designs varied tremendously even within particular groups. For example, Seri women used all sorts of lines, dots, and circles, as well as solid coverage of substantial portions of the face.[4] Facial designs were also sometimes part of full-body painting or costumes. The best examples are the Puebloans' Koshare and Quirana clowns, whose entire bodies, including mouth and eyes, were encircled with alternating black-and-white rings (Figure 6.2; Figure 4.8c shows a possible Mimbres example).

Face painting was done primarily for ceremonial dances and occasionally for curing rituals and battle preparations. Among Pueblo groups, decorations conveyed an individual's ceremonial role, which could in turn be associated with a particular moiety. The colors contributed to these messages and also had deeper symbolic meanings associated with particular kachina deities, celestial bodies, directions, and varieties of corn, all of which ultimately related to the ceremonies' paramount concern with fertility.[5]

Painted designs could also convey other messages. Among the Seri, different genders and families had their own facial designs. Residents of the Humanas pueblos wore nose stripes that marked their ethnic or tribal identity. Similarly, the Yavapai practice of covering their entire bodies with red clay for sun protection may have also conveyed their cultural affiliation.

PREHISTORIC-PERIOD FACIAL DESIGNS

Prehistoric ceramics that depict facial designs include Mimbres bowls and Mimbres, Chacoan, Hohokam, Salado, and Casas Grandes effigies.[6] Among the diverse Classic-period Mimbres (AD 1000–1150) designs, the most popular were cheek tick marks followed by the "Lone Ranger" eye covering (Figure 5.1a–b; Appendix Table 5.1).[7] Moderately frequent designs consisted of various kinds of lines on different parts of the face and solid rectangles or triangles on or by the chin (Figures 5.1c–d).

Among the Chacoans, an undated, complete ceramic effigy had vertical lines on both sides of the face and zigzag lines above and hanging from the lips (Figure 5.2). The designs on other fragmentary, effigy faces dating to the Pueblo II period (AD 900–1150) consisted mostly of varied combinations of lines, sometimes with dots (Figure 5.3).[8] One had only dots arranged in linear and curvilinear patterns (Figure 5.4a). The few Pueblo III-period designs (AD 1150–1300) resembled their predecessors but with a greater emphasis on sets of parallel lines that either hung from a horizontal line or were angular.[9]

Most of the rare Preclassic-period Hohokam designs (pre–AD 1150) consisted of multiple dots, covering the entire face below the eyes (Figure 5.4b; also see Figures I.4, 3.6a).[10] One had small X and plus (+) marks on the lower half of the face beneath a solid, horizontal band. The remaining two faces had solid paint covering the lower half and a line down the nose. In contrast with the Preclassic preference for dots, the rare Classic-period designs (AD 1150–1450) were all different from one another. With its red-on-buff paint, the only clearly local example has a worn-away line down the nose and a pair of horizontal lines with appended tick marks on each cheek (Figure 5.5). Two other examples, one black-on-white and the other polychrome, may be imports (Figures 5.6–7).[11]

Among the few documented Salado designs (AD 1150–1450), one stylistically similar pair had bands encircling the outer edge of the face and crossing horizontally between the nose and lips (Figure 5.8a).[12] One member of the pair had an extra horizontal band on either side of the nose with a fringe.[13] The remaining Salado designs were different from one another. One had dots on the right cheek, a solid covering with a short fringe on the left, and vertical lines on the chin (Figure 5.8b). Another had hatched triangles on each cheek, horizontal lines extending from the outer edge of each eye, and single, diagonal lines with tick marks on each side of the chin. The last had a pair of vertical lines on each cheek; possible extended eyeliner; and a horizontally oriented, hollow rectangle between the nose and mouth with tick marks resembling teeth on the interior.

The Medio-phase Casas Grandians (AD 1200–1450) have the greatest variety of depicted designs (Figures 5.9–5.12; also Figures 3.16, 4.3–4, 4.9–10; Appendix Table 5.2,).[14] Most frequent were a line down the top of the nose, chin tick marks, and stepped cheeks. Of moderate frequency were extended eyeliner, eyeglasses, various kinds of cheek lines, and cheek feathers. Because individual faces were often decorated with several different designs, the entire sample was characterized by

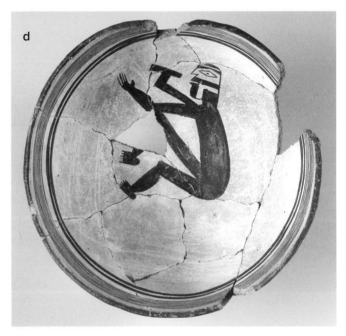

5.1. Mimbres ceramic depictions of facial decoration, southwest New Mexico: (*a*) triple cheek marks; note the figure's tunic and breechcloth; (*b*) Lone Ranger eye covering; Mimbres culture (southwest New Mexico, Galaz archaeological site), classic black-on-white bowl (style III, ca. AD 1000–1150), earthenware with slip and pigments, 2¼ × 5½ in; note the figure's hair decoration; (*c*) extended eye liner, X-mark on cheeks, chin lines bordered by solid triangles; (*d*) bowl, eleventh–mid-twelfth centuries; Mimbres; earthenware with slip; 4¾ × 9¼ inches; note the horizontal band below nose and solid rectangles on chin and lower cheek.

5.2. Chaco male effigy with parallel sets of straight and zigzag lines on face, Chaco Canyon, northwest New Mexico. Also note the figure's sash.

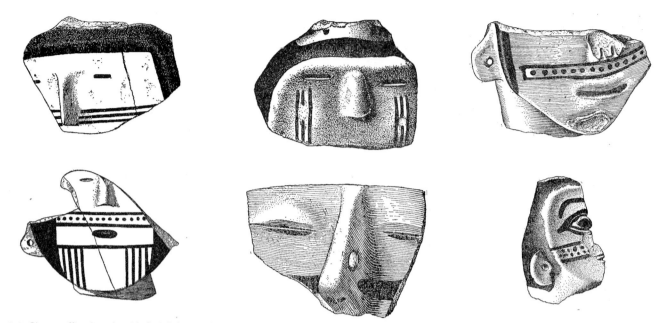

5.3. Chaco effigy heads with facial decorations consisting of various combinations of lines and dots, Pueblo Bonito, Chaco Canyon, northwest New Mexico.

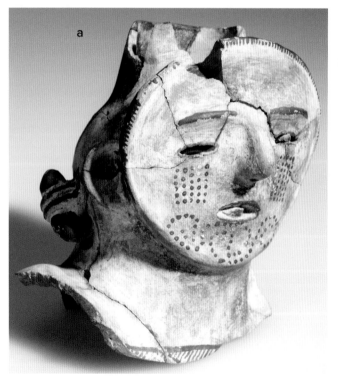

5.4. Effigy heads with dotted facial designs: (*a*) Chaco face with dots in parallel rows and scroll pattern, Pueblo Bonito, northwest New Mexico; also note the figure's hairstyle; (*b*) Hohokam face with dots in random pattern, West Branch site, south-central Arizona.

5.5. Classic-period Hohokam effigy head with facial decoration, Los Muertos, south-central Arizona. The face's red-and-buff colors indicate that it was locally made.

5.6. Classic-period Hohokam effigy head with facial decoration, Las Acequias, south-central Arizona. The face's black-and-white colors suggest that it was imported from the north.

5.7. Classic-period effigy head with facial decoration, Los Muertos, south-central Arizona. The jar has been identified as Tonto Polychrome, which suggests that it may have been imported from the Tonto Basin.

overlapping design combinations. Consequently, Casas Grandes faces exhibited a stylistic coherency despite the diversity of individual designs.

Identity Messages

The distinctive design repertoires used by approximately contemporary groups suggest that facial decoration signaled cultural affiliation. During the pre–AD 1150 period, the Preclassic Hohokam, Pueblo II-period Chacoans, and Mimbres applied different designs. The same was true during the post–AD 1150 period for the Pueblo III-period Chacoans, the Casas Grandians, and to a lesser extent the Classic-period Hohokam and Salado.

5.8. Salado ceramic effigies with facial decoration, Tonto Basin, east-central Arizona: (*a*) female effigy with line bordering lower part of face and connected by two horizontal lines, one of which has appended hooks; (*b*) male effigy with a mix of designs characteristic of other groups; also note the figure's shell earrings.

5.9. Casas Grandes ceramic male effigy with a pair of horizontal lines on each cheek, northern Chihuahua. Compare with Figure 3.16.

5.10. Seated male effigy vessel with raised right knee, crosshatches, dotted bands, and zigzag markings; also note the figure's headband; Casas Grandes, Ramos Polychrome, AD 1280–1450, 16.5 × 12.4 × 14 cm (6½ × 4⅞ × 5½ in).

The few shared designs may reflect intergroup connections. During the pre–AD 1150 period, both the Mimbres and Hohokam decorated the lower halves of their faces with solid paint, and the Mimbres and Chacoans both used extended eyeliner.[15] These patterns are consistent with other evidence for Mimbres ties with both the Hohokam and Chacoans.[16] While the Pueblo II-period Chacoans and Preclassic-period Hohokam both applied dots to their faces, they did so in different ways (Figure 5.4). The absence of any other shared designs suggests that these two groups were not interacting, at least in ways reflected by facial decoration.

Jill E. Neitzel

During the post–AD 1150 period, the Hohokam, Salado, and Casas Grandians drew lines down the nose.[17] The Casas Grandians and Salado also shared hatched triangles.[18] These concurrences evidence connections among the three groups. In contrast, the Pueblo III-period Chacoans did not share any designs with other late-period groups, which suggests even greater isolation than in the preceding period.

Some facial decorations may have connected later groups with their ancestral past.[19] The Casas Grandians shared at least eight designs with their Mimbres predecessors: chin lines, eyeglasses, extended eyeliner, zigzag cheek lines, the Lone

Ranger eye covering, chevrons, chin triangles, and horizontal lines below the nose.[20]
The Pueblo III-period Chacoans shared three designs with the Pueblo II-period
Chacoans: dots between parallel lines, pairs of parallel right-angle lines to the side
of each eye, and sets of three vertical lines extending down from a horizontal line
on either side of the mouth. Perhaps due to the major cultural transformation that
occurred around AD 1150, the Classic-period Hohokam shared just one facial design
with their Preclassic-period predecessors—a line drawn down the nose.[21]

    Facial designs could also signal a person's gender. Among the Mimbres, only
men wore the Lone Ranger eye covering, a solid covering of the lower half of the

face, vertical lines covering the lower half of the face, and pairs of diagonal lines on the cheeks. Only women had parallel, angular lines on the lower sides of their faces. Among the shared designs, women wore virtually all of the examples of vertical cheek marks (single, double, and triple) as well as crosshatching covering the lower half of the face. In contrast, dots or solid lines extending straight down from the eyes were worn mostly by men.

Among the Casas Grandians, Maria Sprehn Malagon found that women wore chin lines more than twice as often as men. In addition, women's lines were black, which she interpreted as tattoos; men's were black and red, which she interpreted as painted decorations.[22] In a later study, Christine and Todd VanPool found that only men adorned their chins with triangles and scrolls and that men and women shared other decorations in varying proportions.[23] In descending order of frequency, more men had weeping eyes, cheek squiggly lines, cheek V-shapes, eyeglasses, and ear ticking; and more women had cheek steps, cheek lines, cheek arrows, and chin ticking.

SYMBOLIC MEANINGS

Analogies with their historic-period descendants suggest that prehistoric Southwesterners decorated their faces primarily on ceremonial occasions and that the designs were imbued with religious symbolism.[24] Hopi ethnographies document designs that were also used prehistorically, and this continuity suggests that design meanings may have also extended into the ancestral past. Ethnohistoric and archaeological evidence from the Basin of Mexico expands the spatial and temporal scales of a few designs and perhaps their associated meanings.

Hopi Religious Symbols

Ethnographers describe the Pueblo religion as centering on a pantheon of kachina spirits, ancestors whose diverse roles related mostly to fertility.[25] In a seasonal cycle of ceremonies, men perform most ritual songs and dances that beseech the spirits to bring rain and bountiful crops (Figure 6.2). The performers' elaborate costumes represent different kachinas, and all aspects of the garments, masks, and face and body paint are imbued with religious symbolism. Paints are prepared in elaborate rituals from sacred plants and minerals and then applied in patterns with cosmic significance that transform the wearer "into a sacred being with a specific role to play."[26]

Hopi kachina mask decorations offer the best analogies for prehistoric facial designs. In profusely illustrated books on Hopi costumes and kachina dolls, I identified 15 mask designs that prehistoric Southwesterners also used to decorate their faces (Appendix Table 5.3); and for seven, I found accounts of their symbolic meanings.[27]

The Hopi mask designs all reference water and fertility—messages that are consistent with the kachina ceremonies' main purpose.[28] They depict weather-related phenomena, such as rain, moisture, lightning, and clouds; stars, which are important to the start of the kachina cycle and the first planting; and corn, the Hopi's most important crop.[29] Other designs that are seemingly unrelated to successful farming (e.g., warriors' marks) decorate kachinas whose roles and dances involve bringing rain, germinating seeds, ensuring successful harvests, and promoting reproduction in general. All of these messages are reinforced by the symbolic meanings that the Hopi associate with designs' colors.

Mesoamerican Religious Symbols

Despite being located more than 1,000 miles south of the present-day United States-Mexico border, three empires that succeeded one another in the Valley of Mexico offer further insights into prehistoric Southwest facial designs. The Southwest groups discussed previously in this chapter coincided with the two later empires, the Toltec (AD 900–1250) and the Aztec (AD 1250 to the Spanish conquest in 1521).[30]

Numerous parallels have been identified between the Aztec and historic-period Pueblo religions, including an overriding concern with fertility and water, the impersonation of deities during religious ceremonies, and the symbolism associated with every aspect of ceremonial regalia.[31] No historic documentation exists for the Toltec religion. However, Aztec codices and Spanish documents record how Aztec emperors appropriated Toltec cosmology and myths and established fictive, ancestral links with the earlier empire. Thus, the Aztec-Pueblo religious parallels probably apply to the Toltecs as well.

The Aztec codices include illustrations of deities and the priestly elite during ceremonies.[32] Surveying these illustrations, I identified five facial designs also used by prehistoric Southwesterners (Appendix Table 5.3). Ernest Christman's study of Aztec gods depicted on Casas Grandes ceramics revealed two more designs that the Aztecs shared with the Mimbres and Casas Grandians.[33] Only the Pueblo II- and Pueblo III-period Chacoans had no facial design matches with the Aztecs.

All but one design used by both prehistoric Southwesterners and the Aztecs also decorated Hopi kachina masks. This design continuity spanning the nineteenth- and early twentieth-century Hopi, the early sixteenth-century Aztecs, and prehistoric Southwest groups may extend even farther back in time. Just as Aztec rulers established ancestral connections with the Toltecs, Toltec rulers did the same for the empire that preceded them. In their architecture and sculpture, the Toltecs referenced the massive city of Teotihuacán, which was the center of the Valley of Mexico's first empire from 150 BC to AD 750.[34]

In published illustrations of Teotihuacán's painted murals, I identified two facial designs that were also used by later groups in both the Valley of Mexico and the Southwest (Appendix Table 5.3).[35] One was the Lone Ranger eye covering that was also used by the Mimbres, Casas Grandians, and Aztecs. The other consisted of dots, which covered the lower half of the face at Teotihuacán, and either the entire face or half of it by the Preclassic Hohokam, the Salado, and the Hopi. These matches evidence continuity in designs and perhaps their symbolic meanings over a span of perhaps 1,400 years.[36]

The two concordances between prehistoric Southwest and Teotihuacán facial designs could be just coincidence, or they could be the result of Teotihuacán's influence on the Toltecs and Aztecs who in turn influenced their prehistoric Southwest contemporaries. Alternatively, Teotihuacán could have influenced contemporary Southwest groups in ways that their descendants perpetuated. Another possibility is that Teotihuacán and Southwest groups shared a cosmology whose history extended even farther back in time.

CONCLUSION

During a journey across the Southwest, our traveler would have seen a wide array of facial decorations whose identity messages reinforced those conveyed by people's physical appearance, clothing, ornaments, and hairstyles. In some groups, women and men applied different designs, and each group's distinctive repertoire expressed its cultural identity. A small number of shared designs showed interaction among contemporary groups; and those shared by ancestral and descendent groups reflected the importance of heritage in defining cultural identity.

Although their specific meanings may have been unknown, a traveler would have recognized many designs as religious symbols, especially if they were being worn on ceremonial occasions. Any one decoration probably had multiple layers of meaning. For example, a zigzag line might be a symbol for lightning, which could be associated with rain and in turn with certain deities and myths. The line's colors would have had their own set of complementary meanings. At their most profound level, virtually all facial designs and their colors shared the same religious preoccupation with water and fertility—the two essentials for survival in the arid Southwest.

Some indigenous Southwesterners continue to decorate their faces on ceremonial occasions today, using the same designs as their prehistoric ancestors. Even though their religious meanings may no longer be known, the designs continue to express the importance of heritage. In doing so, they contribute to the Native American identity being conveyed by the entire ritual costume and performance.

6
LANGUAGE

by JANE H. HILL

Moving across the Southwest, a prehistoric traveler would have encountered people who spoke different languages. Language functions to communicate messages, but the way we speak also conveys information about who we are. Most people are members of multiple groups, many of which have their own distinctive ways of talking. Thus, over the course of a conversation, a person's utterances can reveal, for example, his or her cultural affiliation, community residence, gender, status, and connections with other cultural groups.

One major obstacle severely limits any effort to study the identity messages encoded in the speech of prehistoric Southwesterners: none of them had writing. In the absence of any material evidence, their languages must be investigated indirectly through the discipline of historical linguistics. In this chapter, I use its phylogenetic approach to assess the historical relatedness and origins of the best documented of the Southwest's indigenous languages. Then, I apply the areal approach to define language areas and to examine the distributions of loan words related to the kachina religion.

My analyses reveal two patterns that would have been apparent to our traveler. The first is the presence of two language areas within which the speakers of different languages interacted, sometimes to the point of becoming multilingual. The other is a stark gender difference in the distribution of kachina loan words in the northern language area. While Pueblo men used loan words frequently in rituals, women used them rarely for feast foods. This contrast suggests that our traveler was most likely an adult man who visited distant places not just to trade but also to participate in religious ceremonies.

PHYLOGENETIC LINGUISTICS

Historical linguists use the phylogenetic approach to sort languages into language families, which are groups of languages whose members can be shown to be descended from a single common ancestor.[1] Once a language family has been defined, then the phylogenetic approach seeks to define the characteristics of its ancestral or protolanguage.

Analyzing Language Families

Language families are defined by grouping languages that share either (1) vocabulary with similar meanings and regular sound correspondence, or (2) anomalies in the patterning of structures such as the conjugations of verbs or the declension of nouns.

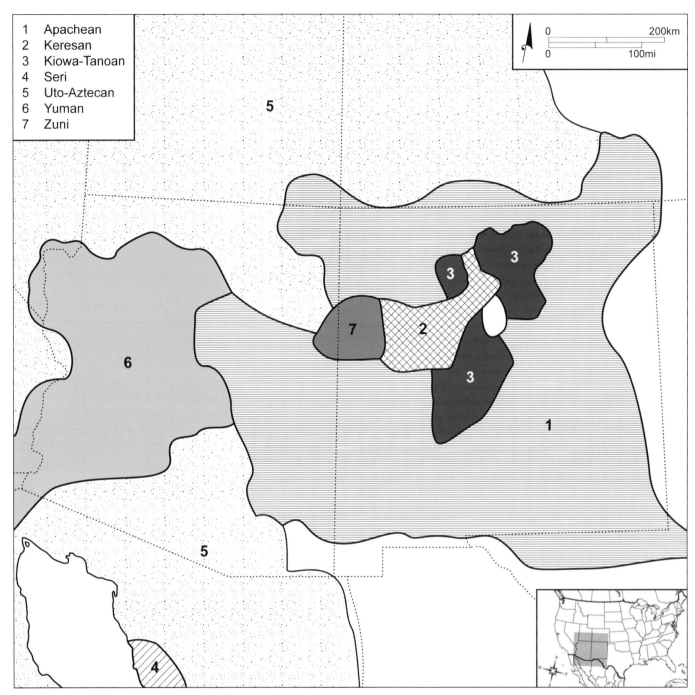

1	Apachean
2	Keresan
3	Kiowa-Tanoan
4	Seri
5	Uto-Aztecan
6	Yuman
7	Zuni

6.1. Map of Greater Southwest language families.

These similarities can be found in successively larger sets of languages, resulting in the definition of smaller families that together comprise a larger family. Once the members of a language family have been identified, their similarities illuminate characteristics of the family's protolanguage.

Various levels of linguistic relatedness are expressed as processes of branching and differentiation from the common ancestral state, similar to models in biological evolution. Two language families that lack a shared, common ancestor are said to be distinct. But comparisons may reveal even deeper roots that preceded the development of the two families' respective protolanguages. The members of a language family can also be sorted into lower-level units—subfamilies or subgroups—by looking for shared innovations that depart from the features of the reconstructed protolanguage.

Generally, speakers of different languages within the same family do not understand each other unless they are bilingual. For instance, as members of the same subfamily (Germanic) of the Indo-European language family, English and German are pretty closely related, but an English speaker would have to study German to understand it. Linguists use the term "dialect" to refer to distinctive regional varieties that retain mutual intelligibility—for instance, the New Zealand dialect of English sounds odd to most Americans, but they have no trouble understanding it, and vice versa, unless some strange local slang is used.

Within language families, there can be tremendous cultural diversity. For instance, Indo-European languages are spoken in south India (Oriya, Marathi); in parts of the Middle East in Afghanistan, Iran, and Kurdistan; in Europe from Russia to Greece to Norway; and in the Americas. Yet clearly, I do not have much in common culturally with most people who speak Oriya or Kurdish!

Most of the time, people who speak the same language share other cultural characteristics. But there are dramatic exceptions. For example, Spanish is spoken by two groups who have almost nothing in common culturally: Indian peasants in Mexico and Madrileño elites in Spain. The reverse case of people who share the same culture necessarily speaking similar languages is notoriously untrue. We can refer loosely to the "Pueblo" culture in the northern Southwest, but about eight mutually unintelligible languages are spoken in the Pueblos.

Southwest Language Families

From the phylogenetic perspective, the Greater Southwest is extremely diverse, with six distinct language families encompassing more than 20 different languages (Appendix Table 6.1). From west to east (roughly), these families include Yuman, Uto-Aztecan, Zuni, Keresan, Kiowa-Tanoan, and Apachean (Figure 6.1).[2] Only

Zuni and Keresan are restricted to the Greater Southwest. The other language families extend well beyond its borders. Yuman reaches the Pacific Coast and includes several languages of Baja California. Kiowa-Tanoan can be found both in New Mexico and on the Great Plains. The Uto-Aztecan family is distributed from El Salvador to Idaho and from the Pacific Ocean to east Texas; and its languages are spoken by such culturally diverse groups as Western Shoshone hunter-gatherers of the North American Great Basin and members of the Aztec civilization in the Basin of Mexico.

The distribution of Apachean offers an excellent example of language family embeddedness. With the exception of one language spoken on the Plains (Lipan), the Apachean languages are spoken exclusively in the Greater Southwest; but this language family comprises the southern portion of the Athapaskan family, whose northern members extend across Alaska and western Canada. Athapaskan is in turn part of the Na-Dene family, which also includes the Northwest Coast languages Tlingit and Eyak. Even more broadly, and, at the deepest level, Na-Dene is probably related to the Yeneseic languages of Siberia.[3]

Southwest Protolanguages

The protolanguages from which each of the Southwest's language families descended vary greatly in their locations and in the timing of their differentiation.[4] Some protolanguages were spoken within the Greater Southwest and their diversification took place there. Others originated elsewhere, were brought to the region by migrants, and once here, diversified.

The language families that diversified from their respective protolanguages most recently are Keresan and Apachean. Given that the distribution of Keresan is restricted to the northern Southwest, it seems likely that its protolanguage originated here as well.[5] The Keresan languages diverged roughly 500 years ago. Although Zuni's timing may be similar, its dates cannot be estimated, because it is an isolate with no known phylogenetic relatives.[6]

Proto-Apachean was brought to the Southwest by immigrants, and its differentiation occurred here. While its ultimate Athapaskan origins were in present-day eastern Alaska and the Yukon Territory of Canada, Proto-Apachean has been dated in the Southwest to roughly 700 years ago based on two sets of evidence.[7] The protolanguage included an expression for "corn," which translates as "enemy-food," and archaeological data suggest that the Proto-Apachean ancestors probably first encountered maize cultivators in the northern plains by the twelfth century.

The Yuman, Kiowa-Tanoan, and Uto-Aztecan protolanguages are much older. The location of the Yuman protolanguage is unknown—differentiation

Jane H. Hill

of its descendant languages occurred no more than 2,000 years ago. Analyses by David Shaul and myself have suggested that one of the Yuman ancestral languages, Proto-Colorado River Yuman, may have been among the languages spoken by the prehistoric Hohokam.

The Kiowa-Tanoan languages are probably indigenous to the Greater Southwest, and their date of initial differentiation has been estimated at 3,000–2,500 years ago.[8] These dates were derived from words for corn that were loaned into Proto-Kiowa-Tanoan from Proto-Northern Uto-Aztecan. Corn first appeared on the Colorado Plateau no earlier than about 3,500 years ago, which means that the loans must date from after a time that Proto-Kiowa-Tanoan was still spoken. Good candidates for speakers of the common ancestral language are the Durango or Eastern Basketmakers. Kiowa, one of the four main branches of Kiowa-Tanoan, is a language of Great Plains bison hunters. Exactly how and when they left the Southwest is uncertain.

Of all the Southwest language families, Uto-Aztecan diverged from its proto-language longest ago.[9] My estimated dates of no earlier than 4,400–4,000 years ago are derived from linguistic and archaeological evidence. Proto-Uto-Aztecan includes words implying knowledge of pottery, and words for "pot" and "clay" with regular sound correspondence are found in daughter languages in several subfamilies of Uto-Aztecan.[10] Since pottery in any area where Proto-Uto-Aztecan might have been spoken is no older than about 4,400 years ago, the protolanguage must have still been spoken at this time.

Elsewhere, I have argued that Proto-Uto-Aztecan was spoken on the northwest edge of Mesoamerica and that it was brought to the Southwest by immigrants. The northern branch of the Uto-Aztecan family may have differentiated initially around 3,500–3,000 years ago, within the emerging Greater Southwest macroregion.[11] These dates were derived from the Proto-Northern Uto-Aztecan words for corn that, as discussed previously, were loaned into Proto-Kiowa-Tanoan.[12] Macroregional dynamics probably contributed to ongoing connections among the Greater Southwest's various northern Uto-Aztecan languages, among several of its southern Uto-Aztecan languages, and between these languages and members of other language families. For example, David Shaul and I think that shared involvement in the prehistoric Hohokam regional system may be the source of similarities among Opatan and Tepiman languages, and between them and Colorado River Yuman.[13]

AREAL LINGUISTICS

Historical linguists use the areal approach to define language areas and to identify loan words. This approach analyzes the distributions of linguistic features that crosscut language boundaries but do not satisfy the criteria for descent from a common ancestor.[14] In defining language areas, special weight is given to features that are relatively specific and uncommon, since very general or common features may simply be shared by chance. Multiple examples of shared specific and uncommon features are better evidence than single features. Loan words—vocabulary that the speakers of one language have adopted from another language—are an important feature used to define language areas, identify more distant connections, and provide insights into the contexts within which these words were diffused.

Language Areas

Language areas are thought to reflect interaction spheres where many speakers manage local language diversity by becoming multilingual. Linguistic resources of all types, originating in any of the region's languages, can move across the region as they are adopted by multilingual speakers. Once such linguistic resources are in circulation, they may become associated with desired identities and be adopted even by monolingual speakers in contexts where manifesting such identities is appropriate. A good example is the use of Italian words on the menus posted by Starbucks stores. They exploit the prior association of Italian, not only with coffee culture but with luxury goods of many types. All over North America, people who otherwise don't know a word of Italian step up to the counter daily and order *grande* and *venti* servings of *latte*. Through such usages customers show that they are skilled consumers of a luxury product.

At least two language areas have been identified in the Greater Southwest.[15] David Shaul and I defined one in its southwest portion based on two unusual innovations in the use of sounds: glide hardening, and the development of retroflex coronals (definitions in chapter notes).[16] These innovations are shared among all the Tepiman (southern Uto-Aztecan) languages, including Upper Piman (Akimel O'odham and Tohono O'odham, formerly "Pima" and "Papago"), Lower Piman, Northern and Southern Tepehuan, and the Colorado River subfamily of the Yuman languages. Glide hardening also spread into the non-Tepiman southern Uto-Aztecan languages of Opata, Eudeve, and Yaqui.[17] In the case of retroflex consonants, the Upper Piman languages and all Yuman languages exhibit both coronal and retroflex stops and spirants. Since these distinctions are widespread in California, where several Yuman languages are located, the direction of spread was surely from Yuman into Tepiman.

Based on the rarity and specificity of these phonological innovations across the Piman-Yuman family boundary, David Shaul and I suggest with some confidence that they represent a genuine language area. Furthermore, we think that these unusual developments might reflect the Hohokam sphere of interaction. If we are correct, the formation of this linguistic area dates to at least AD 750.

Lexical and phonological evidence suggest that all of the Pueblo languages should be considered part of a second language area in the north.[18] Paul Kroskrity observed that all but one of these languages share a pattern of different male and female usage of certain expressive words, greetings, and politeness formulas, although the lexical items involved are entirely different from pueblo to pueblo.[19] Two phonological features are widely shared, but with somewhat different distributions. The first is a glottalized series of stop consonants, which appears in Keresan, Tanoan, and Zuni and which may reflect Zuni borrowing of glottalization from the Keresan and/or Tanoan.[20] The second is the development of a fronted or "palatalized" /kʸ/ as variants of ordinary /k/, which appears in Towa, Zuni, and Hopi and which suggests diffusion from Zuni or Towa to Hopi.[21]

Loan Words

In contrast with chance similarities or shared inherited vocabulary, loan words are not always obvious, and determining their sources can be difficult.[22] A word may be a loan if it contains sounds that do not appear in the nonloan vocabulary, such as the occurrence of /f/ in loan words from Spanish in many American languages. Another diagnostic is if the word is long enough to be internally complex, but cannot be analyzed using the language's morphology, and better still can be analyzed in the source language if this can be identified. For instance, "catastrophe," which is unanalyzable in English, can be analyzed in Greek, where it is κατά "down" + στρέφειν "to turn." Finally, a word may be a loan if it cannot be traced to the borrowing language's protolanguage but can be traced to the source language's protolanguage. An example is English "tamale," which obviously has no etymology in Germanic or Indo-European. It comes from Nahuatl *tamal-li* by way of Spanish, with a Proto-Uto-Aztecan reconstruction *tɨmat-ta.

The vast majority of languages borrow relatively few words—only a handful of languages, including English, have been identified with more than about 10 percent loan vocabulary in their "basic" vocabulary, the 200 or so meanings represented in nearly all languages. While the indigenous Southwest languages are typical in exhibiting relatively few loans, suites of loan words can sometimes be identified. They offer insights into the kinds of relationships and mutual understandings that connected the diverse communities of the Pueblo core and the Puebloans with other peoples in the Greater Southwest.

One early example discussed previously is my proposed loan-word exchange between Proto-Northern Uto-Aztecan and Proto-Kiowa-Tanoan. Occurring at least

6.2. Artist's depiction of historic-period Hopi Kachina dance. Fred Kabotie (Hopi, 1900–1983), *Hopi Tashaf Kachina Dance.* Note the clown kachinas in the lower left and the other dancers' masks, jewelry, kilts, and moccasins. The circle in the upper right sky is discoloration due to chemicals in the paper.

3,000 years ago, this exchange involved the loan of maize-complex vocabulary from Proto-Northern Uto-Aztecan into Proto-Kiowa-Tanoan. In reverse, the names for the Colorado Plateau's economically important wild plants and animals were loaned from Proto-Kiowa-Tanoan into Proto-Northern Uto-Aztecan.[23]

Later loan words crossed the boundaries between the northern Pueblo Southwest and neighboring regions. One example is the Hopi word *tsoongo*, which translates as "pipe for smoking."[24] It ultimately comes from the Yokutsan languages of central California, probably by way of intervening Uto-Aztecan Southern Numic languages that also have the term. In reverse, the Numic languages received the word for "paper bread" from either the Hopi or another Pueblo source. It was from one such source, the Northern Tiwa, that Kiowa speakers on the Plains borrowed their term of "paper bread."

Although the Apachean languages spoken by the eastern Southwest's dominant non-Pueblo groups borrowed almost no words, they did loan some. Paul Kroskrity thinks that the Tewa borrowed a possessive-pronominal suffix from the Apachean possessive prefix *bi-*. Since this borrowing is present in both the Rio Grande and Arizona varieties of Tewa, it presumably dates prior to AD 1700, when the Tewa fragmented after the second Pueblo revolt.[25]

A very widespread loan word in the Southwest and beyond may have been a word for "trading partner, ritual kinsman."[26] Since it appears in every subgroup of Yuman and can be reconstructed to the protolanguage, this term probably originated there. To the west, it has been identified in two California Uto-Aztecan languages; to the east, it is found in another Uto-Aztecan language, Tohono O'odham; and farther east in other language families, Zuni and Keresan. This loan's meaning suggests two modes of loan word diffusion—trade and ritual gatherings; and its wide distribution suggests that both probably contributed to the spread of loan words throughout the Southwest.

LOAN WORDS IN THE KACHINA RELIGION

Pueblo religion centers on a pantheon of kachina spirits, dead ancestors whose diverse roles relate mostly to fertility.[27] As part of a seasonal cycle of ceremonies, predominantly male participants dress in elaborate costumes that represent the spirits and perform ritual songs and dances (Figure 6.2). The multitude of loan words associated with the kachina religion provides strong evidence that ceremonies were a major venue in which people who spoke different languages gathered. This vocabulary sharing, which is widely distributed and often crosses language-family boundaries, probably began around AD 1300–1450, when the kachina cult first spread throughout the northern Southwest.

Inter-Pueblo Loans

Evidence for considerable cross-language family sharing of kachina vocabulary was first recorded by Elsie Clews Parsons in the 1920s.[28] Working with residents of Jemez Pueblo, whose language is part of the Kiowa-Tanoan family, Parsons recorded loan words from three other languages: Tewa, which is also part of the Kiowa-Tanoan family; Hopi, which is part of the Uto-Aztecan family; and Keres, which is part of the Keresan family. Parsons also had an encounter with a Tewa man who was eager to learn Hopi words so that he could use them in composing songs.

Subsequent research has revealed a web of inter-pueblo connections underlying the distributions of kachina loan words.[29] The Tewa man who wanted to include Hopi words in his songs was not an anomaly—the kachina songs of many pueblos are rife with loan words, sometimes strung together at length. For example, in the 1940s, Leslie White described Hopi and Zuni men switching languages as they performed kachina songs.[30] White could not identify which languages were involved; but more recently, Emory Sekaquaptewa and colleagues analyzed a collection of Hopi kachina songs dating from the late nineteenth century to the 1950s and identified entire lines and stanzas sung in Keres, Tewa, and Zuni.[31]

Similar inter-pueblo, cross-language family connections are evident in the names of kachina deities. In fact, the Hopi term *katsina*, which is the source of English "kachina," may be a loan from Keresan. In Hopi, I have enumerated 14 kachina names borrowed from Zuni.[32] Zuni *kokko* appears in Hopi kachina names such as *Kokkopölö* "Kokopelli." Zuni *kokko* may also be the source for the *ko-* element in widespread words for ceremonial clowns, such as Zuni *koyemsi* and the Tanoan and Keresan versions of "koshare." Since kachina spirits were thought to have diverse origins, it may have been appropriate to address them in their different ancestral languages.

The names of the ritual societies associated with different kachinas are also frequently foreign. Parsons reports that the Jemez clown-society name *Kwiraina* is a Keres word.[33] I have identified several other kachina-religion words borrowed into Hopi from Keresan and vice versa; and a number of Keresan religious words also appear in Zuni. While Pueblo groups prefer place names in the local languages, both Hopi and Zuni name the eastern kachina homes with Keresan names.

The multitude of kachina-related loan words in the different languages and language families spoken in the Pueblos confirms the previous identification of the northern Southwest as a language area. It also suggests that kachina ceremonies were a major venue for intergroup interaction. I speculate that the loan-word complex may constitute the "iconization" of the intercommunal, multilingual, and public dimensions of kachina religion.[34] The fact that these rituals were primarily the domain of initiated males suggests that this volume's hypothetical traveler was probably an adult man.

External Loans

In addition to this considerable sharing of ritual vocabulary across language families within the Pueblo world, some kachina loan words can be traced to more distant languages. A number of widely distributed lexical elements may come ultimately from Tepiman (or southern Uto-Aztecan).[35] One example is Zuni *kokko* "kachina" from Tepiman *kok'oi* "the dead," an etymon that can be traced to Proto-Uto-Aztecan. David Shaul and I think that Upper Pima *sima* "bold, mean" might be the source of Zuni *shuma-* in the name of the Shuma'kwe society. The same lexical item can be seen in the name of the Jemez Warrior society—*Soma*.

Another example of a connection between Upper Pimans, Zuni, and the Rio Grande pueblos is the loan chain perhaps starting with Keresan *shiwanna* "rain deities," appearing in Zuni as *shiwanna* "priest," and from Zuni into Upper Piman as *siwañ* "lord of a Great House." One last example of a cross-language family loan can be seen in Hopi and Zuni words that use the same root that translates as to "be afraid"—Hopi *tuutuskya*, which *means* "shrine," and Zuni *teshkwi*, which *means* "household shrine." Both probably derive from a Hopi and ultimately Uto-Aztecan word for "cave."

The southern Uto-Aztecan origins for Zuni words like *kokko* and *shuma-* point to broader interactions between the Pueblos and the residents of the Greater Southwest's other major language area. The fact that these loan words were incorporated into the language of kachina rituals suggests that adult men may have traveled on ceremonial occasions not just within language areas but also between them.

FESTIVE CUISINE

Feasts were another important part of kachina gatherings. Their prototypical cuisine can be traced back as early as AD 1275 and continues to be prepared and served by women today.[36] It includes paper bread (Hopi *piiki*); stews of corn, beans, and meat; dried fruits and squash; and melon slices. In marked contrast to men's rituals, these festive foods exhibit relatively little linguistic borrowing. Only a few loan words have been identified, and only in Hopi do they cross language families.[37]

Paper Bread

Undertaking the research for this chapter, I fully expected to find a rich and broadly distributed loan vocabulary associated with paper bread. I already knew that *piiki* is a loan word in Hopi. I also knew that the preparation of paper bread is a highly skilled, multistage process that requires face-to-face instruction to learn. Thus, I was confident that the rapid and wide spread of this festive food's associated technology in the early fourteenth century must have involved direct interaction among women who spoke different languages.[38] While that conclusion is probably true, my expectations about an extensive loan vocabulary turned out to be incorrect.

The process of making paper bread begins with a technical and exacting procedure for preparing and curing piki stones, tasks that among the Zuni were done by elderly women working in silence, assisted by a male ritual expert.[39] The words for "piki stone" are quite unrelated to one another across languages.[40] All include a morpheme meaning "stone," but in the local language. Hopi has *tuma* "cured piki stone," which may contain the Uto-Aztecan root for "stone," *tɨN*. Zuni has *he'lashnakya a'le* "a large slab of treated sandstone for making paper bread." Arizona Tewa has *mowa-k'u* "bread-stone." Western Keresan (Acoma) has *y'âu-shi* "flat cooking stone"; and Eastern Keresan (Cochiti) has *yo'asha* "comal," which is probably descended from the same Proto-Keresan source as the Acoma word.

To make the bread, corn flour is ground to the optimal fineness (Figure 6.3), diluted to the right consistency, and supplemented with the proper amount of ash. After the piki stones have been heated to the correct temperature, the dough must be deftly manipulated on the stones to avoid burning the bread or the cook's hands (Figure 6.4).[41]

Similar to piki stones, the vocabulary related to paper bread also lacks loan words with one notable exception—Hopi. Given the lack of any evidence that the Hopi term *piiki* has any Uto-Aztecan etymology, I speculate that it originated in Towa, the northwestern-most variety of Tanoan in the Kiowa-Tanoan language family. Other probable loans from Hopi or Towa are found in Numic languages, where, again, we have no evidence that the words have any Uto-Aztecan etymology. For instance, Timpisa Shoshone has *piki* "mesquite flour, especially in blocks"; and Southern Paiute has *piqo-s* "'yant' cake made of the roasted heart of the cabbage-like head of the 'yant' (Agave spp.)."[42]

Except for Hopi, all of the other Pueblos refer to paper bread using terms from their own languages.[43] The Zuni expression, *tow he-le* "ancient round.thing-singular" (often *he-we*, "round.thing-plural") has no resemblants in other languages and may be a ritual euphemism. The Tanoan languages have at least three unrelated words for wafer bread: in Towa, it is *wų bélá* "real bread"; in San Juan Tewa, it is *bùwá*; in Arizona Tewa, it is *mowa*; and in Northern Tiwa, it is *p'òkú-*. The San Juan Tewa and Arizona Tewa words are probably from the same ancestral word. The Eastern Keresan words for "paper bread," Cochiti *mátzi·n* and Santa Ana *matsinis*, do not resemble any terms in other languages spoken in the macroregion. It is possible

that the general Zuni form for bread (not paper bread), *mu-* (usually *mu-we* in the plural) is related to the Tewa *buwa~mbuwa~mowa* group. Zuni would be the source, since in Zuni *mu-we* is morphologically analyzable ("bread-plural"), while the Tanoan words are not.

Some of these local terms may have become loan words for languages spoken by non-Puebloans. John P. Harrington thought that Northern Tiwa *p'ǒkú-* is probably the source of the Kiowa *bouk'ae* "the paper bread of the Pueblo Indians" (and that Tewa *mbuwa-yave* "bread-peeled" is the source for the widespread Southwestern U.S. Spanish word for paper bread, *guayabe*). In reverse, the Spanish *cemita* "bread roll, bun" is the source of Eastern Keresan (Cochiti) *sá·mit* "maize bread" and Laguna

6.3. Hopi maidens grinding corn meal, AD 1906; Edward S. Curtis, photographer. Also note the young women's hairstyles and blankets.

6.4. Hopi woman making paper bread on a piki stone, AD 1906; Edward S. Curtis, photographer. After being cooked, the paper-thin sheets are folded into a rectangular shape for eating. Also note the woman's hairstyle and over-the-shoulder blanket dress.

semiita "bread," which are from the same Spanish word and probably do not refer to "paper bread."

The archaeological, historic, and linguistic evidence concerning paper bread raises questions about the degree to which women traveled during the prehistoric period. Archaeologists have documented the rapid spread of piki bread throughout the Pueblo world in the early AD 1300s. Throughout the historic period, ethnographers have described the production of this festive food as the responsibility of women, who in turn teach the elaborate set of procedures to their daughters, granddaughters, and other younger-generation female relatives. Finally, historical linguists have found piki bread vocabulary to be almost entirely language specific, with few possible loan words.

Together, this evidence suggests that women's travel in the early fourteenth century was responsible for the rapid spread of piki technology. The distances traveled are unknown, as are the reasons for it; but nevertheless, women from different locales were able to interact with one another and in the process share their knowledge about how to make piki bread. The fact that cooking and serving vessels for festive food were circulated intercommunally is further evidence for this face-to-face interaction. But one thing that women from different communities did not share was their paper bread vocabulary. Instead, local terminology was developed and used. This vocabulary may have been a marker of female or group identity that women wanted to preserve in such settings.

Festive Stews

The other major festive food served in conjunction with kachina rituals is stews made by boiling corn, beans, and meat together in a ceramic jar (or a metal kettle today).[44] Similar to paper bread, the terminology referring to both the cooking process and the various ingredients for stews is almost entirely local. Virtually no loan words have been identified, and the only clear examples that cross language-family boundaries occur once again only in Hopi.

Stew Words

In several unrelated Pueblo languages, the word for "stew" contains the word for its preparation method—"boiled."[45] As a cooking method, boiling has a long history in the Southwest, dating back at least to the advent of both ceramic cooking vessels and the farming of corn, beans, and other domesticated plants. Boiling probably dates even earlier to when hot stones were used to heat liquids in sealed basketry. Linguistic evidence supports this view, because in several unrelated languages, the words for festive stews are similar to the "stone" word. However, while boiling foods in general may have a long history, a shift from roasting to boiling as the preferred preparation method for festive foods may have been a late development that coincided with the rapid spread of paper bread.

The words for stew in Hopi, Tewa, and Zuni have the same construction, "ingredient-boiled." Although these words could conceivably be loan translations, the lexical items that fill these slots are in every case local. Thus, it is entirely possible that each community arrived independently at this solution for naming festive stews. As with *piiki*, the Hopi word for stew is a loan, *nöq-kwivi*, which literally means "meat-boiled." The incorporated noun *nöq-* has no Uto-Aztecan etymology, but its source cannot be identified.

For the Kiowa-Tanoan languages, the Tewa "stew" words all share a root that is probably related to a verb for "to boil."[46] They include (1) San Juan Tewa *xį·sǫ̀*, literally "dried.corn-stew," translated as "posole"; (2) Santa Clara Tewa *píví-sę̂·*, literally "meat-boil"; and (3) San Juan Tewa *sæm-bé·* and Santa Clara tewa *sén-bé* "cooking bowl," where *-bé·* is a ball- or pot-shaped object and the first syllable is from "boil."

Zuni also has the "boil" expression: *-leya-nne* "boiled dish" (*-leya-we* means "boiled items," as with *mi-leya-we* "boiled ears of corn") compounded with diverse elements to create names for stews, such as *chu-leya-nne* "hominy stew" (corn .kernel-boiled.dish-singular), *no-leya-nne* "bean-boiled.dish-singular," and *shi-leya-nne* "meat-boiled.dish-singular." Logan Sutton has noted the resemblance between Zuni *–leya-* "boil" and the Tanoan verbs for "to boil," with reflexes in Tewa *saye-* and Taos Tiwa *łiya* "boil" and possibly in Towa *tʸǫ́y'e* "boil".

I have found only one Keresan word in this domain—Santa Ana *c'éwAsčA* "stew."[47] I have no analysis for this word, but it does not include elements for "meat" or "boil." A list of 384 Proto-Keresan reconstructions does not include a word for "stew" or related terms, suggesting that these words may be different in Eastern and Western Keresan.[48]

Vegetable Words

The crucial ingredients for festive stews are corn and beans, whose native words were generally not shared across languages. All of the Pueblo languages have diverse words for different states of corn, such as fresh ear, dried ear, kernel, and hominy; and none of these terms are resemblant among the different languages. Even when one searches the entire maize vocabulary for resemblants among any of the shifting meanings, none are evident. The only exceptions to the local character of "corn" words are ancient loans between Northern Uto-Aztecan and Kiowa-Tanoan.

With the exception of Hopi, the words for "beans" in different languages are also dissimilar.[49] Once again, the Hopi terminology is a loan word. Hopi *mori* "beans" is part of a large family of similar bean words found also in Yuman languages, Siouan, and a number of Uto-Aztecan and other languages of Mexico. Word sharing is absent in the words for beans in other Pueblo languages. The reconstructed term in Proto-Keresan is **gánami*. Zuni has *no-* (usually *no-we*) "bean" and *poka* "bean plant." The Tanoan languages are diverse, with Towa *khyį́* "bean, seed"; Northern Tiwa (Taos) *tǫ́-na*; Northern Tiwa (Picuris) *tà'á-nę*; Arizona Tewa *tú*; and Rio Grande Tewa *tû·*. The Tiwa and Tewa words are resemblant, but do not exhibit regular sound correspondences so do not descend from Proto-Kiowa-Tanoan.[50] Logan Sutton suggests that the Tewa words may ultimately derive by metaphorical innovation from a Tanoan word for "meat."

In addition to being a minor stew ingredient, pumpkin was probably a source of dried slices for festive snacks and of oily seeds for seasoning piki stones. Similar to corn and beans, its vocabulary is disparate across languages. The Hopi say *paatanga* "squash," the Keresan **dâ:ni* "squash," and the Zuni *mo·teyalha* in which the *mo·* element is also in *mo·ki'isi* "necked squash."[51] In the Tanoan languages, the words for "pumpkin" include Towa *wą'hą·*, and a set of related words including Northern Tiwa (Taos) *pó-na*, Northern Tiwa (Picuris) *pà'á-ne*, and San Juan Tewa *po·*.

Meat Words

The other important ingredient of festive stews is meat. Historically, the most frequently used species were turkey, jackrabbit, and deer. Elk and bison were used more rarely. Generally, the more common the species, the more localized the vocabulary. Only for elk and bison did loan words cross language families.

According to James Potter and Scott Ortman, turkey became a major ingredient in prehistoric festive stews during later time periods.[52] In different languages, the words for turkey vary in their degree of similarity.[53] Keresan **cín'A* "turkey" is unrelated to any other Pueblo vocabulary. The words in the Tanoan languages are resemblant: Towa *de'lï'* (today "chicken," but recorded as "turkey" in personal names); Tiwa *diru*, and Rio Grande Tewa *di·*, (without tone). Logan Sutton suggests that these words may be descended from a common ancestral form. However, Kiowa *pę̂·* "turkey" is completely unrelated, with Kiowa being the other major division in the Kiowa-Tanoan language family.

Two possible cross-language family loans have been identified for "turkey." Zuni *tona* resembles Piman *to:wa* and might be part of the Piman-Zuni loan complex.[54] However, since these are clearly sound-imitative forms, they may be a chance resemblance. Catherine Fowler speculates that Hopi *koyongo* "turkey" may be related to Shoshone *kuyuŋwi'yaa'*, Chemehuevi *kuyuita*, and Ute *qwiyut*.[55] These resemblant forms do not show regular sound correspondence, which suggests the spread of a loan from a source outside Uto-Aztecan.

The vocabulary for jackrabbit, the other small animal used in festive stews, shows borrowing within but not across language families.[56] For Keresan, Acoma *pé·ça* and Santa Ana *péṣ'a* are resemblant but do not regularly correspond in their sounds. In Tanoan, Towa *bïdæ·* "jack rabbit" is unrelated to Santa Clara Tewa *kw'án* "jackrabbit" (the latter probably reflects the Proto-Kiowa-Tanoan word, also seen in Kiowa *k'oNm-sO* "jackrabbit"). For "cottontail," Tanoan has cognate words in Northern Tiwa (Picuris) *pìwé-ne* "rabbit"; Rio Grande Tewa *pù·* "cottontail." Hopi *sowi* "jackrabbit" is probably cognate with other Northern Uto-Aztecan words for this animal. Zuni has *pok'a* "jackrabbit" and *shapayok'o* "small jackrabbit."

Festive stews can also include larger mammals, which most frequently are cloven hooved (artiodactyls). The words given to these species tend to be old, tracing to protolanguage origins. With the exception once again of Hopi, no cross-language-family loans have been identified. Kiowa-Tanoan languages all have derivatives of *$t'V_2$ "pronghorn" and *pV_3 "deer." Both the eastern and western Keresan languages have *$k\dot{i}\cdot ci$ "pronghorn" and *$dyán'\acute{e}$ "deer." Zuni has *ma'wi* "antelope" and *na'-le* or *ohho'li* "deer." Hopi has *tsööviw* "pronghorn" and *sowi'ngwa* "deer," names that are unique to that language within Uto-Aztecan, but with no source identified. The "deer" word may be a euphemism based on *sowi* "jackrabbit."

"Elk" and "bison" are the two largest and rarest game animals used in festive stews. Unlike other animals, their names include loans across Pueblo language families. For "elk," Zuni *tsaylusi* and Hopi *tsayrisa* are clearly loans from Keresan *$dy\ddot{i}'\cdot\d{s}A$. The Tanoan forms are different and may reflect a Proto-Kiowa-Tanoan form for "elk": Tewa *tà·-*, Northern Tiwa (Taos) *ti'-*, Southern Tiwa (Isleta) *t\dot{i}-*, and Towa *tôtya·* "bison" (a semantic shift).[57]

The origins for "bison" words are mostly similar to those for "elk."[58] For Hopi, *mosayru* "bison" is once again a Keresan loan from *$m\acute{u}\check{s}\hat{e}\dot{i}\dot{z}A$ "bison." The Proto-Kiowa-Tanoan term for "bison" is the source for Northern Tiwa (Taos) *kòn-*, Tewa *k\d{o}'*, Kiowa *kol-*, and perhaps is related to Proto-Numic *kuhcun-* and Atakapa *cokoñ*, in a loanword complex that is widespread in North America. As was just discussed, Towa *tôtya·* "bison" shares a common ancestor with "elk" words. Only Zuni contradicts this pattern of similar origins for "elk" and "bison" words.[59] Its *si:wolo* "buffalo" is a Spanish loan.

Stew Inferences

The vocabulary for the boiling process and for stew ingredients is mostly local with several notable exceptions. Hopi is distinguished by multiple loan words that originated in other language families. The terms for large mammals are also characterized by cross-language-family loans. For other plant and animal ingredients, the few examples of linguistic borrowing occur within language families, most notably Tanoan.

The preparation of stews for feasts held in conjunction with kachina rituals reveals little about our traveler. Ethnohistoric data indicate that stews were prepared by women, and linguistic data suggest that any interactions these women had with outsiders occurred mostly with neighboring groups who spoke languages within the same language family. The only suggestive archaeological evidence for intercommunal contacts among women is the proposed late replacement of roasted foods by stews, but boiling was not a new technique, and mastery did not require person-to-person instruction.

The Hopi are an intriguing case, because their stew-related vocabulary indicates contacts with other Pueblo and non-Pueblo groups that spoke languages from other language families. Whether it was males or females who engaged in this interaction is unknown. However, the fact that the loan words relate to the female activity of food preparation suggests that Hopi women may have been interacting with outsiders in a way that was different from other Puebloans. For all Pueblo languages, it is noteworthy that the kinds of stew ingredients with cross-language-family loans—elk and bison—would have involved men hunting over the longest distances and thus would have offered the highest potential for meeting foreign-language speakers.

The Entire Feast

Together, the linguistic evidence for the piki bread and stews that women prepared for ceremonial feasts offers insights into the related issues of interaction, gender, and metaphors in the Pueblo world. The vocabularies for these festive foods only rarely exhibit loan words even where it is clear—as in the case of paper bread—that the preparation technique must have spread face-to-face across linguistic boundaries.

There are exceptions to the pattern: the names for the principal festive foods in Hopi, *piiki* and *nöq-kwivi*, are of obscure origin and are surely loans.[60] Also, some words, such as Keresan "jackrabbit," were loaned within language families. But cross-family loans, which are so apparent in kachina rituals, are absent in festive foods. In this semantic domain, there are no striking Keresan loans in Zuni, no loans between Hopi and Zuni, and no loans between Hopi and Keresan. I have noted possible loans between Zuni and the Tanoan languages (for "paper bread" and "boil") that require further investigation. Looking outside the Pueblo languages, there are no festive-food loans that either originate in Tepiman or have spread into it as seen in the ritual vocabularies of various Pueblo languages. The only spread outside the Pueblo languages is to the north, with the diffusion of the "piki" word into Southern Paiute and Tümpisa Shoshone. There its meaning is greatly changed to accommodate local cuisine, which does not include paper bread.

This overall pattern of no cross-language-family sharing raises questions about the one major exception—Hopi. Why does Hopi exhibit non-Uto-Aztecan loan words for paper bread and for the main festive stew ingredient? Are the Hopi lexical items visible as loans to speakers? Does Hopi have a distinctive ideology about local as opposed to intercommunal dimensions in kachina religious practice? Why is Hopi different from Zuni, the other language with no Pueblo relatives? Zuni doesn't have any obvious festive food loans except for the "elk" word.

The general absence of loan words for festive foods and for the prototypical festive cooking implement, the piki stone, suggests that female food preparation for feasts was not a public activity carried out by interethnic groups of multilingual women. This characterization is a marked contrast to men's participation in kachina ceremonies. Consistent with this gender distinction is the fact that the obvious, festive-food loans from Keresan into Hopi and Zuni appear in the most "masculine" part of the festive-food domain, the large game animals of elk and bison.

These linguistic contrasts are probably only one element of a more complex picture. In what must have been a difficult tension between local expenditure and wider intercommunity interests, the female contribution to kachina events may have represented the "local" as much as the "feminine." James Potter and Scott Ortman argue that in feasting "the ideational aspects of community structure may have been expressed through metaphors that took the experiential imagery of domestic food production, procurement, preparation, and consumption as models for the meaning of communal feasts in the context of public ritual."[61]

Their emphasis on metaphors of the "domestic" sphere is supported by linguistic data. We can imagine that, just as the pan-Pueblo loans in the domain of kachina ritual practice are icons for intercommunal connections, locally specific names for festive food, even where the same dishes were prepared in every community, could function as icons for the important local contribution and the prototypical site of domestic consumption. By serving familiar foods, hospitable hosts may have welcomed guests with the Pueblo version of "this is your house," but the food labels clearly referenced local identity.

Festive cuisine offers no clear conclusions about women and travel. The paucity of loan words suggests that women did not travel. But the rapid spread of paper bread and the complex tasks involved in its preparation indicate that women did move from place to place in the late thirteenth century. Furthermore, possible linguistic metaphors related to festive cuisine suggest the use of local language may have served as an indicator of the host group's distinctive cultural identity. Thus, the absence of loan words associated with festive cuisine may say nothing about whether women did or did not travel.

CONCLUSION

The field of historical linguistics offers insights into the Southwest's prehistoric past that are inaccessible to archaeological studies of material remains. By sorting indigenous languages into language families and reconstructing their respective protolanguages, the approach highlights deep historical connections among people who today speak mutually unintelligible languages. Furthermore, maps showing where both protolanguages and the languages comprising different language families were spoken offer clues to past population movements and zones of interaction.

Probably of more significance to this volume's hypothetical traveler are the distributions of shared linguistic features. Their distinct spatial patterns divide the Southwest into two language areas. Located in its southwestern and northern portions, these areas represent interaction spheres within which the speakers of different languages routinely engaged one another. Whatever the nature of these contacts, they resulted in the adoption of varying numbers of foreign words with some individuals becoming bi- or even multilingual.

For both our traveler and people met along the way, speech would have been an indicator of cultural identity, as each tried to figure out who the other was. If our traveler moved within his or her own language area, then other languages might be familiar, even if they were not understood. Also, the cultural identities associated with these other languages may have become fairly nuanced with more frequent contacts and the adoption of varying numbers of loan words. Going outside the language area would bring encounters with speakers of unfamiliar languages, and their associated identity messages would have been more difficult to decode, perhaps being limited to the general assessment of their speakers as just being "foreign." Efforts to associate language with cultural identity may have been affected by gender—differences in loan-word frequency related to the kachina rituals and festive cuisine suggest that men were traveling and encountering foreign languages more than women.

The research presented in this chapter highlights the potential of historical linguistics for gaining new and unexpected insights into the Southwest's prehistoric past. Further work on ritual language will be difficult, because the information is still considered sacred.[62] However, in at least Zuni and Hopi, kachina names seem to be public, so this is a promising area for future research. The cuisine lexicon is currently very sparsely documented except for Hopi. Further research on this domain may also be difficult, given Pueblo sensitivities about sharing language data. Furthermore, this lexicon may be threatened, because in many pueblos only a few elderly women continue to make paper bread.

Today, the ways that the Southwest's native peoples speak continue to signify their identities and their interactions with others but in ways different from the past. As a result of ongoing acculturation, the Southwest's indigenous linguistic and cultural diversity is eroding. In fact, if this volume's traveler were currently traversing the Southwest, he or she would only need to be fluent in English north of the international border and Spanish to the south in order to communicate with virtually everyone met along the way.

Around the world, nearly all small, indigenous languages are "endangered."[63] In the Southwest, some smaller communities now face a situation in which only the elderly are fluent in the language; and data from children entering school suggest that even the largest languages are approaching "moribundity," a stage of attrition when no young children are acquiring the language. Recognizing the important role of language in maintaining their traditional cultural identities, many native communities have moved aggressively to develop language-maintenance projects to arrest the processes of language loss.[64] Speaking English or Spanish is a necessity for their interactions with outsiders—both whites as well as members of other native groups. But maintaining their indigenous languages is a way to sustain a sense of belonging to a distinct and enduring cultural group in the midst of the rapidly changing, modern world.

CONCLUSION

Jill E. Neitzel

Moving short distances from one community to another and greater distances from one area to another, this volume's hypothetical traveler would have observed tremendous diversity in how prehistoric Southwesterners looked and spoke. Variety would have been present even within individual communities. Over the course of an extended journey, personal characteristics would change at different rates, creating a visual and auditory mosaic of embedded and overlapping patterns. At each successive destination, the residents would both resemble and differ from those met previously. And nowhere would stark boundaries separate biologically and culturally homogeneous groups.

While the preceding chapters focus on separate personal characteristics, this is not how our traveler would have assessed people met along the way. Instead, he or she would have observed each stranger's overall appearance and speech and then used this composite impression to draw conclusions about who the person was. Those identities conveyed by multiple personal characteristics would be expressed most strongly.

Here, I conclude our traveler's journey by synthesizing information presented throughout the book on the themes of identity and personal appearance, first reviewing the identity messages that were broadcast most forcefully within communities and between different cultural groups, then describing what the members of the best-documented cultural groups looked like.

IDENTITIES WITHIN COMMUNITIES

Of all of the identities conveyed by a prehistoric Southwesterner's appearance, messages about gender were the most redundant. Everywhere, whether a person was a man or woman was visually obvious from his or her stature, breast size, clothes, and other personal characteristics. On average, men were 2–4.5 inches taller than women, and their breechcloths contrasted with women's fringed aprons. To varying degrees, men and women arranged and decorated their hair differently, and at some times and places, they applied different facial designs. Some individuals broadcast mixed gender messages, signaling femaleness with one characteristic and maleness with another. They may have represented a dual-gender, as has been suggested for Ancestral Puebloans with uneven haircuts, or perhaps they were ceremonial entertainers, similar to historic-period clown kachinas.

Among the most stratified groups, social prominence was also signaled in multiple ways. The highest status individuals were sometimes significantly taller and wore special clothes and ornaments. Their garments were made with intricate, labor-intensive weaves and unusual, eye-catching decorations. Their jewelry was distinguished by its raw materials; the numbers and kinds of beads and pendants strung for necklaces, bracelets, and anklets; the intricacy and craftsmanship of composite pieces; and the numbers of these different kinds of ornaments worn together. Among minimally differentiated groups, individuals with a bit more status signified it in modest ways. Yet even subtle differences in adornment would have been apparent to people who were in regular, face-to-face contact and who were aware of everyone's social roles and activities.

For all groups, ceremonial roles were communicated by participation in ritual processions, dances, and other activities and by the costumes worn on these sacred occasions. Individuals with different roles could be distinguished by their headdresses, masks, hairstyles, body and facial decoration, ornaments, and ritual paraphernalia, such as wooden staffs and inlaid bone spatulas. The materials, colors, and designs of each addition to the performer's body were imbued with powerful symbolic meanings that were expressed repeatedly in the full regalia.

Within communities, gender, status, and ceremonial roles overlapped. Ceremonial leaders were typically men, and in more stratified societies they had high status. Thus, ritual costumes may have also broadcast gender and status messages, and high-status clothing and jewelry may have carried religious meanings related to ceremonial responsibilities.

IDENTITIES IN RELATION TO OUTSIDERS

Cultural affiliation and connections with other groups were broadcast less clearly than gender, status, and ceremonial roles. Some individuals' cultural affiliation could be discerned from just a single characteristic such as Sinagua red argillite nose and lip plugs; Casas Grandes short, sharp haircuts; Hohokam hair pins with carved snakes; and various groups' distinctive sandal styles. But these indicators were not always reliable. Not all of a group's members wore its distinctive ornaments, hairstyles, and sandals. Furthermore, ornaments could be traded and worn by members of other groups, and some unique sandal characteristics were hard to see.

Determining cultural affiliation usually involved an assessment of multiple characteristics. Depending on the time period, Ancestral Pueblo and Hohokam individuals could be distinguished by some combination of their stature; facial features; the weaves, designs, and colors of their fanciest garments; preferred ornament raw materials; and facial designs. Close observation was required for identifying Sinagua and Salado individuals, because many aspects of their appearance blended Ancestral Pueblo and Hohokam characteristics.

A person's connections with other cultural groups were most evident in his or her ornaments, whose raw materials and finished pieces were often obtained through trade. Jewelry made from marine shell reflected ties with the Hohokam or Casas Grandians, perhaps other intermediaries, and ultimately the Gulf of California or Pacific Coast. Turquoise adornments evidenced connections with suppliers and source areas both within and outside the Southwest. While intricate turquoise mosaics could have been obtained through trade, their presence in different groups also reflected widely shared beliefs about how elites should mark their preeminent positions.

Further evidence of a person's connections with other groups might be observed in a garment made from an imported textile or in a hairstyle or facial design that was also worn elsewhere. However, common heritage may be the reason for some shared hairstyles and facial designs. Ancestral connections extending far back in time may account for the similar color and design symbolism seen throughout the Southwest and Mesoamerica.

It is important to note that a single personal characteristic could simultaneously broadcast multiple kinds of identity information. For example, a Mimbres man's *Glycymeris* bracelet may have conveyed his somewhat higher status or special social role within his community and his ties with the Hohokam. Furthermore, the bracelet's designs could signify widely held religious beliefs and an ancestral heritage shared with other Southwest and Mesoamerican groups. Each of this man's other personal characteristics, such as his clothes, hair, facial decoration, and speech also conveyed multiple identity messages. As a result, his overall appearance advertised and reiterated all of the various identities that made him who he was.

WHAT A TRAVELER WOULD HAVE SEEN

Given all of the identity messages that were expressed by a prehistoric Southwesterner's appearance, a traveler could have inferred a lot about who people were just by observing them. But what exactly would our traveler have seen? For even the best-documented groups, composite images of what their members looked like are incomplete due to gaps in the archaeological evidence. Nevertheless, they document distinctive-looking people whose identities our traveler would have recognized.

During the AD 900–1150 period, Chacoans from Pueblo Bonito could be identified by their high stature, round eyes, narrow noses, fancy clothes, predominantly turquoise ornaments, and facial decorations consisting mostly of lines, sometimes with dots. In contrast, the Mimbres were shorter, had more horizontal eyes and broad noses, wore jewelry made mostly of black argillite and shell, and decorated their faces with a wide array of distinctive designs. Although the Hohokam generally had the same stature as the Mimbres, they were distinguished by their predominantly shell adornments, most notably *Glycymeris* bracelets, and by their dotted facial designs.

Within each of these early-period groups, males were 2–3.5 inches taller than females, and, with the exception of blankets, the two genders wore different garments (breechcloths vs. aprons). Among the Chacoans, higher-status individuals were distinguished by their stature, and among the Chacoans and Hohokam, they could be recognized by their fancier clothes and larger quantities and special kinds of jewelry. Among the less socially differentiated Mimbres, individuals with somewhat higher status or special social roles wore more ornaments.

During the AD 1150–1300 period, Ancestral Puebloans could be identified by their modestly higher stature, clothes, and jewelry. Their clothes were distinguished by twilled weaves and combinations of light and dark colors in stripes, bands, and centered designs; and their ornaments were made mostly of argillite and shell with some turquoise. The Hohokam were shorter; their clothing was distinguished by a variety of weaves and multiple color combinations woven into plaids and allover designs. Their jewelry was made mostly of shell, again most notably *Glycymeris* bracelets, followed by black stone. Some of the intermediately located Sinagua were distinguished by their red argillite nose and lip plugs and brightly painted armbands. But their stature was generally the same as the Ancestral Puebloans, and their clothes and adornments were a blend of Ancestral Pueblo and Hohokam characteristics.

Within these intermediate-period groups, males were 3.5 to almost 4.5 inches taller than females. Men continued to wear breechcloths and women wore aprons, but some Hohokam men probably wore kilts and women had wraparound skirts. Among the Sinagua, one high status man was notably taller; and among all groups, high-status individuals were easily identified by their fancier clothes and larger quantities and special kinds of jewelry.

During the AD 1300–1450 period, Ancestral Puebloans could be identified by their narrow faces, clothing, and hairstyles. Their fanciest clothes were decorated in black-and-white tie-dye or polychrome paint. Their hairstyles included two unique arrangements: the uneven sidecut worn by both men and women, and ear whorls worn by women. The Hohokam were distinguished by their clothes; ornaments made predominantly of shell, including the iconic *Glycymeris* bracelets, followed by black stone; some facial designs; and in at least one community, very wide faces. Their fanciest clothes continued to emphasize supplementary weft and negatively patterned white openwork and included the colors blue and green.

Among other AD 1300–1450 groups, the Casas Grandians were distinguished by their predominantly shell jewelry that included relatively few *Glycymeris* bracelets; short, sharp haircuts; and a wide array of distinctive facial designs. The Salado could be recognized by their taller height, clothes that combined Hohokam and Ancestral Pueblo characteristics, and some facial designs. The Mountain Mogollon could be identified by their short stature and very round eyes.

Within these late groups, males were 3 to almost 4.5 inches taller than females. Men continued to wear breechcloths, but some Ancestral Pueblo and probably Hohokam men wore kilts. Women's fringed aprons seem to have disappeared, and Ancestral Pueblo women wore wrap-around dresses. As in previous periods, high-status individuals could be identified by their more finely woven and decorated versions of standard garments and by their larger quantities and special forms of jewelry.

THE JOURNEY ENDS

At the beginning of this book, we asked how far a traveler would have to go in the prehistoric Southwest before encountering people who looked noticeably different. At first, it seemed as if the answer would depend on the trip's starting point, the direction taken, the personal characteristics considered, and the criteria for defining "noticeably different." But it turns out that in many times and places the answer to, "How far would a traveler have to go?" is not far. In fact, our traveler could have seen different-looking people in his or her own community.

Instead of focusing on the question of distance, the preceding chapters have taken a broader view, considering the personal characteristics of people who lived in different parts of the Southwest and the identity messages that those characteristics conveyed. What we have learned is that appearance and speech varied a lot and broadcast considerable information about who people were. Moving across the Southwest, the patterns shifted in a visual and auditory kaleidoscope. To varying degrees, the people at each new destination both resembled and differed from those met previously. Every person's overall appearance would immediately indicate his or her gender, relative status, and perhaps cultural affiliation and connections with other groups. If it was a special occasion, those with ceremonial roles could be easily identified. Over an extended stay, information about religious beliefs and cultural heritage would become more apparent.

Throughout this book, our emphasis has been on groups: what their members looked and sounded like and what identity messages their personal appearance and speech conveyed. But it is important to note that it was individuals who decided, for example, what garments and ornaments to wear, how to arrange their hair, and whether and how to decorate their faces. Although these choices were certainly constrained by group norms, it was the individual who wore the clothes and jewelry; and it was the aggregate of many individuals' choices over time that produced the complicated mosaic of embedded and overlapping patterns evident in the archaeological record.

At the end of our traveler's journey, this book's most important contribution might be its emphasis on prehistoric Southwesterners as people. Ruined architecture and broken pottery have drawn many of us to the study of archaeology, and by analyzing such remains we have been able to document the societies that left them and to develop explanatory models for why these societies developed and disappeared. But archaeology is ultimately concerned with human beings in the past. By looking at personal appearance, speech, and identity, we can see the prehistoric Southwest filled with all kinds of people, individuals who were active agents in their own lives and in the communities and societies of which they were a part.

Appendix

Table 1.1. Male Stature Averages by Period*

Cultural/temporal group	N of Individuals	N of Groups	Mean (cm)
AD 950–1150			
Chaco, Pueblo Bonito North	7	1	166.9
Mogollon Mimbres	>29	5	164.6
Hohokam Preclassic	5	1	164.2
Mogollon Mtn.	10	1	164.1
Ancestral Pueblo	>60	9	162.8
AD 1150–1350			
Sinagua	>20	5	163.8
Salado, Early Classic	42	4	163.5
Ancestral Pueblo	>85	9	163.1
Mogollon Mtn.	>20	1	160.8
Hohokam Classic	31	1	160.0
AD 1350–1450			
Salado Classic	*	1	167.0
Late Prehistoric Pueblo	39	3	163.9
Hohokam Classic	45	5	163.6
Mogollon Mtn.	>95	2	161.8
Sinagua	63	1	157.9

*Not all publications indicate the number of individuals contributing to a mean stature figure.

Table 1.2. Female Stature Averages by Period*

Cultural/temporal group	N of Individuals	N of Groups	Mean (cm)
AD 950–1150			
Chaco, Pueblo Bonito North	7	1	157.5
Hohokam Preclassic	5	1	156.4
Mogollon Mimbres	19	5	155.5
Ancestral Pueblo	33	9	153.7
Mogollon Mtn.	9	1	152.9
AD 1150–1350			
Sinagua	>18	5	153.9
Ancestral Pueblo	>73	10	152.7
Salado, Early Classic	40	4	152.5
Hohokam Classic	26	1	151.1
Mogollon Mtn.	>31	3	150.6
AD 1350–1450			
Salado Classic		1	158.9
Hohokam Classic	39	5	155.7
Late Prehistoric Pueblo	30	2	153.3
Mogollon Mtn.	>90	2	151.3

*Not all publications indicate the number of individuals contributing to a mean stature figure.

Table 1.3. Average Male Facial Metrics by Period*

Site/Group	Affiliation	Bizygomatic Breadth mean	Orbital Breadth mean	Orbital Height mean	Nasal Height mean	Nasal Breadth mean
Pre–AD 900						
AZ Basketmakers	Basketmaker	132.38	39.00	34.23	50.80	25.40
Grand Gulch	Basketmaker	134.78	37.98	34.75	51.37	25.24
Canyon de Chelly	Basketmaker	134.20	37.40	36.50	51.50	25.40
Ridges Basin	Ancestral Pueblo PI	138.20	39.70	34.20	48.40	26.40
AD 900–1150						
Duckfoot Site	Ancestral Pueblo PI	136.20	38.55	35.35	49.95	25.90
Canyon de Chelly	Kayenta PI–II	139.10	38.20	34.50	50.00	25.10
Mesa Verde	Ancestral Pueblo PI–III	136.60	39.00	35.00	51.40	25.40
La Plata Hwy.	Ancestral Pueblo PII–III	137.65	38.38	34.93	49.98	25.50
AD 1150–1450						
Los Muertos	Hohokam Classic	135.33	38.25	34.61	52.75	25.41
Casa Buena	Hohokam Classic	133.75	41.50	36.75	46.75	25.75
Schoolhouse Pt.	Salado Classic		38.87	37.30	49.70	24.50
Chaves Pass	Sinagua	133.83	38.59	32.25	51.37	24.34
Point of Pines	Mogollon	133.90	37.60	35.50	49.80	25.00
Paa'ko	Ancestral Pueblo	133.00	38.30	34.60	49.10	25.60
Pecos	Ancestral Pueblo	132.28	38.64	35.04	50.11	25.35

*Measurements are in mm.

Table 1.4. Average Male Facial Indices by Period

Site	Affiliation	Orbital Index mean	Nasal Index mean
Pre–AD 900			
Grand Gulch	Basketmaker / Eastern	91.33	49.35
AZ Basketmakers	Basketmaker / Western	87.50	50.13
Canyon de Chelly	Basketmaker/Kayenta	97.50	49.30
Ridges Basin	Ancestral Pueblo	86.50	54.50
AD 900–1150			
Mesa Verde	Ancestral Pueblo	89.80	49.60
Canyon de Chelly	Kayenta	90.30	50.20
Pueblo Bonito	Chaco	91.86	48.64
Swarts Ruin	Mimbres	87.50	54.90
AD 1150–1450			
Canyon de Chelly	Kayenta	94.00	51.80
Puye	Ancestral Pueblo	90.00	48.71
Paa'ko	Ancestral Pueblo	90.30	52.10
Los Muertos	Hohokam Classic	90.83	48.57
Casa Buena	Hohokam Classic	88.64	55.13
Point of Pines	Mogollon	94.50	50.00
Schoolhouse Point Mesa	Salado	88.41	49.27
Chaves Pass	Sinagua	91.50	47.38
Pecos	Ancestral Pueblo	90.73	54.36

Table 1.5. Male Femur Robusticity Averages by Period*

End date	Site	N of Individuals	Mean
Pre–AD 900			
775	5LP110, 111, BMIII	1	11.87
550	SU Site Mogollon	4	12.50
AD 900–1150			
1150	Mesa Verde NP, PI–II	8	12.02
1150	Black Mesa	14	12.35
1150	Lowry Ruin	7	12.73
1100	Alkali Ridge	7	12.75
980	Dolores, PI	6	13.22
AD 1150–1350			
1300	Mesa Verde NP, PIII	9	11.70
1325	Rocky Point Salado	2	12.04
1350	La Plata Valley	10	12.06
1300	Starkweather Ruin, Mogollon	8	12.48
1250	LA 3333	5	13.03
1300	Yellow Jacket	2	13.76
AD 1350–1450			
1400	Cochiti (LA 70)	9	12.00
1450	Grand Canal Ruin, Hohokam	6	12.14
1425	Alfred Herrera	16	12.20
1450	Tonto Basin, Salado	5	12.60

* Ancestral Pueblo sites, unless otherwise noted.

Table 1.6. Female Femur Robusticity Averages by Period*

End date	Site	N of Individuals	Mean
Pre–AD 900			
550	SU Site, Mogollon	2	11.64
775	5LP110, 111, BMIII	1	11.64
700	Yellow Jacket	1	12.64
810	Ridges Basin PI, early	6	12.86
500	Tamarron Site (5LP326)	1	13.30
AD 900–1150			
900	Alkali Ridge	2	11.48
1150	Mesa Verde NP, PI–II	1	12.07
1150	Black Mesa	19	12.13
1150	Lowry Ruin group	3	12.24
1100	Yellow Jacket (5MT1, 3)	2	12.54
1000	Pena Blanca	4	13.10
980	Dolores sites PI, late	9	13.13
AD 1150–1350			
1300	Mesa Verde NP, PIII	4	11.24
1300	Starkweather Ruin, Mogollon	6	11.32
1350	La Plata Valley sites	7	11.70
1300	Yellow Jacket	2	11.73
1250	LA 3333	11	12.00
1325	Rocky Point (AZ:9:365/908), Salado	2	12.37
AD 1350–1450			
1425	Alfred Herrera	10	11.40
1450	Grand Canal Ruin, Hohokam	3	11.59
1400	Cochiti (LA 70)	4	11.90
1450	Tonto Basin, Salado	5	12.46

* Ancestral pueblo sites, unless otherwise noted.

Table 1.7. Cranial Modification in Ancestral- and Historic-Period Pueblo Groups

Site/group	Pecos Stage	Lambdoidal	Occipital	Not Modified	Obelionic
Pre–AD 900					
Darkmold Site	BMII			X	
Mesa Verde, La Plata, Mancos Canyon, Yellow Jacket	BMIII			X	
Ridges Basin	Early PI			X	
La Plata 13, 18, 25	PI	X		X	
AD 900–1150					
Dolores	PI–PII	X			
Lowry Ruin	PII	X			X (1)
Mesa Verde Site 34	PII	X	X		
Chaco	PII	X	X		
AD 1150–1450					
Mancos Canyon, Yellow Jacket	PII–III	X			
Mesa Verde	PII–III	X	X		X (1)
Canyon de Chelly	PII–III	X			
Alkali Ridge	PII–III	X	X		
Post–AD 1450					
San Cristobal	PIV–H	X	X	X	
Hawikku	PIV–H		X	X	
18th-Century Hopi	H		X		
Taos Pueblo 1930s	H		X	X	

Table 1.8. Cranial Modification in Other Major Cultural Groups

Site / Group	Period*	Lambdoidal	Occipital	Not Modified	Obelionic
Gallina					
Largo Gallina, Rosa Phase	1			X	
Largo Gallina PIII	2	X			
Llaves Valley sites, Cañada Simon I	1–2	X			x (5)
Sinagua					
Ridge Ruin	1	X	X		
Winona	1	X	X		
Lizard Man	2	X	X	X	
Mogollon, AZ Mountains					
Bear Village, Forestdale Phase, 600–800	0	x	x	x	
Point of Pines	2–3	X	X		
Grasshopper	2–3	X	X	X	
Mimbres					
NAN Ranch Ruin	2		X		
Salado					
Tonto Creek, Preclassic	1		X	X	
Tonto Creek, Early Classic	1–2	x	x	x	
Rocky Pt., Murray Wash	2		X		
Roosevelt Platform Mound sites	2–3		X	X	
Hohokam					
Grand Canal	2		X		

*Periods:
0 = Pre–AD 900
1 = AD 900–1150
2 = AD 1150–1300
3 = AD 1300–1450

Table 2.1. Distribution of Loom-Woven Fabrics to AD 1300

	A	B	C	D	E	F	G	H	I
Ancestral Pueblo	X	X				?	T	**	**
Sinagua	X	X	X	X	X	X	X	X	X
Salado	**	**			X	X	X	X	X
Mogollon	**	**			X	X	X		
Hohokam	**				X		X	X	X

Key:
A various twills
B twill tapestry
C loom-woven, plain-weave tapestry
D gauze weave with supplementary weft
E plain weave with rag weft
F plain weave with supplementary weft
G gauze weave
H weft-wrap openwork
I warp-face or warp-float plain weave (belting)
X present
** rare
T probable trade piece
? undetermined (supplementary weft or embroidery)

Table 2.2. Distribution of Applied-Color Decoration Techniques on Finished Fabrics to AD 1300

	A	B	C	D	E
Ancestral Pueblo	X		X	?	
Sinagua	T	**	X		
Salado		**	**		**
Mogollon					
Hohokam	**		**	**	

Key:
A negative painting
B painted solid color (no design)
C tie-dye
D other resist dye (batik?)
E stamping

X present
** rare
T probable trade piece
? undetermined (resist dye or negative painting)

Table 2.3. Distribution of Primary Textile Design Layouts and Motifs to AD 1300

	A	B	C	D	E	F	G	H
Ancestral Pueblo	X	X	X	(P)				
Sinagua			X	X	X	X	X	
Salado			X	X	X	X	X	X
Mogollon							**	**
Hohokam					X	X	X	X

Key:
A horizontally banded and striped designs
B centered layout with terraced motifs arranged in offset quartering (fourfold rotation)
C triangle motif with hypotenuse parallel to weft
D triangle-and-hook motif
E uncentered layout with allover patterning

F steeply pitched triangle motif
G scroll-with-hook motif
H finite design layout with isolated motifs
X present
** rare
P on painted textiles only

Table 3.1. Jewelry and Other Grave Goods in Burial #14, Pueblo Bonito, Chaco Canyon, North-Central New Mexico, AD 1020*

Jewelry Worn	Other Jewelry	Other Grave Goods
Chest ornament w/ 1,980 turquoise beads **Right wrist** 1+ bracelet w/ 617 beads, 147 pendants, 4 sets, all turquoise; and 1 shell and 2 stone beads **Left wrist** 1+ bracelet w/ 2,388 beads, 194 pendants, all turquoise; and 5 shell pendants **Right ankle** 1 anklet w/ 324 beads, 5 pendants, all turquoise **Left ankle** 1 anklet w/ 434 beads, 8 pendants, all turquoise; and 9 shell and stone beads	**Abdomen** cache w/ 2,642 beads, 172 pendants, 3 sets, all turquoise; and 5 jet inlays **By right knee** 26 complete and 15 fragmentary *Glycymeris* (?) bracelets; 2,150 beads, 174 pendants, all turquoise, in turquoise inlaid basket; and 78 beads and 68 pendants, all shell; and 1 stone pendant **Nearby** red stone inlay, shell ornament fragments, small turquoise sets	1 shell trumpet 4 complete *Haliotis* shells 1 valve of bivalve shell 1 cylindrical basket inlaid with 1,214 turquoise pieces pieces of turquoise matrix remains of turquoise and shell mosaic on basketwork

*Akins 1986:117

Table 3.2. Jewelry and Other Grave Goods in the Most Jewelry-Rich Burials at the Galaz Site, Mimbres River, Southeast New Mexico, AD 1000–1130*

Burial Pit #	Jewelry Worn[1]	Other Jewelry	Other Grave Goods
2-267	**Neck** 243.8 cm black stone beads 170 turquoise beads 3 turquoise pendants **Left arm** 3 *Glycymeris* bracelets **Ankles** 512 shell beads 142 red shell beads 16 red stone beads 1 red stone pendants	2 shell and turquoise pendants	
15-235	**Neck** 327.7 cm shell beads 21 turquoise beads 8 turquoise pendants		
2-256	**Neck** 600 red stone beads 535 black stone beads **Neck** 230+ shell beads **Ears** 2 shell/turquoise inlay earrings		
2-200		1100 black stone beads 200+ *Olivella* beads 17 dark stone beads	
15-305		274.3 cm shell beads 6 *Glycymeris* bracelets 2 shell pendants	1 palette

*Anyon and LeBlanc 1984:394–95, 396–97, 402–03, 410–11, 416–17
[1]cm refers to length of bead string.

Table 3.3. Jewelry and Other Grave Goods in Feature #1679, La Ciudad, Phoenix Basin, South-Central Arizona, AD 950–1150*

Jewelry	Other Grave Goods
65 shell beads 20 *Glycymeris* bracelets 1 bilobed shell bead	2 *Laevicardium* shells 1 unidentified shell 1 palette 1 obsidian projectile point 1 piece hematite 3 r/b bowls 4 miniature r/b bowls 1 miniature r/b jar 1 miniature plainware jar

*McGuire 1992:185

Table 3.4. Jewelry and Other Grave Goods with Richest Individual in Burial #16 at Aztec West, San Juan River, North-Central New Mexico, AD 1150–1300*

Jewelry Worn	Other Jewelry	Other Grave Goods
Left leg *Olivella*-shell anklet	**Above body** "…skeleton…completely covered from throat to thighs with beads, abalone shell, and mosaic pendants" (Morris 1924:155–156). **In deposit between feet of Burial #16's two adults and corner of room** necklace of approx. 400 *Olivella* beads, 3 *Conus*-shell beads, 2 shell disks with some mosaic pieces attached, approx. 31,000 extremely small, black disk beads (in bird effigy jar)	**In deposit between feet of Burial #16's two adults and corner of room** 4 b/w bowls 1 polychrome bowl 1 b/w water jar w/ handles 1 b/w pitcher 2 b/w mugs 2 b/w bird effigy vessels (one contains the 31,000 beads mentioned to left) galena crystals and bits of stone in bird effigy vessel with 31,000 beads 1 b/r dipper 1 unbaked small corrugated pot 2 polishing stones

*Morris 1924:154–161

Table 3.5. Jewelry and Other Grave Goods in the Most Jewelry-Rich Burials at Pueblo Grande, Phoenix Basin, South-Central Arizona, AD 1150–1450

Period/Burial #	Jewelry	Other Grave Goods
Early Classic (AD 1150–1300) #184	1154 other stone beads 56 turquoise beads 1 turquoise tessera 40 shell beads	38 unmodified/raw shell 2 ceramic vessels bulk ceramics chipped stone groundstone environmental/subsistence/sample
Late Classic (AD 1300–1450) #1428	1595 other stone beads 25 shell beads 3 shell pendants 5 turquoise pendants 3 turquoise beads 3 turquoise tesserae	12 unmodified/raw shell 1 spindle whorl 11 ceramic vessels bulk ceramics chipped stone groundstone faunal bone environmental/subsistence/sample
Late Classic (AD 1300–1450) #2319	1441 shell beads 1 *Glycymeris*-shell bracelet 3 turquoise pendants 1 turquoise bead 1 bone ornament (?)	2 unmodified/raw shell 2 spindle whorls 2 bone awls 6 ceramic vessels bulk ceramics chipped stone groundstone faunal bone environmental/subsistence/sample

*Mitchell n.d., 1994:242, 248

Table 3.6. Jewelry and Other Grave Goods in the Magician's Burial at Ridge Ruin, Coconino Plateau, North-Central Arizona, AD 1150–1175*

Jewelry Worn	Other Jewelry	Other Grave Goods
Head cap made of 3,6000 extremely small shale beads and several hundred shell beads	**By right foot** 1 lignite button, necklace of mountain-lion claws and teeth	**At same level as Magician's body** 1 abalone shell, 3 marine shells, 1 rim of large shell, mass of specular iron crystals on shell fragments
Nose 1 red argillite nose plug w/ circular turquoise inlays	**By left side** 1 lizard-shaped shell pendant; 2 painted stone pendants; 3 turquoise-and-shell mosaics in shapes of a circle, a bird, and an ear	1 large inlaid bone awl, 1 ceremonial stick w/ shell on end, 1 stick w/ inlay, 1 inlaid stick ornament
Ears turquoise pendant earrings inlaid w/ shell	**By right side of head** 1 turquoise-and-shell mosaic pendant; 1 turquoise-and-shell mosaic bird-in-flight attached to a *Glycymeris* bracelet; 1 12-cm-tall basketry armband covered w/ 1,500 pieces of turquoise inlay and additional orange, red, and black inlay	1 painted wood hand on stick, 1 painted wood deer foot on stick, 1 carved painted stick, 9 painted sticks
Right wrist 1 bracelet w/ 73 turquoise beads		5 b/w bowls, 2 polychrome bowls, 1 red pitcher
Left wrist 1 bracelet with 2 turquoise grasshopper heads		1 coiled basket, 2 sets of painted basket fragments
Knees loops of *Conus* tinklers	**By left side of head** 2 shell pendants	1 obsidian blade, 2 large knife blades
		scattered mass of copper ore
Legs strings of *Conus* tinklers (probably attached to lower body clothing)	**25 cm above body** 2 painted green stone pendants	reeds filled with paint, gourd with paint inside, skin sacks with paint, hematite paint fragments
		mass of hair, mass of string
		25 cm above Magician's body 1 painted wooden stick w/ carved deer foot on end, 1 painted wooden stick w/ carved human hand on end, 1 stick
		3 b/w bowls, 1 b/w jar, 1 red jar, 1 crushed b/w bowl
		From top of burial pit's collapsed roof hundreds of miniature wooden bows and reed shafts w/ 420 projectile points

*McGregor 1943

Table 3.7. Jewelry and Other Grave Goods in the Most Jewelry-Rich Burials at Site RB568, Kayenta, Northeast Arizona, AD 900–1100*

Burial #	Jewelry	Other Grave Goods
50	Necklace (?) of 50,400 red/black stone beads 2 turquoise pendants 1 wood pendant w/ 17 turquoise mosaic insets 1 painted wood bracelet painted wood bracelet frags.	5 painted jars[†] 1 painted bilobe jar 2 gray jars 3 painted bowls* 1 unidentified bowl 1 painted bowl frag. 1 gray jar frag. 1 painted ladle 8 bone awls 1 bone awl frag. 3 manos 1 metate 3 textile frags. 2 pieces cordage matting maize and vegetable remains unknown organic material rodent bone twigs 5 clumps of charcoal

26	Armband of 39,000 black/red stone beads
	  w/ a few turquoise disks
	necklace of 80–90 turquoise beads and
	  pendants
		2 painted jars
		1 painted jar colander
		2 painted bowls
		1 painted ladle
		mano frags.
		metate frag.
		cloth frag. (?)
		squash seeds

*Crotty 1983:32–33, 79, 83–85
[†]Possible color combinations include: black-on-white, black-on-orange, black-on-red, polychrome.

Table 3.8. Jewelry and Other Grave Goods in the Most Jewelry-Rich Burials at Paquimé, Chihuahua, Northwest Mexico, AD 1200–1450*

Burial #	Jewelry	Other Grave Goods
384/385	2,321 shell disk beads 875 whole-shell beads 850 gray slate disk beads 54 jet disk beads 33 siltstone disk beads 14 turquoise disk beads 13 felsite disk beads 8 red slate disk beads 7 other stone beads 1 ricolite disk bead 2 copper tinklers	2 polychrome bowls 2 polychrome jars 1 polychrome effigy jar 1 polychrome miniature bowl textile fragment (?) pigment crayons wood paho fragment unidentified plant remains
314	638 shell beads 608 whole-shell beads	
157	1,122 whole-shell beads	

*Ravesloot 1988:22, 86–87, 88

Table 3.9. Jewelry and Other Grave Goods in the Most Jewelry-Rich Burials at Point of Pines and Grasshopper Pueblos, AD 1275–1400, Mogollon Mountains, East-Central Arizona*

Site/Burial #	Jewelry Worn	Other Jewelry	Other Grave Goods
Point of Pines B-271		564 disk beads[†] 159 whole-shell beads	2 corrugated bowls 1 corrugated jar
Point of Pines B-128		556 disk beads	
Point of Pines B-148		43 whole-shell beads	2 corrugated bowls 1 crystal
Point of Pines B-121		1 *Glycymeris* bracelet 150 *Glycymeris* bracelet frags. 1 disk bead	4 corrugated bowls 1 b/w bowl 1 plain bowl 3 corrugated jars 1 b/w pitcher
Grasshopper #140	**Left arm** 8 *Glycymeris* bracelets **Left ear** earring with 3 turquoise ear bobs **Right ear** earring with 4 turquoise ear bobs		**In pit w/ body** 2 modified *Cardium* shells (containers?) 15 polychrome bowls 3 b/r bowls 1 b/w jar 1 polychrome plate 74 projectile points 3 knives 1 turquoise and shell-inlaid bone awl 1 plain bone awl 1 bone wand 1 bone rasp/noise-maker 1 bone tool 1 mortar w/ ground hematite 1 mortar/rubbing stone w/ hematite ground hematite stains azurite powder mat **In pit above body** 1 polychrome jar 1 b/w jar 2 red jars 11 polychrome bowls 1 red bowl 54 projectile pts. 2 bone awls ground hematite sherds

*Arizona State Museum catalog, Griffin 1967
[†]Material of disk beads not specified in ASM catalog.

Table 3.10. Jewelry and Other Grave Goods in Most Jewelry-Rich Burials at Arroyo Hondo and Tijeras Pueblos, Middle Rio Grande River Valley, North-Central New Mexico, AD 1300–1425*

Site/Burial #	Jewelry	Other Grave Goods
Arroyo Hondo 12-18-8-VII-1	Necklace of 177 juniper-seed beads 4 jet beads 1 turquoise bead 1 shell pendant 1 shell pendant frag.	
Arroyo Hondo 12-11-8-2-13	1 turquoise bead	1 corrugated water jar 1 corn cob
Tijeras Pueblo B2	1 shell pendant 1 stone bead	5 broken pots sherds lithics
Tijeras Pueblo B22	1 stone pendant	1 polishing stone 1 shaft smoother sherds lithics
Tijeras Pueblo B36	1 shell bead	1 obsidian point sherds lithics 1 corn cob
Tijeras Pueblo B52	1 bone bead	sherds lithics worked bone

*Palkovich 1980, Maxwell Museum of Anthropology catalog

Table 4.1. Mimbres Hairstyle Data*

	Females	Males	Unknown	Total
Double side bun	15		2	17
Single back bun		11	18	29
Long in back		9	2	11
Pulled back horizontally, tied at end, sometimes with ornament	2		3	5
Fringe top and back of head		2	1	3
Side pony/pig tails		1		1
Fringe on top, side ponytails with fringed balls on end			1	1

*Data compiled from the Mimbres Pottery Image Data Base (MimPIDD).

Table 4.2. Casas Grandes Hairstyle Data*

	Females	Males	Unknown	Total
In front of ears	10	1	2	13
Behind ears		9	1	10
Cheek curl		1	3	4

*Data compiled from published ceramic effigy illustrations.

Table 4.3. Pueblo IV-Period Ancestral Pueblo Hairstyle Data*

	Awat'ovi/Kawaika'a	Pottery Mound/Kuaua	Total	Sex Identifications[†]
Long on sides/back	10	26	36	2f, 6m
Uneven sides	3	13	16	3f, 5m
Medium on sides/back	8	1	9	2m
Ear whorls	1	7	8	6f
Long in back, wrapped at end	7		7	1 f, 1m
Side bob	5		5	2f
Single back bun		2	2	1f
Sideways "M" on sides of head		2	2	2f
Comma on sides of head		1	1	2f

*Data compiled from published kiva mural illustrations.
[†]f = female; m = male

Table 4.4. Mimbres Hair-Decoration Data*

	Females	Males	Unknown	Total
Single feather	3	36	27	66
Double feather	1	6	4	11
Total single/double feather	**4**	**42**	**31**	**77**
Headband	18	7	9	34
(# w/ pattern)	(12)		(7)	(19)
Hat	11	7	9	27
(# w/ pattern)	(10)	(3)	(2)	(15)
Total headband/hat	**29**	**14**	**18**	**61**
(# w/ pattern)	**(22)**	**(3)**	**(9)**	**(34)**
Antler		3	2	5
Animal head		1	2	3
Ring of triangles			3	3
Feather			2	2
Ring of half circles			1	1
Conical hat with triangle on top		1		1
Total headdresses		**5**	**10**	**15**
Decorated ornament at end of horizontal tied-back hair	1		2	3

*Data compiled from the Mimbres Pottery Image Data Base (MimPIDD). Note: some individuals wore more than one hair decoration. This table does not include hair wraps for double and single buns.

Table 4.5. Casas Grandes Hair-Decoration Data*

	Females	Males	Unknown	Total
Headband with empty squares with dot	4	5	12	21
Other headbands	5	5		10
Hat		1		1
Headband or hat	3	5	14	22
Total headband/hats	**12**	**16**	**26**	**54**
Snake headdress		1	2	3
Stepped crown	1	1	1	3
Flat circles			2	2
Duck bill			1	1
Total headdresses	**1**	**2**	**6**	**9**

*Data compiled from published ceramic effigy illustrations. Note: some individuals had more than one decoration.

Table 4.6. Pueblo IV-Period Ancestral Pueblo Hair-Decoration Data*

	Awat'ovi/Kawaika'a	Pottery Mound/Kuaua	Total	Sex Identifications[†]
Red stripe down hair	15	16	31	1f, 8m
Elaborate, multifeather headdress		18	18	1f, 8m
Other elaborate headdress		6	6	1f
Total headdresses		**24**	**24**	**2f, 8m**
2–4 feathers	9	6	15	1f, 4m
2 long feathers w/ 3–5 short feathers	3		3	2m
Total simple feather combination	**12**	**6**	**18**	**1f, 6m**
Single feather		11	11	3f, 1m
Headband only[‡]	5	1	6	1m

*Data compiled from published kiva mural illustrations.
[†]f = female; m = male
[‡]This table does not include headbands with other decorations.

Table 5.1. Mimbres Facial Designs*

Design	Frequency
1–3 cheek tick marks	16
Lone Ranger eye band	14
Crosshatch/vertical lines across bottom half of face	7
Negative straight/angular line on face sides	6
Solid triangle/rectangle on chin sides	5
Horizontal black band/pair straight lines across face below nose	5
X-mark on cheeks	3
Parallel right-angle lines on sides of jaw	3
Vertical chin lines	2
Vertical tears below eye	2
Solid line/band vertical below eyes	2
Zigzag line on cheeks	1
Eyeglasses	1
Solid gray covering bottom half of face	1

*Data compiled from the Mimbres Pottery Image Data Base (MimPIDD).

Table 5.2. Casas Grandes Facial Designs*

Design	Frequency
Line down top of nose	56
Chin tick marks	55
Solid steps on cheeks	45
Extended/droopy eye liner	28
Solid triangle chin, side, forehead	16
Eyeglasses	16
Parallel straight lines on cheeks	15
Parallel zigzag lines on cheeks	15
Cheek feathers or feather-like	14
Chevrons	9
Curl/scroll on cheek	9
Lone Ranger eye band	8
Vertical line either side of nose	7
Solid rectangle on side of face	7
Lip ticking	6
Single horizontal line either side of nose	4
Solid band/long, narrow rectangle	3
Dots in lines	3
Angular line and solid triangle/rectangle	3
Diagonal series solid rectangles	2
Circle outline on chin	2
Solid rectangle on side of face	2
Vertical lines between upper lip and chin	2
Triangle line above/around mouth	2
Barbed lines	1
Solid wide line across chin	1
Solid triangle on either side of chin	1
Solid triangle above lip	1
Solid triangle covering forehead to chin	1

*Data compiled from published ceramic effigy illustrations.

Table 5.3. Other Occurrences of Prehistoric Southwest Facial Designs*

Design	Hopi Kachinas	Aztec Codices	Teotihuacán Murals	Hopi Symbolism
Cheek lines—vertical pair	X			warrior's marks, decorate kachinas who sing for rain, perform in bean dance
Cheek lines—vertical triple	X	X		
Cheek triangle—hatched	X			hatching w/in frame = water, decorates kachinas who support seed generation, ensure harvest, perform in bean dance and water-serpent ceremony
Chin lines	X	X[†]		
Chin triangle	X			
Dots—random	X		X	stars = moisture, corn kernels, fertility
Dots—pattern	X			
Extended eyeliner	X	X		decorates kachina who is messenger to rain god
Horizontal lines from mouth	X			
Horizontal line from nose		X		
Lone Ranger eye band	X	X	X	
Plus (+) marks	X			stars = moisture, decorates kachina who is messenger to rain god
Solid lower half face	X	X		
Stepped cheeks—solid	X			clouds, corn (if stepped squares hollow)
Triangle encircling face	X			
Zigzag lines	X	X[†]		lightning = water, decorates kachina who is messenger to rain god

*Data compiled from published illustrations.
[†]Match found in Christman 2002.

Table 6.1. Languages Comprising Greater
Southwest Language Families

Language Family	Languages
Apachean	Chiricahua
	Jicarilla
	Kiowa Apache
	Lipan
	Mescalero
	Navajo
	Western Apache
Keresan	Eastern Keres
	Western Keres
Kiowa-Tanoan	Kiowa
	Tewa
	Tiwa
	Towa
Seri*	Seri (Comcaac)
Uto-Aztecan	Eudeve
	Hopi
	Opata
	Northern Tepehuan
	Southern Tepehuan
	Upper and Lower Piman
Yuman	Cocopa
	Kiliwa
	Maricopa
	Mohave
	Quechan
	Upland Yuman
	Yavapai
Zuni	Zuni

*The Seri language family is not discussed in this chapter.

Notes

Preface and Acknowledgments

1. Research by ethnohistorians, ethnographers, and archaeologists has shown that prehistoric Southwesterners did in fact travel. Riley (1976, 1982) summarizes ethnohistoric data on 16th-century long-distance trade. Chapters in Snead et al. (2009) contain ethnographic and archaeological evidence for trails traveled by historic-period groups (Hopi, Tohono O'odham, indigenous residents of the Pajarito Plateau in north-central New Mexico) and their prehistoric-period ancestors. Underhill (1938, 1946) describes how the historic-period Tohono O'odham undertook four-day ritual pilgrimages to the Gulf of California to obtain salt and spiritual power. A series of ethnographic studies document how the historic-period Hopi traveled far, both for trade and for ritual pilgrimages to collect salt and to visit sacred places and shrines (Colton 1964, Fewkes 1906, Geertz and Lomatuway'ma 1987, Glowacka et al. 2009, Titiev 1937). Tohono O'odham and Hopi ancestors—the Hohokam and Ancestral Puebloans—probably made similar journeys.
2. Due to reproduction quality issues, a few of the images were not included in the book.

Introduction

1. Barth (1969) conducted the seminal cultural anthropological study of identity. More recent examples can be found in Holland et al. (1998), and Weinreich and Saunderson (2013). Early studies by archaeologists using ethnographic data include Wobst (1977) and Hodder (1982).
2. Early attempts to divide the prehistoric Southwest into culture areas can be found in Kidder (1924), Gladwin and Gladwin (1929), and Haury (1936).
3. Wilcox (1979) first proposed the regional system concept for the Hohokam, and the concept was subsequently applied to the Chacoans (Crown and Judge 1991) and Salado (Crown 1994).
4. McGregor (1943) conducted perhaps the best-known mortuary study to highlight a particular individual. Mitchell and Brunson-Hadley (2001) include mortuary studies that focus on status differences in cases from throughout the Southwest. Gender roles have been investigated using grave goods by Crown and Fish (1996) and Howell (1995), and skeletal analyses by Benson (1986), Hawkey (1988), and Merbs and Vestergaard (1985).
5. In chapter 2, Ann Stodder discusses an example of cranial modification used to identify migrants at Point of Pines Ruin.

6. Good examples of archaeological research on identity and migration in the Southwest can be found in Clark (2001, 2007).

7. Joyce (2005) provides an overview of archaeological approaches to the body in the sense that it is the site of lived experience.

8. Haury (1950:467–68) states that the burial of the man depicted in Figure I.3 could be older than the proposed AD 1000–1400 date range. The man's grave goods included a human hair wig.

9. The clothes, jewelry, and facial decoration of the man in Figure I.4 are a composite of archaeological evidence collected from different Hohokam sites in the Lower Salt and Middle Gila River valleys.

10. Excellent overviews of the prehistoric Southwest's major chronological sequences can be found in Cordell and McBrinn (2012), Lekson (2009), and Stephen Plog (2008).

    Earlier Hohokam Preclassic periods include the Colonial (AD 700–900) and Pioneer periods (AD 450–700). They were preceded by the Early Agricultural (1000 BC–AD 450) and Archaic periods (7000–1000 BC).

    Earlier Ancestral Pueblo periods include the Pueblo I (AD 700–900) and Basketmaker III (AD 500–700) and II periods (1500 BC–AD 700). These were preceded by the Archaic period (7000–1500 BC).

    As in Figure I.7, the dates for these earlier periods are approximate and open to dispute but over greater temporal ranges.

Chapter 1: Physical Variation

1. DNA analysis has been done on a slowly growing number of prehistoric Southwest skeletons (e.g., Carlyle 2005; Carlyle et al. 2000; Snow et al. 2010). Because it involves the destruction of small amounts of bone or tooth, DNA analysis requires the approval of culturally affiliated descendant groups, in addition to adequate funding.

2. Nonmetric variation in dentition can discern biological differences across a region (Durand et al. 2010, Scott and Turner 1997, Turner 1999, Turner and LeBlanc 2010), within a locality (McClelland 2010), or within a single community (McClelland 2003). Analyses of nonmetric skeletal traits can also be very effective in looking at biological distance between small groups of people.

    These low-tech, nondestructive, analytical methods, underutilized for many years, are coming back into common use. But not all students have the opportunity for training in the recording and analysis of nonmetric trait data, and many researchers use the somewhat limited list of primary traits in the osteometric standards (Buikstra and Ubelaker 1994) instead of the longer lists of traits productively used by previous generations of researchers (e.g., Bennett 1975, Birkby 1973, El-Najjar 1974, Hooton 1930).

    Nonmetric traits are not unrelated to phenotypic variation, but like mtDNA haplotypes, trigonid crests on tooth crowns, and suture patterns on the skull vault, such traits do not exactly pop out at the visitor from another valley!

3. Today, terms like "descriptive historicism," "diffusionism," "racial typology," "migrationism" (Armelagos and Van Gerven 2003:61), and "reductionist" (Martin 1998) are used to decry the outdated implications of early research by Hooton (1930), Hrdlicka (1931, 1935), Seltzer (1936, 1944), and others who pioneered the study of population biology in the Southwest. Hooton's typological groups in the Pecos population include Pseudo-Australoids and Negroids, among others, and two decades later Neuman (1952)

concluded that variation in Southwest cranial morphology was the result of an influx of people from the Louisiana Gulf coast.

    While it now seems incredible that people actually thought that, it is worth remembering that the residents of Los Muertos, the Hohokam site excavated by the Hemenway Expedition, were thought to be related to the Incas (Matthews et al. 1893), and that archaeological sites were given names like Aztec Ruin and Montezuma's Castle because it seemed to the earliest archaeologists that the ancestors of the local indigenous people could not have constructed these sophisticated buildings.

4. One consequence of early racial interpretations and the imperative to respect the wishes of descendant communities regarding the study of human remains is that it is now considered unseemly for physical anthropologists to array a group of skulls in the laboratory or museum and look at the differences between them. Space constraints in museums are an additional problem for this approach. Even if photography is not explicitly prohibited (and it often is), there is little incentive to take the traditional series of skull photographs in standard anatomical planes. The publication of such photographs is extremely rare in the U.S. today.

    Yet the dismissal of early physical anthropology ignores the fact that the painstaking univariate analyses of craniometric data did establish the biological continuity of prehistoric inhabitants of the region (e.g., Basketmaker and Pueblo I periods) and prehistoric- and historic-period Southwest people.

    Today, researchers who study human remains from a particular region can indeed recognize typical facial features and detect differences between people from communities up and down the Rio Grande Valley, for example. Cranial dimensions and facial features *do* have their place in the study of prehistoric people in social as well as ecological and economic contexts. Furthermore, such research could allow us to recover the notion of individuation in bioarchaeology.

5. Stodder (2006) provides an overview of stature trends.

6. Appendix Tables 1.1–2 show pooled stature estimate data from 62 sites or multisite localities with occupation end dates in the three periods under consideration here. The number of individuals in a stature data set and the range of variation across all the measured individuals are not always reported in publications, but the data here are based on a minimum of 435 females and 527 males.

    Like the robusticity data, there is considerably more information presented here for Ancestral Pueblo (Anasazi) skeletal assemblages than for other groups. This is due in part to my own research focus on the Colorado Plateau but also a result of different mortuary practices, especially the use of cremation by the Hohokam (and other groups at certain times and places), which affect skeletal preservation and data recovery. Another issue that affects meta-analysis of stature data is the use of different formulas to estimate stature based on skeletal elements. These data are all based on measurements of complete femora or tibiae and the formula published by Genovés (1967), since this has been the most common method (almost exclusively) used in regional publications over the past several decades (see Malville 2008 for discussion).

7. Available data suggest that overall health declined in groups in the areas colonized by Spaniards (Bruwelheide et al. 2010; Morgan 2010; Stodder 1990, 2006).

8. Akins (1986), Lumpkin (1976), and Malville (2008) present analyses of skeletal and grave-good data from Chaco great houses (and Appendix Tables 1.1–2).

9. McGregor (1943) described the Magician's burial, and Neitzel (2012) presents a recent overview of research on this individual. The Magician's grave goods are discussed in Chapters 3, 4, and 5.

10. This perusal of univariate data is not presented as a study in the variation of facial features. It is instead a deconstruction of the multivariate approach that simultaneously uses multiple measurements to detect biological distance patterning. We see faces as complexes of features, and a multivariate study specifically designed to elucidate the different trends in facial features would be a worthwhile exercise in meta-analysis.

    Many early multivariate studies of prehistoric Southwest crania were less than edifying in terms of finding substantial biological distance between skeletal populations from different sites, time periods, or regions. Current analytical methods are now better suited for craniometric data (accommodating the typically small and incomplete data sets generated from the study of poorly preserved remains). But in the current research emphasis on understanding social and economic networks in the prehistoric Southwest, we now approach the topic of biodistance as illuminating large- and small-scale networks, rather than identifying small, isolated populations scattered across the plateau and desert.

    Researchers are moving towards an improved understanding of how we can integrate biomolecular with craniometric data (Heather Smith 2009).

11. The sources for the craniometric data in Appendix Tables 1.3–4 are courtesy of Nancy Akins and Scott Ortman (La Plata Highway data, Akins forthcoming), Katherine Weisensee (Pecos, Peabody Museum data), Barnes 1988 (Casa Buena), Bennett 1973 (Point of Pines), Douglas and Stodder 2010 (Ridges Basin), El-Najjar 1974 (Canyon de Chelley, Paa'ko), Hoffman 1993 (Duckfoot), Regan and Turner 1997 (Schoolhouse Point Mesa), Seltzer 1944 (originally in Hrdlicka 1931) (Grand Gulch Basketmakers, Pueblo Bonito, Puye, Los Muertos, Chaves Pueblo, Hawikku).

12. Hooton's work (1930) contains the Pecos craniometric data and his interpretations of Pecos population history. Weisensee (2008) and Weisensee and Jantz (2010) have reanalyzed these data.

13. A recent movement to include systematic recording of a series "macromorphoscopic traits" of the face and skull vault, defined by forensic anthropologist Joseph Hefner (Hefner 2009, 2011; Hefner et al. 2014), is very useful in capturing aspects of the face and skull that are not readily measurable. These traits include interorbital breadth (narrow, medium, broad), shape of the nasal aperture (bowed, teardrop, rounded), shape of the eye orbit (rectangular, circular, rhomboid), and 13 others. Some were recorded by early Southwest researchers and such recording is still done by researchers in Oceanic and Asian population history. But they fell out of the North American skeletal collection repertoire many decades ago. Forensic anthropology is leading the way back to this methodology for use in estimating "peer-perceived ancestry" in medico-legal contexts, the language of which is carefully framed to distance current applications from the race-oriented approach of the 1900s (Hefner et al. 2014:588). Along with nondestructive, three-dimensional laser scanning of brow ridge and chin shape, these systematic data will be extremely useful in characterizing facial features, especially in skeletal assemblages for which photographic documentation is prohibited.

14. The formula for the femur robusticity index is (anterior-posterior midshaft diameter +

mediolateral midshaft diameter × 100 / bicondylar femur length). Ruff (2006, 2010) discusses how environment can affect skeletal morphology.

15. See Auerbach (2011) for discussion of body mass and stature in ancient North Americans. Stodder (2006) provides an overview of femur robusticity trends.

    The robusticity comparisons require a caveat: they were undoubtedly affected by the very small numbers of individuals representing some cultural groups and site assemblages (see Appendix Tables 1.3–4). As in the earlier discussion of stature, there is relatively little metric skeletal data for Hohokam assemblages because many Hohokam were cremated, and skeletal preservation in many inhumations is very poor.

16. The very first observers of prehistoric Southwest human remains noted skulls with modified shapes. See Retzius's (1893) report on the remains from Nordenskiold's excavations at Mesa Verde, the Matthews et al. (1893) report on human remains from the Hemenway Expedition's work at Los Muertos, and Bessels (1876) study of human remains from the early USGS expeditions.

    The quantification and study of the dimensions of the head and face is the oldest tradition in biological anthropology, but the nearly ubiquitous use of cradleboards by prehistoric Southwesterners modified the shape of the cranial vault such that standard measurements could not be taken. This was a source of great frustration to early anthropologists. In his report on the human remains from Lowry Ruin, Von Bonin (1936, in Stewart 1937:169) wrote that the modification of the back of the skull vault "played havoc with the shape of the brain case so that for purposes of comparison only the face can be used."

17. Hrdlicka (1935:250) did not see the creation of a particular head shape as the main objective of cradleboards, but he did think that Pueblo people must have favored certain shapes. Otherwise, in his view, they would not have persisted in the practice. Bessels (1876) noted that cranial asymmetry is not consistent with the cliff dwellers' aesthetic, as seen in architecture and ceramics. Head shape is not discussed in ethnographic works addressing Pueblo notions of beauty (Hrdlicka 1906), dress, and ornamentation (Stevenson et al. 1987), or in the detailed account of Hopi cradles and infant care by Dennis and Dennis (1940).

18. See Piper (2002) for extensive discussion of prehistoric Southwest cradleboards and their use.

19. The quotes describing different kinds of cranial modification are from Erik Reed (1949:106).

20. Nelson and Madimenos (2007, 2010) point out the ambiguity in definitions of horizontal (lambdoidal) and vertical (occipital) modifications (many reports include a designation of "intermediate" modification) and suggest there are probably other individuals with obelionic modification that was recorded as occipital modification or "none of the above." Lambdoidal and occipital modifications were certainly far less noticeable than frontal and annular cranial modifications, which dramatically alter the forehead and overall shape of the skull. These more extreme forms of modification signaled group identity in terms of social standing, occupation, or particular roles in the Pre–Inca Chiribaya of Peru, for example (Lozada 2011).

21. The sources for the craniometric data in Appendix Tables 1.7–8 are courtesy of Nancy Akins (La Plata Highway), Barnes 1988 (Casa Buena), Bennett 1973 (Point of Pines),

Douglas and Stodder 2010 (Ridges Basin), El-Najjar 1974 (Canyon de Chelly, Paa'ko), Hoffman 1993 (Duckfoot), Katherine Weisensee (Pecos, Peabody Museum data), Regan and Turner 1997 (Schoolhouse Point Mesa), Seltzer 1944 (originally in Hrdlicka 1931; AZ Basketmakers, Chaves Pueblo, Grand Gulch, Hawikku, Los Muertos, Pueblo Bonito, Puye).

22. Haury (1985:256) discusses skull form at Bear Village. Erik Reed (1949) discusses the inclusion of skull modification in the definition of the Mogollon culture area.

23. Haury (1985) considers the significance of co-occurring skull forms. Bennett (1973) presents interpretations of the Point of Pines remains. Ezzo et al. (1997) use strontium isotope analysis to confirm the presence of immigrants at Grasshopper Pueblo. Strontium isotopes are used to compare place of origin with place of burial and thus track people across the landscape. Similar to DNA analysis, isotope analysis involves the destruction of small amounts of bone or tooth and thus requires approval of culturally affiliated descendant groups.

24. Hays-Gilpin (2002) documents the antiquity of Hopi ear whorls.

25. Woolf (2005) discusses Native American albinism.

26. Hammond and Rey (1940:68) present this account of migrant workers. Merbs (1992) and Schillaci (1999) describe coccidioidomycosis.

27. Rakover and Cahlon (2001:59) examine cultural differences in the perception of facial features.

Chapter 2: Clothing

1. Hendrickson (1995), Schevill et al. (1996), and Weiner and Schneider (1989) address the expressive potential of cloth and clothing.

2. Although this chapter discusses the Ancestral Puebloans of the Colorado Plateau and the Mogollon, Sinagua, Salado, and Hohokam south of the Mogollon Rim as if they were distinct cultural groups, I recognize that these terms are archaeological constructs that inadequately address the spatial and temporal variation of prehistoric Southwest groups.

3. Kent (1957, 1983a) and Teague (1998) describe the thousands of archaeological textiles recovered from alcoves and dry caves of the Colorado Plateau and other parts of the Southwest. Webster (1997, 2000, 2012) discusses the Colorado Plateau's Pueblo I- and IV-period textile remains, which are more limited due to the lesser use of dry caves during these periods.

4. Brody (2004: Figs. 30, 38, Pl. 2) illustrates the valuable clothing information provided by Mimbres bowls. The kiva murals of Awat'ovi, Kawaika'a, Pottery Mound, and Kuaua are well documented by Dutton (1963), Hibben (1975), and Watson Smith (1952). Webster (2007a) compares the ceremonial clothing recorded in these murals.

5. For examples of prehistoric yucca use in different regions of the Southwest, see Haury (1950), Hays-Gilpin et al. (1998), Kent (1983a), Kidder and Guernsey (1919), King (1974), Martin et al. (1952), Elizabeth Morris (1980), O'Neale (1948), and Teague (1998: 13–14). See Webster (1997, 2000, 2007b:295–299) for late prehistoric use of yucca in the Zuni area.

6. For information on the adoption of cotton from Mexico and its use south of the Mogollon Rim, see Kent (1983a:27–28) and Teague (1998:19–20). For the cultivation and

weaving of cotton in this region during the late prehistoric period, see Haury (1934, 1945a:172), Kent (1954, 1983a:27–36), Paul Martin et al. (1952:130, Fig. 69b), and Steen et al. (1962).

7. For information on prehistoric cotton cultivation and use on the Colorado Plateau, see Hall and Dennis (1986:134–138), Kent (1957; 1983a:27–35), Magers (1986:245, 272), and Teague (1998:19–21, 26). Webster (2012:178–179) discusses cotton evidence at Pueblo I-period sites in northeast Arizona. Bohrer (2006:739), Osborne (2004:435–441), and Webster (2006:1011–1012; 2008:185) discuss the lack of evidence for cotton production at Mesa Verde and in the San Juan Basin.

8. Castetter and Bell (1942:198), Huckell (1993:176–180), Stephen (1936:825–827), and Stevenson (1915:92) discuss cotton symbolism among historic-period Southwest groups.

9. For examples of Basketmaker and Pueblo I-period hair use in weaving on the Colorado Plateau, see Kent (1983a: Fig. 25), Morris and Burgh (1954:67), and Nusbaum (1922:88–89). Evidence is lacking for the use of hair fibers in the southern deserts during this early time period. For hair use on the Colorado Plateau during the late prehistoric period, see Kent (1983a:26–27) and Magers (1986:237, 241). For hair use south of the Rim during the late period, see Dixon (1956:27, Fig 17), Haury (1950:392, 434, 440–441), Hough (1914:72–76, Fig 150), King (1974:80), Steen et al. (1962:92–93), and Teague (1996:170, 172; 1998:11).

10. For information on the use of fur- and feather-wrapped yarns in the Southwest, see Haury (1950), Kent (1983a:26), Magers (1986:236), Osborne (2004), Rohn (1971: Fig. 183), and Webster (2006:1002–1003; 2008:178, 183).

11. The extremely rare use of asbestos fibers is discussed by Kelly and Webster (2010: Fig 1, Table 1), Kent (1983a:27), Stubbs (1959), and Teague (1998:13).

12. Emery (1966), Kent (1983a), and Teague (1998) discuss finger weaving structures and techniques. Kent (1957:Chart 12, 602; 1983a:60–65) describes the braiding rhythms used in different regions of the Southwest.

13. Teague (1998:116–123) discusses the introduction of the loom into the southern Southwest and the effects of different loom forms on the characteristics of woven cloth.

14. Webster (1997:414–415, 434–439, 457–458, 468–474, 484–485, 511) discusses the archaeological evidence for the use of the upright loom in the Rio Grande Valley.

15. Kent (1983a) and Teague (1998) describe loom-woven fabric structures used in the Southwest. The plain-weave estimate of 85 percent is from Kent (1983a:125).

16. For information about yucca plain-weave fabrics in the Zuni area, see Webster (1997:233–235, 258–261) and (2000:193–194, Tables 10.2, 10.3).

17. Emery (1966:84–85, 181, Figs 111–113, 250–252) describes the fabric structure of weft-wrap openwork and gauze.

18. Kent (1983a:153, 215) and Teague (1998:78, 177) discuss Mesoamerican connections for Southwest fabrics.

19. Prehistoric pigments and dyes are discussed by Kent (1983a:36–43). Early colors were probably obtained primarily from mineral pigments and less often from organic materials. More research is needed on the chemical identification of prehistoric colorants.

20. For a discussion of tie dye in the Southwest, see Kent (1983a:192–195), Teague (1998:135, 141–142), and Webster et al. (2006). In addition to tie-dye, an unpublished cotton

fragment from Casa Grande in southern Arizona appears to be decorated with a circular motif in a resist technique similar to batik. The catalog number of this fragment is National Museum of Natural History A-170137 (Smithsonian Institution).

21. For a discussion of preferred color palettes in different regions of the Southwest, see Kent (1983a:36–44; 209–215).

22. The use of blue and green in yarns and woven textiles is discussed by Kent (1983a: Pl. 7, pp. 42–43), McGregor (1931:3–4), and Teague (1998:132–133). Examples are provided by Keith Anderson et al. (1986:200, Fig. 11.2c), Hough (1914:83), Steen et al. (1962:122), Walt (1978), Wasley (1962), and Webster et al. (2006: Table 1, Fig 1e).

23. For additional information about design layouts and motifs used in different regions of the Southwest, see Kent (1983a:201–220) and Teague (1998:143–158).

24. The offset-quartered layout used to decorate painted blankets on the Colorado Plateau has precedence in the ceramic designs of the Hohokam and Mogollon and farther south in Mexico. See Haury (1945b:28–29) and Kent (1983a:211–213).

25. Webster et al. (2006) discuss the metaphorical meanings of the dot-in-square motif and its use in tie-dyed fabrics.

26. For information about the ritual uses of blue and blue-green in the Southwest, see Plog (2003), Vivian et al. (1978), Wasley (1962), Webster (2011), also *Hopi Color-Direction Symbolism*, (n.d.) http://www.as.wvu.edu/~scmcc/colordirections.pdf (accessed March 31, 2016).

27. Webster et al. (2006) discuss the metaphorical meanings of the dot-in-square motif and its use in tie-dyed fabrics.

28. For contemporary Hopi interpretations of stepped and hooked triangles as symbols for clouds and rain, see Webster and Loma'omvaya (2004:86).

29. For mural depictions of men and perhaps women wearing short, decorated blankets around their shoulders, see Watson Smith (1952: Figs. 17n,p, 81a,b, Pl. 1) and Webster (2007a:195, Fig. 9.2d).

30. Kent (1983a:227–228) discusses a long, rectangular cotton blanket from Ventana Cave made from two narrow loom-woven fabrics.

31. We do not know if yucca and rag-weft blankets were used as articles of dress or only as burial shrouds.

32. The elaborately decorated turkey-feather blanket from Mesa Verde is described and illustrated by Osborne (2004:56, Fig. 42).

33. The Sinagua rabbit-fur blanket is part of the Dyck Collection at the Verde Valley Archaeology Center.

34. For more information about styles of women's aprons, see Kent (1983a:243–246).

35. Ezell (1983: Fig. 4) documents historic-period O'odham women wearing free-hanging bark skirts and loom-woven, cotton, plain-weave fabrics as wrap-around skirts.

36. It is unknown when women on the Colorado Plateau started wearing their blankets as wrap-around dresses. The earliest direct evidence is for the period AD 1350–1540 from the Pottery Mound kiva murals (Hibben 1975: Fig. 74; Webster 2007a:195, Fig. 9.9a; see also Figure 2.12a), but women could have adopted this style much earlier. We lack specific information about how blankets were worn south of the Mogollon Rim.

37. For more information about men's breechcloths, see Kent (1983a:239–243, 245–256). Kent (1983a:243) suggests that late prehistoric breechcloths were undecorated because they were often hidden beneath kilts.

38. Hough (1914:72, Figs. 149, 150) illustrates and briefly describes the cordage breech covering from the Upper Gila region.

39. For more information about kilts and their depiction in the kiva murals, see Dutton (1963: Figs. 30–32, 56, 64), Hibben (1975: Figs. 30, 65, 72, 75, 86), Kent (1962:156–157, Pl. 5a, 1983a:235–239), King (1974:84–85), Watson Smith (1952: Figs 52a, 76b, 71a, Pl1), and Webster (2007a:169–170, 183, Figs 9.2d, 9.3, 9.4, 9.10–9.13).

40. The Ancestral Pueblo negative-painted or resist-dyed shirt is from the site of Poncho House.

41. The openwork braided shirt was recovered from White House in Canyon de Chelly.

42. For more information about shirts and tunics and their depiction in the kiva murals, see Hibben (1975: Fig. 60), Kent (1957:597–600; 1983a:65, 230–231, Figs. 30, 137g–i), Osborne (2004:37–43), and Watson Smith (1952: Figs. 50c, 66c, 88a, Pl. F).

43. Kent (1957:603; 1983a: Fig. 34) and Teague (1998:cover, Fig. 3.22) describe the spectacular lace-like shirt found near Tonto Ruins.

44. The asbestos sash from Awat'ovi is described by Stubbs (1959).

45. The feather-pile band from Aztec Ruins is unpublished (cat. # AMNH 29.0/5283).

46. For information on different sandal styles worn in the Southwest, see Cosgrove (1947: 82–98), Dixon (1956: Figs 16, 19), Haury (1950:433–439, 464, 466–467, Fig. 102, Pl. 46), Kankainen (1995), Kidder and Guernsey (1919:158, Pl. 39a), Martin et al. (1952:235, 240, 266–272, 276–277, Figs. 97–100), Morris and Burgh (1954:65), Osborne (2004), Steen et al. (1962:24–25, Pl. 12b), and Yoder (2010). Based on early photographs of indigenous people from Mesoamerica and the Southwest that show many women going barefoot, it is likely that men wore sandals more often than women in the prehistoric Southwest.

47. The square heel on diagonally plaited sandals worn south of the Rim was made by folding the weaving elements toward the upper surface and anchoring them to the heel with a crosswise strip of yucca.

48. For more information about the twined sandals worn on the Colorado Plateau, see Hays-Gilpin et al. (1998) and Webster (2008:163).

49. For more information about the Hohokam sandals that resemble a coiled braid, see Fulton (1941:25–26, Fig. 4, Pl. VIIB), Haury (1950:433–439, 467, Fig. 102, Pl. 46), King (1965:114), and Sayles (1937:160, Figs. 60, 61). Their method of manufacture is still open to question.

50. For more information about the finely woven twill-plaited sandal with the H-shaped braided strap worn in central Arizona and northern Mexico, see Haury (1934:64–68, Pl. XLII), King (1974:90, Fig. 87, 88), Steen et al. (1962:25, Pl. 12a), and Webster (2007b:307, Fig. 16.7i).

51. For more information on the prehistoric use of leggings, see Dixon (1956: Fig. 17), Dorothea Kelly (1937:Pl. XII), Kent (1957:589; 1983a:50–51, Figs. 17, 18), Magers (1986: 239), Elizabeth Morris (1980:97–98, 114, Figs. 58e, 73), Rohn (1971:112, Fig. 132), and Webster (2006:1002–1003, Figs. 46, 85a; 2008:176, 183, Fig. 9.5d).

52. The Aztec feather band is at the American Museum of Natural History (cat. # 29.0/5283). The remains of several northern flicker (*Colaptes auratus*) quill bands are known from Pueblo Bonito (cat. numbers National Museum of the American Indian 055246 and American Museum of Natural History H/175, H/192, H/202, H/204, and H/214). All are unpublished.

53. At Painted Cave, a painted polychrome blanket was associated with a woman, and another painted blanket was found with an infant (Haury 1945b:22–24, Pls. 10–12). At Mesa Verde, a decorated turkey-feather blanket with a geometric design was also associated with an infant (Osborne 2004:24, 37, Fig. 12).

54. Kivas were ceremonial chambers in which both prehistoric- and historic-period Puebloans conducted religious rituals. Kiva murals are undoubtedly sacred, illustrating Pueblo religious beliefs and practices.

55. Information about costume depictions in the Pueblo-period IV kiva murals is taken from Dutton (1963), Hibben (1975), and Watson Smith (1952). Regional comparisons of ritual clothing are summarized from Kent (1983a:228–229) and Webster (2007a).

56. The possible hide tunic depicted at Kuaua may represent a warrior tunic (see Dutton 1963: cover jacket and Fig. 54; Webster 2007a:192).

57. Although men are usually identified as the wearers of decorated kilts, a rectangular fabric decorated in gauze weave was associated with the burial of a young girl from the Verde Valley (Kent 1983a:237), and an unpublished rectangular fabric decorated in supplementary weft or embroidery was associated with another young girl from the Verde Valley. The warps in the first example run in the long direction similar to modern Pueblo kilts. The warps in the second example run in the short direction similar to the kilt from Hidden House.

58. For legwear depicted in the kiva murals, see Dutton (1963: Figs. 6, 32, 64–66), Hibben (1975: frontispiece, Figs. 2, 3, 72, 86), and Watson Smith (1952: Figs. 50f, 52b, 61b, 67a, 71, 80b, 81). For footwear depictions, see Dutton (1963: Figs. 1, 6, 24, 31, 32), Hibben (1975: frontispiece, Figs. 30, 45, 47, 71, 86), Watson Smith (1952: Figs. 51c, 67, 69a, 71, 72b, 81). The footwear depictions may represent moccasins.

59. For a discussion of Mexican influences in Southwest textiles, see King (1979:275) and Teague (1998:98–101, 151–158, 171, 177–184). For southern origins of the off-set quartered layout in Ancestral Pueblo painted textiles, see Haury (1945b:28–29) and Kent (1983a: 213). For the southern origins of the tie-dye technique and its significance in Mesoamerica, see Anawalt (1990, 2000), Teague (1998:141–142), and Webster et al. (2006).

60. For more information about the post-contact changes in Pueblo clothing and the importance and ongoing evolution of precontact clothing styles and designs among the Pueblos, see Webster (1997, 2000, 2001) and Webster and Loma'omvaya (2004).

61. Kent (1983b: title page, 49–71, Figs. 5, 10, 11, 37) and Roediger (1941:122, Pls. 1, 31, 38) discuss historic-period Pueblo women's mantas. Keegan (1999:62, 99, 142, 144, 146–152, 158–159) shows how the manta dress serves as a symbol of Pueblo female social identity.

Chapter 3: Ornaments

1. Jernigan (1978) provides the most comprehensive and best-illustrated overview of jewelry throughout the prehistoric Southwest.

2. This chapter does not consider differences in the jewelry worn by women and men. Munson (2000) and Shafer (2003) document differences among the Mimbres, and Crown and Fish (1996) and Randall McGuire (1992) for the Hohokam.

3. Mortuary analyses have a long tradition in Southwest archaeology, as illustrated by the work of Akins (1986), Geoffrey Clark (1969), Crown and Fish (1996), Howell (1995), Randall McGuire (1992), Mitchell and Brunson-Hadley (2004), Neitzel (2000), Ravesloot (1988), Rice (2016), and Whittlesey (1978). Early research focused primarily

on comparisons of different individuals' grave goods to determine the degree of social stratification in the community or the broader society.

    The underlying assumption of all mortuary analyses is that the way a person is treated at death reflects his or her status when alive (Binford 1971, Brown 1971, Carr 1994, Chapman et al. 1981, O'Shea 1984, Tainter 1978). Thus, a person with the most and/or the fanciest grave goods would have been the most prominent in life. The potential fault in this logic is that the agendas of surviving family members and others may affect the numbers and kinds of grave goods included in a deceased individual's grave.

4. When possible, I distinguish the ornaments that an individual wore at the time of interment from those that were added as grave goods. Even if the individual never wore all of his or her mortuary jewelry at one time when alive, together it reflects status and other identities. I assume that all worn jewelry belonged to the deceased and that everyone wore at least some unknown fraction of their mortuary jewelry when they were alive. Ornaments that were added to the grave may not have belonged to the deceased, but they are material indicators of the respect that others afforded him or her.

    For graves containing multiple burials, it may be impossible to distinguish jewelry added at the time of one individual's interment from that added with other individuals, or that was deposited later as ritual offerings. Simply dividing the ornament total by the number of bodies may mask variation, inflating the status of some and deflating the status of others.

5. The grave goods in burials excavated at Pueblo Bonito and other Chaco Canyon sites are tabulated in Akins (1986, 2003), Judd (1954), and Pepper (1909, 1920). Pueblo Bonito's Burial #14 was located beneath a plank floor next to another burial (#13) of an adult man who had fewer grave goods. Above the floor in the room's fill, were the mostly disturbed skeletons and grave goods of 12–14 other men and women, along with an infant and child. The room also contained numerous other offerings, including more than 300 ceremonial sticks and a variety of other ritual objects. Akins's (2003:103) most recent age-at-death estimate for the man in Burial #14 has him living longer than she previously thought (Akins 1986:163).

6. Mathien (1997) describes the diversity of Chaco jewelry.

7. The turquoise necklace and two pairs of turquoise ear pendants were deposited in the floor of a burial room located in a different part of the site from Burial #14. In addition to being draped around the neck, turquoise bead necklaces could be wrapped around the wrist to create multistrand bracelets, as in Burial #14.

8. Prehistoric Southwest copper bells are described by Di Peso et al. (1974), Fred Hawley (1953), Richard Nelson (1986), Palmer et al. (1998), Plog et al. (1982), Sprague (1963), and Vargas (1995).

9. Comparisons of Galaz Ruin's mortuary jewelry are hampered by the lack of standardized data recording. For most burials, ornament counts are reported. But for the two most prolific, bead strand lengths were measured, probably because of their extraordinarily high numbers of beads. In this discussion, I used the three burials with the longest strands and the two with the highest quantities of counted beads.

10. Jernigan (1978:111, 115, 119, 121) describes Mimbres zoomorphic pendants. Mimbres shell and stone jewelry may have also depicted animals in silhouette enclosed within a circle, an ornament type seen at other later Mogollon sites (Jernigan 1978:55).

11. Gilman (1990) reports that 80–90 percent of all Mimbres burials lack jewelry.

12. Mentions of richer Preclassic-Hohokam cremations can be found in Antieau (1981), Haury (1976), Sayles (1937), Wasley and Johnson (1965), and Woodward (1931).

13. Prehistoric Southwest turquoise sources are described in Haury (1976), Hull et al. (2008), Hull et al. (2014), Mathien (1981, 2000), Richard Nelson (1981), Northrop (1975), Sigleo (1975), Snow (1973), Vokes and Gregory (2007), Weigand and Harbottle (1993), and Weigand et al. (1977).

14. Prehistoric Southwest shell trade is described in Bayman (1996, 2002), Bradley (1993, 2000), Brand (1938), Colton (1941), Ann Howard (1983), Randall McGuire (1985), McGuire and Downum (1982), McGuire and Howard (1987), McGuire and Schiffer (1982), Richard Nelson (1981, 1986), Seymour (1988), Tower (1945), and Vokes and Gregory (2007).

15. Because of their ubiquity in the Lower Salt and Middle Gila River valleys, some researchers (e.g., Bayman 2002) think that *Glycymeris* bracelets were a marker of Hohokam cultural identity that was sometimes traded to others. The Mimbres *Glycymeris* bracelets depicted in Figures 2.7 and 3.3 would have been Hohokam imports.

    For Mimbres jewelry, shell may have been as important or more so than black stone (see Appendix Table 3.2).

16. James Bayman (2002) thinks that Hohokam mosaic pendants were leadership insignia.

17. Mills (2008) describes Chacoan ritual deposits. Anyon and LeBlanc (1984) do the same for the Mimbres.

18. Plog (2003:671) summarizes Pueblo color symbolism. Also see Mitchell (1994:181–186).

19. Mathien (1997:1153) and Mattson (2011:4–5) discuss early jewelry in the north, and Vokes (1998) and Vokes and Gregory (2007:333) in the south. The dates for the Basketmaker III period are AD 500–750, the Late Archaic/Basketmaker II period 1,000 BC–AD 500, and the Early Ceramic Period AD 50–500.

20. Blanton et al. (1996) define the corporate and network leadership strategies. Renfrew (1974) and Drennan (1991) previously discussed the organizational implications of different kinds of remains left by prehistoric chiefdoms.

21. Neitzel (2003) includes discussions of Pueblo Bonito's size and location. Lekson (1986) documents the sizes of great houses in Chaco Canyon.

22. Jerry Howard (2006) and Nicholas and Feinman (1989) document the expansion of Hohokam irrigation.

23. Jerry Howard (2006) summarizes changes in Hohokam settlement patterns.

24. Hegmon (2002) provides an overview of Mimbres archaeology.

25. Shafer (2003:159) thinks sodalities may be evidenced by the association of Mimbres males with particular kinds of jewelry.

26. The grave goods in burials excavated at Aztec Ruins are tabulated in Earl Morris (1924). Comparing burials from Aztec's West Ruin is difficult due to the practice of interring multiple individuals together. The burial numbers refer not to individual burials, but to all of the individuals interred in a single room. For example, #16 included two adults and three children found in Room 41 of the Ruin's East Wing. One of the adults was the most jewelry-rich, unlooted individual discussed here. The other was immediately adjacent and had a strand of beads on his leg.

27. Earl Morris (1924:155–161) does not identify the materials of the beads and mosaics that covered this individual's body.

28. During the early Classic period, roughly 75 percent of bodies were buried directly in pits, and roughly 25 percent were cremated. The cremains were placed in a jar that was then buried in an area separate from the inhumations. The most jewelry-rich individual was an inhumation.

29. Reports of richer Classic-period Hohokam burials can be found in Cushing (1890), Fewkes (1912), Richard Nelson (1981), and Wilcox (1987).

30. The Magician's burial is also discussed by Ferguson and Loma'omvaya (2011), Neitzel (2012), and O'Hara (2008).

31. Lac, the material used as the backing for the ornaments illustrated in Figures 3.8 and 3.9, is an insect secretion.

32. Whittaker and Kamp (1992) describe Sinagua armbands.

33. Crotty (1983: Figure 16) illustrates Burial #50's beads strung in a necklace.

34. Mattson (2011:11) reports that 78 percent of the individuals interred in and around Aztec's West Ruin lacked ornaments. Mitchell (1994:139) reports that 83 percent of Pueblo Grandes' burials lacked stone and shell beads—the most frequent ornament type; and 90 percent lacked *Glycymeris* bracelets—the second-most frequent ornament type. McGregor (1941:271) reports that six of Ridge Ruin's other burials (42%) had no grave goods. For the five that did, he does not identify the kinds of items. Five burial numbers (1,2,5,8,15) are not accounted for. If they were in fact burials and had no grave goods, then at least 65 percent of the site's burials lacked jewelry. Crotty's (1983:76–85) data indicate that 90 percent of RB568's burials contained no jewelry.

35. Bayman (2002) describes the change in shell ornament manufacture during the Hohokam Classic period.

36. Crotty (1983:33) calculated this labor estimate for beads at RB568.

37. Bayman (2002) discusses the role of mosaic shell pendants as leadership insignia.

38. Mitchell (1994:186–197) discusses the symbolism of Hohokam zoomorphic forms.

39. Bayman (2001) discusses the ritual use of *Conus* shell tinklers.

40. Mitchell (1994:185) describes Pueblo Grande's 40 skeletons with color stains, which were probably the remains of body paint applied as part of mortuary rites.

41. Earl Morris (1919, 1921) published the first descriptions of Aztec Ruins. Further discussion can be found in Lister and Lister (1996) and Paul Reed (2008, 2011). Jerry Howard (2006) describes Hohokam settlement patterns and organization in the Lower Salt River valley.

42. An intriguing question is the degree to which centralized leadership changed when Aztec Ruins replaced Pueblo Bonito as the Chacoans' primate settlement.

43. Dean (2000, 2002) summarizes Kayenta settlement patterns. Ridge Ruin's largest, roughly contemporaneous Sinagua site was nearby Wupatki with roughly 100 rooms (Anderson 1990, Pilles 2000).

44. The clothes, jewelry, hairpin, and facial decoration of the man in Figure 3.11 are a composite of archaeological evidence from archaeological sites collected from different Hohokam sites in the Lower Salt and Middle Gila River valleys.

45. The mosaics and necklace shown in Figure 3.11 were recovered from a cache in the floor of Casa Grande's Compound A (Clemensen 1992:89, Figure 26; Huffman 1925:83). The cache also contained a pair of shell pendants, possibly earrings. In the cache, the large bird and frog were tilted upright against one another, with the smaller bird, pendants,

and beads below them. The birds were inlaid on wood, and the frog, which the original excavators called a turtle, on shell.

46. Kopper (1986:235) illustrates similar frog-shaped turquoise mosaics from the Sinagua site of Limestone Ruin, the Salado site of Keystone Ruin, and the Mountain Mogollon site of Kinishba.

47. Another adult woman (#121) from Point of Pines was interred with 150 *Glycymeris* bracelet fragments, but the number of complete bracelets that they represent is unknown.

48. The burial number of the Arroyo Hondo man with ritual artifacts is 12-19-1-V-1.

49. Crotty (1995) analyzed jewelry depictions in Ancestral Pueblo kiva murals.

50. Bradley (1993, 1996) describes Paquimé's role in Southwest shell trade.

51. Whalen (2013) discusses the ritual significance of Paquimé's two shell-storage rooms. Also see Bradley (1993) and Rakita (2001).

52. Whittlesey (1984) and Reid and Whittlesey (1982) think that Grasshopper Pueblo's mortuary jewelry was part of ritual costumes and signaled sodality membership.

53. Palkovich (1980:135–136) identified two individuals at Arroyo Hondo with paint on the bones that was probably the remains of body paint applied as part of mortuary rites.

54. The rich Mimbres infant had a nine-foot strand of shell beads.

55. Paquimé had approximately 2,000 rooms; Point of Pines Ruin had over 800; Arroyo Hondo roughly 1,000; and Tijeras Pueblo roughly 200.

The nonresidential architecture at late Mountain Mogollon and Ancestral Pueblo sites consisted of great kivas, kivas, and plazas.

56. Jerry Howard (2006) describes changes in Hohokam settlement patterns.

57. For information of historic-period jewelry, see Adair (1944), Bassman and Bassman (2006), Bedinger (1973), Frank (1990), and Simpson (1999).

Chapter 4: Hair

1. Leach (1958) wrote the seminal study on the cultural meanings of hair. Subsequent studies by anthropologists and historians include Aldred (1957), Bartman (2001), Choi (2006), Delaney (1994), Gitter (1984), Hershman (1974), Mageo (1994), Powell and Roach (2004), Rosenthal (2004), Sieber and Herreman (2000), Slobodin (1981), Strathern (1989), Weitz (2001), and Williamson (1979).

2. Brief descriptions of historic-period hairstyles and decorations are scattered throughout a vast literature that spans more than 400 years, from sixteenth-century accounts by Spanish explorers to twentieth-century ethnographies by cultural anthropologists. The most comprehensive synthesis can be found in the two Southwest volumes of the Smithsonian Institution's *Handbook of Native American Indians* series (Ortiz 1979a, 1983). Some chapters mention hairstyles and decorations, occasionally with information on gender and special-occasion coiffures.

The specific *Handbook* chapters are Apache (Basso 1983; Opler 1983a, b; Tiller 1983), Coahuiltecans (T. N. Campbell 1983), Cochiti (Lange 1979a), Cocopa (Alvarez de Williams 1983), Guarijio (Thomas Hinton 1983), Hopi-Tewa (Connelly 1979, Frigout 1979, Stanislawski 1979), Isleta (Ellis 1979a), Maricopa (Harwell and Kelly 1983), Mohave (Kenneth Stewart 1983), Navajo (Emerson 1983, Witherspoon 1983, Wyman 1983), Northern Tepehuan (Pennington 1983b), Pelones (T. N. Campbell 1983), Pima (Ezell 1983), Piros (Schroeder 1979), Pojoaque (Lambert 1979), Quechan (Bee 1983), San Ildefonso (Edelman 1979), Santo Domingo (Lange 1979b), Seri (Bowen 1983), Southern

Periphery: East (Griffen 1983), Southern Tiwas (Schroeder 1979), Tanos (Schroeder 1979), Taos (Bodine 1979), Walapai (Thomas McGuire 1983), Yavapai (Khera and Mariella 1983), Zia (Schroeder 1979), and Zuni (Schroeder 1979).

3. Evidence that Pueblo influence extended to non-Pueblo groups can be seen in a published photograph of a Jicarilla Apache woman with whorls (Tiller 1983: Fig. 7). None of the descriptions of non-Pueblo women with whorls indicate that the women were young, and some photographs suggest that at least some were not.

4. Bowen (1983) states that Seri women and men both wore their long hair either loose or in one or two braids. He does not specify the gender associations of other Seri styles.

5. The Hohokam individual in Figure 3.6b may be wearing a prehistoric version of the helmet-like hairstyle.

6. Dixon (1956:8) describes the preserved Sinagua coiffure.

7. Haury (1950:440–442, Pls. 47–48) describes and illustrates the preserved Desert Hohokam wig from Ventana Cave. The individual interred with it is shown in this volume's Figure I.3.

8. I identified 51 bowls depicting 67 people with clearly visible hairstyles in the Mimbres Pottery Image Digital Data Base (MimPIDD) maintained by Harvard University's Peabody Museum of Archaeology and Ethnology. The sex of some of these individuals was determined based on visible genitalia and clothing—aprons for women and sashes for men.

9. In published illustrations of Casas Grandes effigy vessels, I found 26 individuals with clearly visible hairstyles (Christman 2002; Di Peso 1977; Di Peso et al. 1974; Nielsen-Grimm and Stavast 2008; Phillips and Van Pool 2009a, b; Melissa Powell 2006; and Townsend 2005). The sex of some of these individuals was determined based on visible genitalia.

10. DiPeso (1974:479) also noted these gender differences in whether hair was worn in front of or behind the ears. Furthermore, he observed that women wore bangs, while men pulled their hair back off the forehead.

11. In published illustrations of Pueblo IV-period kiva mural drawings from the Ancestral Hopi site of Aawat'ovi, the Ancestral Keresan site of Kawaika'a, and the Ancestral Tiwa sites of Pottery Mound and Kuaua, I documented the hairstyles of 86 individuals (Hibben 1975, Schaafsma 2007, Watson Smith 1952). For a few cases, I determined sex using visible genitalia, but more often I relied on gender references in the published illustrations' captions. Identified males in kiva murals outnumber identified females by more than three times. The murals depict ceremonial scenes with human-like figures either imitating or representing kachina deities.

12. In Appendix Table 4.3, I call these possible poofed-out, unraveled ear whorls the sideways M and the side comma.

13. Webster (2007a:182) has associated the uneven side cut with dual gender individuals.

14. Hays-Gilpin (2002) documents examples for earlier ear whorl depictions.

15. Fewkes (1910) and Florence Hawley (1940) describe Hopi butterfly and squash-blossom symbolism.

16. In the Mimbres Pottery Image Digital Data base (MimPIDD), I found 97 bowls depicting 140 people with hair decorations. These numbers do not include hair bun ties.

17. In published illustrations of Casas Grandes effigy vessels, I documented hair decorations on 61 Casas Grandes effigies (Christman 2002; Di Peso 1977; Di Peso et al. 1974;

Nielsen-Grimm and Stavast 2008; Phillips and Van Pool 2009a, b; Melissa Powell 2006; and Townsend 2005). The sex of some of these individuals was determined based on visible genitalia and hairstyles—women with hair in front of the ears, men with hair behind the ears. Christman (2002) thinks painted, elongated triangles on heads may represent feathers. I did not include them in my tally.

18. Philips and VanPool (2009a, b) have called headdresses consisting of a circle inside a square "crowns." Since no effigies with headdresses had visible genitalia, their gender identifications are based on their hairstyles. One effigy with the female style of hair in front of the ears wore the step crown decorated with a checkerboard pattern; but in published illustrations one man also wore this hairstyle.

19. In published illustrations of Pueblo IV-period kiva mural drawings from the Ancestral Hopi site of Aawatovi, the Ancestral Keresan site of Kawaika'a, and the Ancestral Tiwa sites of Pottery Mound and Kuaua, I documented the hair decorations of 70 individuals (Hibben 1975, Schaafsma 2007, Watson Smith 1952).

20. The search for regional differences must be tempered by the fact that the Ancestral Tiwa murals depict more than twice as many examples of hair decoration as the Ancestral Hopi murals.

21. Jernigan (1978:136–137) describes and illustrates Mimbres hairpins.

22. Jernigan describes and illustrates pins worn by the Preclassic Hohokam (1978:77–79, 239–240), the Chacoans (1978:184–185), and the Sinagua (1978:136–140). The Sinagua straddle the AD 1150 dividing line, but are discussed in the earlier period here.

23. Odegaard and Hays-Gilpin (2002) describe Chaco, Sinagua, Salado, and Classic-period Hohokam basket caps.

24. McGregor (1943:281–283) describes and illustrates the Magician's beaded cap.
    According to osteologist Kimberly Spurr (personal communication 2015), the facial reconstruction in Figure 4.15 is inaccurate, and an accurate one is not possible due to the condition of the Magician's bones.

25. Dixon (1956:32–33) describes the Sinagua turban.

26. Simms and Gohier (2010:17, 19) illustrate and describe Fremont rock art depicting feather headdresses and also provide a historic-period example.

27. Jernigan (1978:77–79, 136–140, 184–185, 192, 209, 239–241) describes and illustrates post–AD 1150 hairpins.

28. Di Peso (1974:484–485) describes and illustrates Casas Grandes hairpins.

29. Osborne (2004:34–36) describes the Mesa Verde caps. Kidder and Guernsey (1919:100, Pl. 34a) describe the example from northeast Arizona.

30. Odegaard and Hays-Gilpin (2002) describe Chaco, Sinagua, Salado, and Classic-period Hohokam basket caps.

31. Randall McGuire (1992:153) describes Preclassic-period Hohokam hairpins as marking courtyard group leaders. Reid and Whittlesey (1982) and Whittlesey and Reid (2001) think that pins signaled sodality membership among the Mountain Mogollon and the Tonto Basin Salado.

32. *The Handbook of North American Indians*, Vol. 10, includes two photographs of Indian-school students with cut hair: Walapai children at the BIA school in Kingman, AZ (Thomas McGuire 1983: Figure 4), and Navajo children at the Carlisle Institute in Carlisle, PA (Emerson 1983: Fig. 2).

Chapter 5: Facial Decoration

1. For an overview of infant facial recognition studies, see Slater and Quinn (2001) and Pascalis and Slater (2003).

2. Studies of prehistoric facial designs depicted on ceramics, kiva murals, rock art, and clay figurines depend on the assumption that the designs are representative of those worn by their respective groups' members. Research is also constrained by the small numbers of groups with artistic representations of people, of human depictions by these groups, and of depicted individuals with decorated faces.

3. The two Southwest volumes of the Smithsonian Institution's *Handbook of North American Indians* (Ortiz 1979a, 1983) contain information on historic-period facial designs as part of short discussions of clothing and adornment and brief mentions of body decoration.

   Specific chapters discuss the Apache (Lamphere 1983, Tiller 1983), Coahuiltecans (T.N. Campbell 1983), Cochiti Pueblo (Lange 1979a), Cocopa (Alvarez de Williams 1983), Havasupai (Schwartz 1983), Hopi (Frigout 1979), Humanas (Schroeder 1979), Isleta Pueblo (Ellis 1979a), Jemez (Sando 1979), Karankawa (Newcomb 1983), Laguna Pueblo (Ellis 1979b), Maricopa (Harwell and Kelly 1983), Mohave (Kenneth Stewart 1983), Navajo (Wyman 1983), Papago (Fontana 1983, Griffith 1983), Pima (Dunnigan 1983, Ezell 1983), Quechan (Bee 1983), San Ildefonso Pueblo (Edelman 1979), San Juan Pueblo (Ortiz 1979b), Santo Domingo Pueblo (Lange 1979b), Seri (Bowen 1983), Southern Periphery: East (Griffen 1983), Taos (Bodine 1979), Tarahumara (Merrill 1983, Pennington 1983a), Walapai (Thomas McGuire 1983), Yavapai (Khera and Mariella 1983), Zia (Hoebel 1979), and Zuni (Tedlock 1979).

   Colorado River groups with facial tattoos include the Walapai, Mohave, Quechan, and Cocopa. Groups in adjacent areas include the Yavapai, Maricopa, and Pima. The two northwest-Mexico groups are the Seri and Tarahumara.

4. Bowen (1983:246) illustrates the variety of Seri women's facial designs.

5. Plog (2003:671) summarizes Pueblo color symbolism.

6. Facial decorations are also evident on Pueblo IV-period Ancestral Pueblo kiva murals but are not included in this analysis, which focuses only on ceramic depictions.

   In my data recording, I considered only design appearance and its facial location. I did not compare design colors and could not distinguish tattoos from face paint, because potters from different regions used different palettes. Classic-period Hohokam, Salado, and Casas Grandes vessels were polychrome (red/orange, black, white); those of the Mimbres and Chacoans were black and white; and those of the Preclassic Hohokam were red and buff. Given the diverse colors used by historic-period groups, I expect that black-on-white and red-on-buff ceramics, and possibly polychrome ceramics as well, do not reflect the entire range of colors that prehistoric peoples used to decorate their faces.

7. I found 58 decorated faces with 14 different designs in the Mimbres Pottery Image Digital Data Base (MimPIDD), maintained by the Peabody Museum of Archaeology and Ethnology at Harvard University.

8. In published and unpublished illustrations, I found 14 decorated faces on rare Chaco effigy vessels (Franklin 1982; Irwin-Williams and Shelley 1980; Judd 1954; Pepper 1906, 1920; Phillips and VanPool 2009a; and Aztec Ruins cat #'s 3209, 6991). Eight from

Pueblo Bonito dated to the Pueblo II period and five from other sites dated to the Pueblo III period (Aztec Ruin, Salmon Ruin, Bis sa'ani, and an unprovenienced Mancos Black-on-white effigy jar). One unprovenienced effigy jar from Chaco Canyon was undated.

9. One difference is that the Pueblo III-period Chaco facial designs were generally depicted more sloppily on ceramic effigies than the Pueblo II-period examples.

10. In published and unpublished illustrations, I found 11 decorated faces on rare Hohokam effigy vessels and a ladle handle (Faught 1995; Ferg 1997; Gladwin et al. 1937; Hammack 1974; Haury 1945a, 1976; Huntington 1986; Kopper 1986:229; and Peabody Museum of Archaeology and Ethnology collections for Las Acequias [cat #46-73-10/52018] and Los Muertos [cat #46-73-10/44327 and #46-73-10/44320]).

11. Black-on-white ceramics are typical of the northern Southwest, and the identification of the vessel in Figure 5.7 as Tonto Polychrome suggests that it may have originated in the Tonto Basin.

12. In published illustration, I found five decorated faces on rare Salado effigy vessels (Crown 1994, McKusick and Young 1997, Moulard 1984, Vint 2000).

13. The other member of the stylistically similar pair had a similar horizontal band with a fringe across its chest.

14. In published illustrations of Casas Grandes effigy vessels, I found 140 decorated faces with 29 different designs (Christman 2002; DiPeso 1977; Di Peso et al. 1974; Malagon 2001; Narez 1991; Nielsen-Grimm and Stavast 2008; Phillips and C. VanPool 2009a, b; and VanPool and VanPool 2006, 2007).

15. The Chaco-Mimbres match was not a complete duplicate. The Chaco face with extended eyeliner was accompanied by a characteristic Chaco design: a horizontal pair of parallel lines with dots in between, that was not used on any Mimbres faces. Similarly, the several Mimbres examples of extended eyeliner were accompanied by designs not used by the Chacoans.

16. Hegmon and Nelson (2007) and Lekson (2009) discuss Mimbres connections with the Hohokam and Chacoans.

17. None of the Hohokam, Salado, or Casas Grandes duplicates was complete—the faces with corresponding designs also had other decorations that were not used by their counterparts.

18. Two effigy jars from Dutch Ruin, a Salado site in the Upper Gila River valley, offer further evidence of Salado-Casas Grandes interaction (Lekson 2002:28). These vessels have been identified as Ramos Polychrome, the ceramic type associated with the Casas Grandians. I did not include their facial designs in my sample Salado sample, because they could be Casas Grandes imports, especially the one depicting a male smoker with the typical Casas Grandes short, sharp haircut.

19. The few designs that later groups shared with earlier, nonancestral groups suggest that we should think about the prehistoric Southwest in terms of networks in both space and time. The Mimbres shared parallel right-angle lines on the lower cheek with the Pueblo III-period Chacoans and tick marks under the eyes and chin lines with the Salado. The Pueblo II-period Chacoans and Casas Grandians both used extended eyeliner, as did the Mimbres. The Preclassic Hohokam and Salado also had a partial match—the earlier allover dot pattern decorated portions of two Salado faces. The preponderance of

Mimbres links may be a function of that group's larger sample size; or they could reflect indirect influence through Casas Grandes connections with other later groups; or they could indicate that in comparison to other early groups, the Mimbres had a disproportionate impact on the post–AD 1150 period, most strongly on the Casa Grandians and to a lesser extent on other groups.

20. A number of researchers have argued for links between the Mimbres and Casas Grandians (Schollmeyer et al. 2009:174). In addition to the matches in my samples, over half of the designs recorded by VanPool and VanPool (2006) were also present in my Mimbres sample. None of these duplicates were complete—the faces with corresponding designs also had other decorations that were not used by their counterparts.

21. The very small Preclassic- and Classic-period Hohokam sample sizes may have also contributed to there being just one correspondence between the two periods.

22. Sprehn's (Malagon 2001) research was inspired by ethnographic accounts of women along the Colorado River and elsewhere having vertical lines tattooed onto their chins during puberty rituals. She analyzed 11 female and 12 male Casas Grandes effigies.

    Sprehn also observed one woman with a solid oval on her chin and one young woman with vertical bars on her cheeks. One additional finding was that young women decorated their cheeks mostly with chevrons, and adult women with stepped terraces. She thought that these cheek designs were painted decorations, because they often included the color red.

23. VanPool and VanPool (2006) compared eleven facial decorations, as well as a series of other characteristics, in a sample of 40 female and 50 male effigies.

24. Archaeologists have a long history of relying on the Southwest's well-studied historic-period Native groups for explanations of archaeological remains. Although this heavy reliance on ethnographic analogy has been justifiably criticized for a variety of reasons, the approach may be most applicable to religion, which is generally the most conservative aspect of culture. In the northern Pueblos, its use is supported by evidence of religious continuity between the prehistoric and historic periods (e.g., the use of kivas).

25. Parsons (1933a, 1939) wrote seminal studies of Pueblo Indian religion. Also see Bunzel (1932), Cushing (1988), Fewkes (1892), Kroeber (1916), Loftin (1991), Ortiz (1969), Schaafsma (1999), Sekaquaptewa (1976), Stevenson (1904), Tedlock (1979), Washburn (1980), and Waters (1963). Discussions and illustrations of Hopi kachinas can be found in Colton (1959), Earle (1971), Fewkes (1903), and Parsons (1936).

26. This description of face and body paint was made for the Zuni by Bunzel (1932:868).

27. Kachina dolls are small wooden representations of kachinas that were once made for native children and are now avidly collected by outsiders.

    A methodological question is how similar matching designs have to be. For example, I could find no exact matches for horizontal lines extending from either side of the nose for the Hopi; but I did find numerous examples on kachina masks of straight lines angled downward from the nose, which I did not identity as a match. Similarly, the Chacoans also had horizontal lines extending from the nose, which in my previous comparisons I did not consider to be matches with the Mimbres, Casas Grandes, or Aztecs because of the lines' numbers and widths (e.g., multiple thin lines, and a single broad band).

28. For an overview of the symbolism of Pueblo designs, see Crown (1994). Also see Colton (1959), Fewkes (1903), and Secakuku (1995).

29. Ford (1980:26–28) uses historic-period evidence on the propagation of different varieties of corn to conclude that Pueblo color symbolism developed in the prehistoric period.

30. Davies (1978) describes the Toltec empire. Michael Smith (2011) and Townsend (2009) describe the Aztec empire.

31. Parsons (1933b) discusses Aztec-Pueblo parallels. For more recent, broader scale discussions, see Schaafsma (1999) and Randall McGuire (2012).

32. Spranz (1973) shows depictions in the Aztec codices of Aztec gods and their priestly impersonators.

33. Christman (2002) discusses possible symbolic meanings of Casas Grandes ceramic designs.

34. Descriptions of Teotihuacán can be found in Berrin and Pasztory (1993), Cowgill (1997), Headrick (2007), and Pasztory (1997).

35. For information of Teotihuacán murals, see Arthur Miller (1973) and Pasztory (1976).

36. The span of 1,400 years was calculated using Teotihuacán's median date.

Chapter 6: Language

1. For an overview of the Comparative Method that historical linguists use to define language families, see Lyle Campbell (2004).

2. I do not discuss Seri, another language family from northwest Mexico, in this chapter. I also neglect dialect variation. For instance, Hopi has four dialects, which are mutually intelligible without difficulty.

3. Vajda (2010) discusses links between Na-Dene and the Yeneseic languages of Siberia.

4. Historical linguists use two methods to estimate the dates for the initial differentiation of family members from their protolanguage: (1) linguistic paleontology, which links a time-diagnostic cultural element to the reconstructed vocabulary (lexicon) of a protolanguage; and (2) the notoriously imprecise lexicostatistics, which assumes that a core vocabulary changes at a constant rate through time (glottochronology).

   In Hill (2011a), I discuss the reasoning underlying the dates for differentiation of language-family members from their respective protolanguages. The estimated dates, citations, and dating techniques are:

   Keresan: "about 500 years" or AD 1500 (Miller and Davis 1963:310; lexicostatistics);
   Zuni: no estimate is possible as the language is an "isolate";
   Apachean: 700 years (Ives and Rice 2006; linguistic paleontology);
   Yuman: "does not exceed two millennia" (Hale and Harris 1979:172; lexicostatistics);
   Kiowa-Tanoan: 3000–2500 BP (Hale and Harris 1979; lexicostatistics), (Hill 2008a; linguistic paleontology);
   Uto-Aztecan: no earlier than 4400–4000 BP (Hill 2012; linguistic paleontology); 4250 BP (Gray 2010; lexicostatistics);
   Northern Uto-Aztecan: about 3500–3000 BP (Hill 2008a; linguistic paleontology).

5. Swadesh (1967) and Rood (1973) suggested a link between Keresan and the Caddoan languages of the Great Plains, but the data are scant and the claim has been firmly rejected by Lyle Campbell (1997).

6. Newman's (1964) linkage of Zuni to the "Penutian" languages of California has been refuted by (Callaghan 1997, Lyle Campbell 1997, Hill 2007). According to Hill (2007), Zuni had probably been more or less isolated from any possible phylogenetic relatives for a very long time.

7. Ives and Rice (2006) discuss the arrival of Proto-Apacheans into the Southwest. Sapir (1936) discusses "corn" words in Proto-Apachean.

8. Hill (2008a) considers the Kiowa-Tanoan protolanguage; a detailed reconstruction appears in Sutton (2014).

9. Hill (2001, 2008a, 2008b) discusses the Uto-Aztecan protolanguage, including is contacts with speakers of Proto-Oto-Chinantecan, an Otomanguean language. Contrary to Fowler (1983), who thinks that the Uto-Aztecan protolanguage was located within the Greater Southwest, Hill (2001, 2008a) thinks that migrants brought Uto-Aztecan into the Southwest where northern Uto-Aztecan subsequently emerged. Gray's (2010) estimate date of 4250 BP for Uto-Aztecan divergence falls within my proposed range (Hill 2012).

10. Hill (2012) discusses the use of pottery for dating the Uto-Aztecan protolanguage.

11. The recent evolution of the Hopi and the Southern Numic languages in the Uto-Aztecan language family reflects historical processes specific to the Southwest. Hopi and the languages of the Chemehuevi-Southern Paiute-Ute dialect continuum in Southern Numic may be examples of northern Uto-Aztecan languages that were affected by ongoing connections after their initial divergence. Opata, Eudeve, and the Tepiman languages may be examples of southern Uto-Aztecan languages that were affected by ongoing connections after their initial divergence.

12. Shaul (1985), Lyle Campbell (1997), and Hill (2008a) have found many problems with Whorf and Trager's (1937) suggestion of deeper relationships between Kiowa-Tanoan and Uto-Aztecan. If there is a relationship, it is one of extreme antiquity, probably dating at the latest to the earliest stage of the Middle Archaic, a period when these two groups may have been no more closely related to one another than they were to many other Native American language groups.

13. Shaul and Hill (1998) discuss of Tepiman, Yuman, and Hohokam linguistic connections.

14. Features that crosscut phylogenetic boundaries but do not satisfy the criteria for descent from a common ancestor are the residue left from application of the Comparative Method.

15. Shaul and Hill (1998) discuss the southwest language area and its possible Hohokam origins.

16. In glide hardening, the glides or semivowels (such as /w/ and /y/, pronounced without closure in the oral cavity) become spirants or stops (with closure in the oral cavity). In Tepiman languages, *y became /d/, *w became /g/. In "retroflexion," the coronal consonants /t/, /d/, /l/, and /s/, pronounced with the tongue closure at least as far forward as the hard palate, have developed variants in which the tongue is pulled back ("retroflexion"). In the Tepiman languages, Uto-Aztecan *kw "develarized," becoming /b/, a sound that preserves only the labial feature of the original "labio-velar" consonant.

17. Bright (1978) and Langdon and Silver (1984) have different views about the direction of the spread of these phonological innovations.

18. Shaul (1980) has divided the eastern and western Pueblos into two separate language areas. In the east, Tanoan and Keresan languages share contrasts among plain, aspirated, and glottalized stops and also have contrastive tone. However, glottalized or ejective consonants are not a specifically Southwestern phenomenon—they appear in many other North American languages outside the Southwest. In the west, Hopi and Zuni share grammatical similarities that are fairly common and widely spread features and

thus are not good markers for a language area. For example, the shared Hopi and Zuni grammatical switch reference clearly comes from farther west, from a switch-reference area that includes much of aboriginal California, several of the Great Basin Numic languages, and the Upper Piman languages. Shaul (2014) is a detailed study of areal relations across the entire Southwest.

19. Kroskrity (1983) contrasts Pueblo male and female lexical usage. The exception for different male and female usage is Zuni, for which he found no information. According to Sims and Valiquette (1990), the gender distinction in Laguna Keres goes beyond the lexical, involving regular patterning of vowel length that is important in "cue words" that indicate the speaker's emotional stance.

20. Shaul (1982) discusses Zuni glottalized consonants. Both Keresan and Tanoan have plain, aspirated, and glottalized stops. Keresan, with the most complex consonant system, also has glottalized glides and nasals. But in Zuni, the only glottalized consonants are stops, which appear mainly in words with a sound-symbolic dimension.

21. Towa exhibits /ky, /khy, and /k'y/, but only in word-initial position and never on prefixes. Zuni has only /ky/ and /k'y/, which appear before the vowels /a/, /e/, /i/, in affixes, and as stems (see Hale 1967). Hopi exhibits /ky/, appearing before the vowels /a/ and /e/, in word-initial position only. The Hopi lexicon with initial /ky/ is small and mainly includes affectively charged and ceremonially significant lexicon.

22. Bowern et al. (2011) and Haspelmath and Tadmor (2009) provide a general overview of loan words.

23. Hill (2008a) discusses loan-word exchange between Proto-Northern Uto-Aztecan (PNUA) and Proto-Kiowa-Tanoan. This hypothesis is evaluated in Ortman (2012).

24. Hill (2011b) discusses the Hopi loan word *tsoongo*.

25. The search for loans in Apachean requires the attention of specialists, since the very complex morphophonology of the languages makes it difficult to spot loan forms. All Apachean specialists agree that the languages hardly ever borrow words from other languages, although anecdotal information suggests this may be changing in modern forms of Navajo. Kroskrity (1985) discusses Tewa-Apache loan words.

26. Yuman examples of the loan word "trading partner, ritual kinsmen" include Kiliwa -*ki7* "be sibling-in-law"; Cocopa *ki-* "masculine element in *kiyi·* "great-grandfather" and *kixká·* "daughter's husband"; Mojave *ki7iyii* "friend" (used by a male speaker about a Yuma or Maricopa man or woman); Yavapai -*kiñ* "stem in great-grandchild, younger cousins." In the California Uto-Aztecan languages of Luiseño, the loan word translates as *kihaat* "child, youth"; and in Cupeño, it is *kiimal* "boy" (-*mal* is the diminutive suffix). In Tohonno O'odham, the loan word is *kihɨ* "some kind of relative"; and in Zuni, it is *kixe* "ceremonial brother." Keresan *-*kî·ni* "friend" and perhaps San Juan Tewa *k'ema* "friend" extend the loan through the Pueblo groups.

27. Schaafsma (2010) discusses Pueblo kachinas.

28. Parsons (1925b) discusses her work at Jemez pueblo.

29. Kroskrity (1993, 2000) argues that loan words were extremely rare among the Pueblo languages due to a language ideology of "indigenous purism" in which everyday speech was modeled on the language of the kiva, where the use of loan words was supposedly discouraged. However, in making this argument, Kroskrity (who did not work at all on language in religion, following the wishes of his Arizona Tewa collaborators) neglected a

long history of reports of loan material precisely within the ritual register of the kachina religion.

30. White (1944) describes code-switching in Hopi and Zuni kachina songs.

31. Sekaquaptewa et al. (2015) analyze Hopi kachina songs.

32. Hill (2007) discusses Zuni ceremonial language and its connections with Hopi.

33. Parsons (1925b) describes the Jemez clown and warrior societies.

34. Gal and Irvine (1995) discuss "iconization."

35. Hill (2007) and Shaul and Hill (1998) discuss kachina-Tepiman connections.

36. Potter (2000) and Potter and Ortman (2004) discuss the archaeological evidence for intercommunal feasting.

37. Zuni has spotty loans from both Keresan and Piman for food items that are not specifically festive foods. From Keresan *'iṣat'I* "grease, lard," Zuni has *'isha-* "fat." From Keresan *sk'à·shɨ* "fish," Zuni has *k'ashshita.* The Zuni word for "chile," *k'ola,* is from Piman *ko'okol* "chile," a word with a solid Uto-Aztecan etymology (Hill 2007). However, Zuni apparently does not have any Keresan or Tepiman loan words within the specifically "festive food" complex except for a word for "elk" from Keresan.

38. Adams (1991) describes the rapid spread of paper bread technology.

39. Cushing (1920) describes Zuni bread making.

40. Eriacho and Gonzales (1998) record the Zuni *he'lashnakya a'le* "a large slab of treated sandstone for making paper bread." The first word is obviously the same as Cushing's (1920:323) *hel'-äsh-na-k'ia*; *a'le* is "stone"-singular. The modifier *he-l'-asha-nakia* means "bread-singular?-make-instrument." Wick Miller (1965:162) recorded the Keresan (Acoma) *y'âu-shi* "flat cooking stone" (from *y'âu-* "stone"). Lange (1959:116) recorded *yo'asha* "comal" in a paragraph quoted from Bandelier; this is probably the same as the Acoma word.

41. A Penn Museum video showing a contemporary Hopi woman making piki bread can be seen at http://www.youtube.com/watch?v=JnjwLzVr5qM (accessed March 29, 2016).

42. Dayley (1989) discusses Timpisa Shoshone etymology. Sapir (1931) discusses Southern Paiute etymology.

43. My speculation goes like this: the Southern Tiwa word for "bread" is *p'akhu.* Northern Tiwa has *p'ökú-na* "loaf of bread" (Trager 1946). If the vowels in the word were nasal, according to Hale (1967), the Towa (Jemez) word would be *p'įkhį,* a possible source for the Hopi word (and for Southern Paiute *piqo* "yant cake"). However, this item is not recorded for Towa (for which we have very scanty lexical resources). Furthermore, neither Trager (1946, for Northern Tiwa) nor Frantz (1985, for Southern Tiwa) recorded nasal vowels in the "bread" words in those languages. Tanoan vocalism is notoriously intractable, however, and I believe that this is a line of investigation worth pursuing.

44. Potter and Ortman (2004) discuss the ingredients of festive stews and the replacement of roasting by boiling as the preferred preparation method. Spielmann (2004) documents trade in ceramic vessels used in feasts.

45. Etymologies for "stew" are from: Towa (Harrington 1910, Yumitani 1998); San Juan Tewa (Harrington 1947, Martinez 1982); Arizona Tewa (Harrington 1910); Southwestern U.S. Spanish (Harrington 1910); Kiowa (Harrington 1928); Cochiti (Lange 1959); Santa Ana (White 1942); Keresan in general (Spencer 1946:231); and Laguna (Lachler 2006). Note that transcriptions have been adapted, with ï for schwa.

46. Speirs (1966) translated San Juan Tewa *xú·sè̖*, literally "dried.corn-stew"; Hoijer and Dozier (1949) translated Santa Clara Tewa *píví-sè̖·* as "meat-boil." No Tiwa words for "stew" appear in the published literature. According to Lange (1959:120), Towa *zétá* "posole" (Yumitani 1998:42) may refer to corn gruel (the meaning of "posole" at Cochiti). So it may not belong in the "meat stew" set (Lange 1959:120). It does not include a reflex of the Tanoan "boil" word.

47. Davis (1964) discusses the Santa Ana word *c̓éwAs̓čA* "stew."

48. Miller and Davis (1963) includes the list of 384 Proto-Keresan reconstructions.

49. Hill (2001) discusses the roots of Hopi loan words for beans. Hill (2008a) discusses the ancient loans between Northern Uto-Aztecan and Kiowa-Tanoan. Miller and Davis (1963) reconstruct the Proto-Keresan word for beans.

50. The Tiwa and Tewa resemblants do not exhibit sound correspondences in Hale's (1967) system. However Logan Sutton (personal communication December 16, 2012) believes that they may be cognate.

51. Eriacho and Gonzales (1998:65) describe the etymology of Zuni squash words.

52. Potter and Ortman (2004) discuss the increased importance of turkey.

53. Parsons (1925b) discusses Towa words for turkey; and Henderson and Harrington (1914) discuss Tewa and Rio Grande words.

54. Zuni has *towo* "to make a thundering sound" (Hill 2007:26), so Zuni *to-* and Piman *to:-* may be a chance resemblance.

55. Fowler (1983) discusses the connections of Hopi *koyongo* "turkey."

56. Miller and Davis (1963) discuss Keresan resemblants for jackrabbit. The Tanoan references for jackrabbit are: Towa (Yumitani 1998:20), Northern Tiwa and Rio Grande Tewa (Martinez 1982; Speirs 1966), and Santa Clara Tewa (Henderson and Harrington 1914; Hoijer and Dozier 1949).

57. Hill (2008a) discusses Tanoan words for "elk."

58. Taylor (1976) discusses Proto-Kiowa-Tanoan origins for "bison" words throughout North America.

59. Newman (1958) discusses the Zuni word for buffalo.

60. *nöq-kwivi* is a loan blend where the element *kwivi* does have a Uto-Aztecan etymology, but *nöq-* does not.

61. Quote is from Potter and Ortman (2004:184).

62. Only a very sparsely documented ritual lexicon has been recorded, and neither Pueblo indigenous scholars nor the broader Pueblo public desire to share more linguistic data. A good deal of data can be found in some older sources. Although this information is not usually transcribed with sufficient precision for phylogenetic linguistic analysis, it can be useful for areal approaches.

63. Leanne Hinton (2001) discusses the decline in indigenous Pueblo languages.

64. Debenport (2015), Pecos and Blum-Martinez (2001), and Sims (2001) describe projects to prevent further loss of indigenous Southwest languages.

References

Adair, John
1944   *The Navajo and Pueblo Silversmiths*. University of Oklahoma Press, Norman.

Adams, E. Charles
1991   *The Origin and Development of the Pueblo Katsina Cult*. University of Arizona Press, Tucson.

Akins, Nancy J.
1986   *A Biocultural Approach to Human Burials from Chaco Canyon, New Mexico*. Reports of the Chaco Center No. 9. U.S. Department of the Interior, National Park Service, Santa Fe, NM.

2003   The Burials of Pueblo Bonito. In *Pueblo Bonito: Center of the Chacoan World*, edited by J.E. Neitzel, pp. 95–103. Smithsonian Books, Washington, D.C.

Forthcoming   Human Remains. In *Early Coalition Period Occupation in the Eastern Galisteo Basin, Santa Fe County, New Mexico: The Pithouse Village at LA 3333 in the Wildhorse Community*, edited by R. N. Wiseman. Archaeology Notes. Office of Archaeological Studies, Museum of New Mexico, Santa Fe.

Alred, Cyril
1957   Hair Styles and History. *Metropolitan Museum of Art Bulletin, New Series* 15(6):141–147.

Alvarez de Williams, Anita
1983   Cocopa. In *Southwest*, edited by Alfonso Ortiz, pp. 99–112. Handbook of North American Indians, Vol. 10, William C. Sturtevant, general editor. Smithsonian Institution, Washington, D.C.

Anawalt, Patricia R.
1990   The Emperor's Cloak: Aztec Pomp and Toltec Circumstances. *American Antiquity* 55(2):291–307.

2000   Textile Research from the Mesoamerican Perspective. In *Beyond Cloth and Cordage: Archaeological Textile Research in the Americas*, edited by P. B. Drooker and L. D. Webster, pp. 205–228. University of Utah Press, Salt Lake City.

Anderson, Bruce A. (editor)
1990   *The Wupatki Archaeological Inventory Survey Project: Final Report*. Professional Paper No. 35. Southwest Regional Office, Division of Anthropology, Southwest Cultural Resources Center, Santa Fe, NM.

Anderson, Keith M., Gloria J. Fenner, Don P. Morris, George A. Teague, and Charmion McKusick
1986   *The Archeology of Gila Cliff Dwellings*. Western Archeological and Conservation Center Publications in Anthropology 36. Tucson, AZ.

Antieau, John M.

1981   *The Palo Verde Archaeological Investigations of Hohokam Settlement at the Confluence: Excavations along the Palo Verde Pipeline.* Museum of Northern Arizona Research Paper No. 20. Flagstaff.

Anyon, Roger, and Steven A. LeBlanc

1984   *The Galaz Ruin: A Prehistoric Mimbres Village in Southwestern New Mexico.* University of New Mexico Press, Albuquerque.

Armelagos, George J., and Dennis P. Van Gerven

2003   A Century of Skeletal Biology and Paleopathology: Contrasts, Contradictions, and Conflicts. *American Anthropologist* 105(1):53–64.

Auerbach, Benjamin M.

2011   Reaching Great Heights: Changes in Indigenous Stature, Body Size and Body Shape with Agricultural Intensification in North America. In *Human Bioarchaeology of the Transition to Agriculture*, edited by R. Pinhasi and J.T. Stock, pp. 203–233. Wiley-Blackwell, Chichester, UK.

Barnes, Ethne

1988   Inhumations Recovered from Casa Buena: Skeletal Analysis. In *Excavations at Casa Buena: Changing Hohokam Land Use along the Squaw Peak Expressway*, Vol. 2, edited by J. B. Howard, pp. 619–692. Soil Systems Publications in Archaeology No. 11, Phoenix, AZ.

Barth, Fredrik

1969   *Ethnic Groups and Boundaries: The Social Organization of Culture Difference.* Little, Brown, Boston.

Bartman, Elizabeth

2001   Hair and the Artifice of Roman Female Adornment. *American Journal of Archaeology* 105(1):1–25.

Bassman, Theda, and Michael Bassman

2006   *Zuni Jewelry.* 3rd ed. Schiffer Publishing, Atglen, PA.

Basso, Keith H.

1983   Western Apache. In *Southwest*, edited by Alfonso Ortiz, pp. 462–488. Handbook of North American Indians, Vol. 10, William C. Sturtevant, general editor. Smithsonian Institution, Washington, D.C.

Bayman, James M.

1996   Shell Ornament Consumption in a Classic Hohokam Platform Mound Community Center. *Journal of Field Archaeology* 23(4):403–420.

2001   The Hohokam of Southwest North America. *Journal of World Prehistory* 15(3):257–311.

2002   Hohokam Craft Economies and the Materialization of Power. *Journal of Archaeological Method and Theory* 9(1):69–95.

Bedinger, Margery

1973   *Indian Silver: Navajo and Pueblo Jewelers.* University of New Mexico Press, Albuquerque.

Bee, Robert L.

1983   Quechan. In *Southwest*, edited by Alfonso Ortiz, pp. 86–98. Handbook of North

American Indians, Vol. 10, William C. Sturtevant, general editor. Smithsonian Institution, Washington, D.C.

Bennett, Kenneth A.

1973 *The Indians of Point of Pines, Arizona: A Comparative Study of their Physical Characteristics*. The Anthropological Papers of the University of Arizona 23. Tucson.

1975 *Skeletal Remains from Mesa Verde National Park, Colorado*. Publications in Archeology 7F, Wetherill Mesa Studies. U.S. Department of the Interior, National Park Service, Washington, D.C.

Benson, S.L.

1986 Activity-Induced Pathology in a Puebloan Population: Grasshopper, Arizona. Unpublished M.A. thesis, Department of Anthropology, Arizona State University, Tempe.

Berrin, Kathleen, and Esther Pasztory

1993 *Teotihuacán: Art from the City of the Gods*. Thames and Hudson, New York.

Bessels, Emil

1876 The Human Remains Found near the Ancient Ruins of Southwestern Colorado and New Mexico. *Bulletin of the Geological and Geographic Survey of the Territories* No. 3, pp. 47–63. Electronic edition: The Making of America Series, University of Michigan, http://www.hti.umich.edu/cgi/b/bib/bibperm?q1=ABB3707 (accessed March 31, 2016).

Binford, Lewis R.

1971 Mortuary Practices: Their Study and Their Potential. In *Approaches to the Social Dimensions of Mortuary Practices*, edited by J.A. Brown, pp. 6–29. Memoirs of the Society for American Archaeology No. 25. Washington, D.C.

Birkby, Walter H.

1973 Discontinuous Morphological Traits of the Skull as Population Markers in the Prehistoric Southwest. Unpublished Ph.D. dissertation, Department of Anthropology, University of Arizona, Tucson.

Blanton, Richard E., Gary M. Feinman, Stephen A. Kowalewski, and Peter N. Peregrine

1996 A Dual-Processual Theory for the Evolution of Mesoamerican Civilization. *Current Anthropology* 37(1):1–14.

Bodine, John J.

1979 Taos Pueblo. In *Southwest*, edited by Alfonso Ortiz, pp. 255–267. Handbook of North American Indians, Vol. 9, William C. Sturtevant, general editor. Smithsonian Institution, Washington, D.C.

Bohrer, Vorsila L.

2006 Cultivated Plants from Salmon Pueblo In *Thirty-Five Years of Archaeological Research at Salmon Ruins*, Vol. 3: *Archaeobotanical and Other Analytical Studies*, edited by P. F. Reed. Center for Desert Archaeology, Tucson, AZ, and Salmon Ruins Museum, Bloomfield, NM.

Bowen, Thomas

1983 Seri. In *Southwest*, edited by Alfonso Ortiz, pp. 230–249. Handbook of North American Indians, Vol. 10, William C. Sturtevant, general editor. Smithsonian Institution, Washington, D.C.

Bowern, Claire, Patience Epps, Russell Gray, Jane Hill, Keith Hunley, John Ives, Patrick McConvell, and Jason Zentz

2011   Does Lateral Transmission Obscure Inheritance in Hunter-Gatherer Languages? *PloS One* 6(9):e25195. Doi:10.1371/journal.pone.0025195.

Bradley, Rona J.

1993   Marine Shell Exchange in Northwest Mexico and the Southwest. In *The American Southwest and Mesoamerica: Systems of Prehistoric Exchange*, edited by J. E. Ericson and T. G. Baugh, pp. 121–158. Plenum, New York.

1996   The Role of Casas Grandes in Prehistoric Shell Exchange Networks within the Southwest. Unpublished Ph.D. dissertation, Department of Anthropology, Arizona State University, Tempe.

2000   Networks of Shell Ornament Exchange: A Critical Assessment of Prestige Economies in the North American Southwest. In *The Archaeology of Regional Interaction: Religion, Warfare, and Exchange across the American Southwest and Beyond*, edited by M. Hegmon, pp. 167–188. University Press of Colorado, Boulder.

Brand, Donald D.

1938   Aboriginal Trade Routes for Sea Shells in the Southwest. *Yearbook of the Association of Pacific Geographers* 4(1):3–10.

Bright, William

1978   Sibilants and Naturalness in Aboriginal California. *Journal of California and Great Basin Anthropology Papers in Linguistics* 1:39–64.

Brody, J. J.

2004   *Mimbres Painted Pottery, Rev. ed.* School of American Research Press, Santa Fe, NM.

Brown, James A. (editor)

1971   *Approaches to the Social Dimensions of Mortuary Practices.* Memoirs of the Society for American Archaeology No. 25. Washington, D.C.

Bruwelheide, Karin S., Douglas W. Owsley, and Richard L. Jantz

2010   Burials from the Fourth Mission Church at Pecos. In *Pecos Pueblo Revisited: The Biological and Social Context*, edited by M. Morgan, pp. 129–160. Papers of the Peabody Museum of Archaeology and Ethnology Vol. 85. Harvard University, Cambridge, MA.

Buikstra, Jane E., and Douglas H. Ubelaker

1994   *Standards for Data Collection from Human Skeletal Remains.* Arkansas Archeological Survey Research Series No. 44. Fayetteville.

Bunzel, Ruth L.

1932   *Zuni Kachinas: An Analytical Study.* 47th Annual Report of the Bureau of American Ethnology for the Years 1929–1930, pp. 837–1086. Washington, D.C.

Callaghan, Catherine

1997   Evidence for Yok-Utian. *International Journal of American Linguistics* 63(1):18–64

Campbell, Lyle

1997   *American Indian Languages: The Historical Linguistics of Native America.* Oxford University Press, New York.

2004   *Historical Linguistics: An Introduction.* 2nd ed. MIT Press, Cambridge, MA.

Campbell, T. N.

1983   Coahuiltecans and Their Neighbors. In *Southwest*, edited by Alfonso Ortiz, pp. 343–

358. Handbook of North American Indians, Vol. 10, William C. Sturtevant, general editor. Smithsonian Institution, Washington, D.C.

Carlyle, Shawn W.

2005   Discerning the Origins of the Anasazi with Mitochondrial DNA Haplogroups. In *Biomolecular Archaeology: Genetic Approaches to the Past*, edited by D. M. Reed, pp. 93–127. Center for Archaeological Investigations Occasional Paper No. 32. Southern Illinois University, Carbondale.

Carlyle, Shawn W., Ryan L. Parr, M. Geoffrey Hayes, and Dennis H. O'Rourke

2000   Context of Maternal Lineages in the Greater Southwest. *American Journal of Physical Anthropology* 113(1):85–101.

Carr, Christopher

1994   A Cross-Cultural Survey of the Determinants of Mortuary Practices. In *The Pueblo Grande Project*, Vol. 7: *An Analysis of Classic Period Mortuary Patterns*, edited by D. R. Mitchell, pp. 7–69. Soil Systems Publications in Archaeology No. 20. Phoenix, AZ.

Chapman, Robert, Ian Kinnes, and Klavs Randsborg (editors)

1981   *The Archaeology of Death*. Cambridge University Press. Cambridge, UK.

Castetter, Edward F., and Willis H. Bell

1942   *Pima and Papago Indian Agriculture*. Inter-Americana Studies, Vol. 1. University of New Mexico Press, Albuquerque.

Choi, Na-Young

2006   Symbolism of Hairstyles in Korea and Japan. *Asian Folklore Society* 65(1):69–86.

Christman, Ernest H.

2002   *Casas Grandes Pre-Columbian Pottery Decoded: Of Gods and Myths*. Tutorial Press, Albuquerque, NM.

Clark, Geoffrey A.

1969   A Preliminary Analysis of Burial Clusters at the Grasshopper Site, East-Central Arizona. *Kiva* 35(2):57–86.

Clark, Jeffrey J.

2001   *Tracking Prehistoric Migrations: Pueblo Settlers among the Tonto Basin Hohokam*. The Anthropological Papers of the University of Arizona 65. Tucson.

2007   A San Pedro Valley Perspective on Ancestral Pueblo Migration in the Hohokam World. In *The Hohokam Millennium*, edited by S. K. Fish and P. R. Fish, pp. 98–105. School for Advanced Research Press, Santa Fe, NM.

Clemensen, A. Berle

1992   *Casa Grande Ruins National Monument, Arizona: A Centennial History of the First Prehistoric Reserve 1892–1992*. U.S. Department of the Interior, National Park Service, Washington, D.C.

Colton, Harold S.

1941   Prehistoric Trade in the Southwest. *Scientific Monthly* 52(4):308–319.

1959   *Hopi Kachina Dolls with a Key to their Identification*. Rev. ed., 1970. University of New Mexico Press, Albuquerque.

1964   Principal Hopi Trails. *Plateau* 36(3):91–94.

Connelly, John C.

1979   Hopi Social Organization. In *Southwest*, edited by Alfonso Ortiz, pp. 539–553.

Handbook of North American Indians, Vol. 9, William C. Sturtevant, general editor. Smithsonian Institution, Washington, D.C.

Cordell, Linda S., and Maxine E. McBrinn

2012 *Archaeology of the Southwest*. 3rd ed. Left Coast Press, Walnut Creek, CA.

Cosgrove, C. Burton

1947 *Caves of the Upper Gila and Hueco Areas in New Mexico and Texas*. Papers of the Peabody Museum of American Archaeology and Ethnology 24(2). Harvard University, Cambridge, MA.

Cowgill, George L.

1997 State and Society at Teotihuacán, Mexico. *Annual Review of Anthropology* 26: 129–161.

Crotty, Helen K.

1983 *Honoring the Dead: Anasazi Ceramics of the Rainbow Bridge–Monument Valley Expedition*. University of California Museum of Cultural History, Los Angeles.

1995 Anasazi Mural Art of the Pueblo IV Period, AD 1300–1600: Influences, Selective Adaptation, and Cultural Diversity in the Prehistoric Southwest. Unpublished Ph.D. dissertation, Department of Art History, University of California, Los Angeles.

Crown, Patricia L.

1994 *Ceramics and Ideology: Salado Polychrome Pottery*. University of New Mexico Press, Albuquerque.

Crown, Patricia L., and Suzanne K. Fish

1996 Gender and Status in the Hohokam Pre-Classic to Classic Transition. *American Anthropologist* 98(4):803–817.

Crown, Patricia L., and W. James Judge

1991 *Chaco and Hohokam: Prehistoric Regional Systems in the American Southwest*. School of American Research Press, Santa Fe, NM.

Cushing, Frank H.

1890 Preliminary Notes on the Origin, Working Hypothesis, and Primary Researches of the Hemenway Southwestern Archaeological Expedition. *Congrès International des Américanistes*, Compte Rendu de la Septième Session, Berlin 1888, pp. 151–194. Berlin.

1920 *Zuñi Breadstuff*. Indian Notes and Monographs 8. Heye Foundation, Museum of the American Indian, New York.

1988 *The Mythic World of the Zuni*, edited by Barton Wright. University of New Mexico Press, Albuquerque.

Davies, Nigel

1978 *The Toltecs: Until the Fall of Tula*. University of Oklahoma Press, Norman.

Davis, Irvine

1964 *The Language of Santa Ana Pueblo*. Anthropological Papers No. 69. Bureau of American Ethnology, Washington, D.C.

Dayley, Jon

1989 *Tümpisa (Panamint) Shoshone Dictionary*. University of California Publications in Linguistics No. 116. Berkeley.

Dean, Jeffrey S.

2000 Northeastern Arizona, AD 1150–1350. In *The Prehistoric Pueblo World, AD 1150–1350*, edited by M. A. Adler, pp. 29–47. University of Arizona Press, Tucson.

2002   Late Pueblo II–Pueblo III in Kayenta-Branch Prehistory. In *Prehistoric Culture Change on the Colorado Plateau: Ten Thousand Years on Black Mesa*, edited by S. Powell and F. E. Smiley, pp. 121–157. University of Arizona Press, Tucson.

Debenport, Erin
2015   *Fixing the Books: Secrecy, Literacy, and Perfectibility in Indigenous New Mexico.* School of Advanced Research Press, Santa Fe, NM.

Delaney, Carol
1994   Untangling the Meanings of Hair in Turkish Society. *Anthropological Quarterly* 67(4):159–172.

Dennis, Wayne, and Marsena G. Dennis
1940   Cradles and Cradling Practices of the Pueblo Indians. *American Anthropologist* 42(1):107–115.

Di Peso, Charles C.
1974   *Casas Grandes: A Fallen Trading Center of the Gran Chichimeca*, Vol. 2. Northland Press, Flagstaff, AZ.
1977   Casas Grandes Effigy Vessels. *American Indian Art Magazine* 2(4):31–37, 90.

Di Peso, Charles C, John B. Renaldo, and Gloria J. Fenner
1974   *Casas Grandes: A Fallen Trading Center of the Gran Chichimeca*, Vol. 6. Northland Press, Flagstaff, AZ.

Dixon, Keith A.
1956   *Hidden House: A Cliff Ruin in Sycamore Canyon, Central Arizona.* Museum of Northern Arizona Bulletin No. 29. Flagstaff.

Douglas, Michele T., and Ann L. W. Stodder
2010   Skull Morphology in the Animas-La Plata Skeletal Series. In *Animas-La Plata Project*, Vol. 15: *Bioarchaeology*, edited by E. Perry, A. L. W. Stodder, and C. Bollong, pp. 197–222. SWCA Environmental Consultants, Phoenix, AZ.

Drennan, Robert D.
1991   Pre-Hispanic Chiefdom Trajectories in Mesoamerica, Central America, and Northern South America. In *Chiefdoms: Power, Economy, and Ideology*, edited by T. K. Earle, pp. 263–287. Cambridge University Press, Cambridge, UK.

Dunnigan, Timothy
1983   Lower Pima. In *Southwest*, edited by Alfonso Ortiz, pp. 217–229. Handbook of North American Indians, Vol. 10, William C. Sturtevant, general editor. Smithsonian Institution, Washington, D.C.

Durand, Kathy R., Meradeth Snow, David G. Smith, and Stephen R. Durand
2010   Discrete Dental Trait Evidence of Migration Patterns in the Northern Southwest. In *Human Variation in the Americas*, edited by B. M. Auerbach, pp. 113–134. Center for Archaeological Investigations Occasional Paper No. 38. Southern Illinois University, Carbondale.

Dutton, Bertha P.
1963   *Sun Father's Way: The Kiva Murals of Kuaua, A Pueblo Ruin, Coronado State Monument, New Mexico.* University of New Mexico Press, Albuquerque.

Earle, Edwin
1971   *Hopi Kachinas.* 2nd ed., revised. Museum of American Indians, Heye Foundation, New York.

Edelman, Sandra A.

1979 San Ildefonso Pueblo. In *Southwest*, edited by Alfonso Ortiz, pp. 308–316. Handbook of North American Indians, Vol. 9, William C. Sturtevant, general editor. Smithsonian Institution, Washington, D.C.

Ellis, Florence Hawley

1979a Isleta Pueblo. In *Southwest*, edited by Alfonso Ortiz, pp. 351–365. Handbook of North American Indians, Vol. 9, William C. Sturtevant, general editor. Smithsonian Institution, Washington, D.C.

1979b Laguna Pueblo. In *Southwest*, edited by Alfonso Ortiz, pp. 438–449. Handbook of North American Indians, Vol. 9, William C. Sturtevant, general editor. Smithsonian Institution, Washington, D.C.

El-Najjar, Mahmoud Y.

1974 People of Canyon de Chelly: A Study of Their Biology and Culture. Unpublished Ph.D. dissertation, Department of Anthropology, Arizona State University, Tempe.

Emerson, Gloria J.

1983 Navajo Education. In *Southwest*, edited by Alfonso Ortiz, pp. 659–671. Handbook of North American Indians, Vol. 10, William C. Sturtevant, general editor. Smithsonian Institution, Washington, D.C.

Emery, Irene

1966 *The Primary Structures of Fabrics*. The Textile Museum, Washington, D.C.

Eriacho, Wilfred, Sr., and Rena Gonzales

1998 *Bena:we Dana:we/Word Categories*. Zuni Public School District No. 89, Zuni, NM.

Ezell, Paul H.

1983 History of the Pima. In *Southwest*, edited by Alfonso Ortiz, pp. 149–160. Handbook of North American Indians, Vol. 10, William C. Sturtevant, general editor. Smithsonian Institution, Washington, D.C.

Ezzo, Joseph A., Clark M. Johnson, and T. Douglas Price

1997 Analytical Perspectives on Prehistoric Migration: A Case Study from East-Central Arizona. *Journal of Archaeological Science* 24(5):447–466.

Faught, Michael K.

1995 *Archaeological Testing, Limited Data Recovery, and an In-Place Archaeological Site Preservation Plan for the Madera Reserve Property Development in Green Valley, Pima County, Arizona*. Old Pueblo Archaeology Center Archaeology Report No. 94-2. Tucson, AZ.

Ferg, Alan

1997 *Baby on Board: Hohokam Mother-and-Child Effigy Vessels from the Middle Santa Cruz River Valley*. Old Pueblo Archaeology: Bulletin of Old Pueblo Archaeology Center No. 8. Tucson, AZ.

Ferguson, T. J., and Micah Loma'omvaya

2011 Nuvatukya'ovi, Palatsmo Niqw Wupatki: Hopi History, Culture, and Landscape. In *Sunset Crater Archaeology: The History of a Volcanic Landscape*, edited by M. D. Elson, pp. 144–186. Anthropological Papers 37. Center for Desert Archaeology, Tucson, AZ.

Fewkes, Jesse W.

1892   A Few Summer Ceremonials at the Tusayan Pueblos. *Journal of American Ethnology and Archaeology* 1:1–160.

1903   Hopi Katsinas, Drawn by Native Artists. Twenty-first Annual Report of the Bureau of American Ethnology, Washington, D.C.

1906   Hopi Shrines near the East Mesa. *American Anthropologist* 8(2):346–375.

1910   The Butterfly in Hopi Myth and Ritual. *American Anthropologist*, new series 12(4):576–594.

1912   *Casa Grande, Arizona*. Twenty-eighth Annual Report of the Bureau of American Ethnology, pp. 25–179. Washington, D.C.

Fontana, Bernard L.

1983   History of the Papago. In *Southwest*, edited by Alfonso Ortiz, pp. 137–148. Handbook of North American Indians, Vol. 10, William C. Sturtevant, general editor. Smithsonian Institution, Washington, D.C.

Ford, Richard I.

1980   The Color of Survival. *Discovery* 1(80):17–29. School of American Research, Santa Fe, NM.

Fowler, Catherine S.

1983   Some Lexical Clues to Uto-Aztecan Prehistory. *International Journal of American Linguistics* 49(3):224–257.

Frank, Larry

1990   *Indian Silver Jewelry of the Southwest*. 2nd ed., revised. Schiffer Publishing, West Chester, PA.

Franklin, Hayward H.

1982   Ceramic Analysis of Nineteen Sites in the Bis sa'ani Community. In *Bis sa'ani: A Late Bonito Phase Community on Escavada Wash, Northwest New Mexico*, Vol. 3, edited by C. D. Breternitz, D. E. Doyel, and M. P. Marshall, pp. 873–934. Navajo Nation Papers in Anthropology No. 14. Window Rock, AZ.

Frantz, Donald G.

1985   Syntactic Constraints on Noun Incorporation in Southern Tiwa. *Proceedings of the Eleventh Annual Meeting of the Berkeley Linguistics Society* 11:107–116.

Frigout, Arlette

1979   Hopi Ceremonial Organization. In *Southwest*, edited by Alfonso Ortiz, pp. 564–576. Handbook of North American Indians, Vol. 9, William C. Sturtevant, general editor. Smithsonian Institution, Washington, D.C.

Fulton, William S.

1941   *A Ceremonial Cave in the Winchester Mountains, Arizona*. Amerind Foundation Technical Report No. 2. Amerind Foundation, Dragoon, AZ.

Gal, Susan, and Judith T. Irvine

1995   The Boundaries of Languages and Disciplines: How Ideologies Construct Differences. *Social Research* 62(4):967–1001.

Geertz, Armin W., and Michael Lomatuway'ma

1987   *Children of Cottonwood: Piety and Ceremonialism in Hopi Indian Puppetry*. University of Nebraska Press, Lincoln.

Genovés, Santiago

1967   Proportionality of the Long Bones and Their Relation to Stature among Mesoamericans. *American Journal of Physical Anthropology* 26(1):67 77.

Gilman, Patricia

1990   Social Organization and Classic Mimbres Burial in the Southwest United States. *Journal of Field Archaeology* 17(4):457–469.

Gitter, Elisabeth

1984   The Power of Women's Hair in the Victorian Imagination. *Proceedings of the Modern Language Association* 99(5):936–954.

Gladwin, Harold S., Emil W. Haury, E. B. Sayles, and Nora Gladwin

1937   *Excavations at Snaketown I: Material Culture.* Gila Pueblo, Medallion Papers No. 25. Globe, AZ.

Gladwin, Winifred, and Harold S. Gladwin

1929   *The Red-on-Buff Culture of the Gila Basin.* Gila Pueblo, Medallion Papers No. 3. Globe, AZ.

Glowacka, Maria, Dorothy Washburn, and Justin Richland

2009   Nuvatukya'ovi, San Francisco Peaks: Balancing Western Economies with Native American Spiritualities. *Current Anthropology* 50(4):547–561.

Gray, Russell

2010   How Old Is Uto-Aztecan? Paper presented at the Meeting on Dynamics of Hunter-Gatherer Language Change, University of Arizona, March 6, 2010. Tucson.

Griffen, William B.

1983   Southern Periphery: East. In *Southwest*, edited by Alfonso Ortiz, pp. 329–342. Handbook of North American Indians, Vol. 10, William C. Sturtevant, general editor. Smithsonian Institution, Washington, D.C.

Griffin, P. Bion

1967   A High Status Burial from Grasshopper Ruin, Arizona. *Kiva* 3(2):37–53.

Griffith, James S.

1983   Kachinas and Masking. In *Southwest*, edited by Alfonso Ortiz, pp. 764–777. Handbook of North American Indians, Vol. 10, William C. Sturtevant, general editor. Smithsonian Institution, Washington, D.C.

Guernsey, Samuel J., and Alfred V. Kidder

1921   *Basket-Maker Caves of Northeastern Arizona; Report on the Explorations, 1916–17.* Papers of the Peabody Museum of American Archaeology and Ethnology 8(2). Harvard University, Cambridge, MA.

Hale, Kenneth L.

1967   Toward a Reconstruction of Kiowa-Tanoan Phonology. *International Journal of American Linguistics* 33(2):112–120.

Hale, Kenneth L., and David Harris

1979   Historical Linguistics and Archaeology. In *Southwest*, edited by Alfonso Ortiz, pp. 170–177. Handbook of North American Indians, Vol. 9, William C. Sturtevant, general editor. Smithsonian Institution, Washington, D.C.

Hall, Robert L, and Arthur E. Dennis

1986   Cultivated and Gathered Plant Foods. In *Archeological Investigations at Antelope*

House, edited by D. P. Morris, pp. 110–141. U.S. Department of the Interior, National Park Service, Washington, D.C.

Hammack, Laurens C.

1974   Effigy Vessels in the Prehistoric American Southwest. *Arizona Highways* 50(2):33–34.

Hammond, George P., and Agapito Rey

1940   *Narratives of the Coronado Expedition, 1540–1542.* Coronado Historical Series Vol. 1. University of New Mexico Press, Albuquerque.

Harrington, John Peabody

1910   On the Etymology of Guayabe. *American Anthropologist* 12(2):344.

1928   Vocabulary of the Kiowa Language. Bureau of American Ethnology Bulletin 84. Government Printing Office, Washington, D.C.

1947   Three Tewa Texts. *International Journal of American Linguistics* 13(2):112–116.

Harwell, Henry O., and Marsha C. S. Kelly

1983   Maricopa. In *Southwest*, edited by Alfonso Ortiz, pp. 71–85. Handbook of North American Indians, Vol. 10, William C. Sturtevant, general editor. Smithsonian Institution, Washington, D.C.

Haspelmath, Martin, and Uri Tadmor

2009   *Loanwords in the World's Languages: A Comparative Handbook.* De Gruyter Mouton, Berlin.

Haury, Emil W.

1934   *The Canyon Creek Ruin and the Cliff Dwellings of the Sierra Ancha.* Gila Pueblo, Medallion Papers No. 14. Globe, AZ.

1936   *The Mogollon Culture of Southwestern New Mexico.* Gila Pueblo, Medallion Papers No. 20. Globe, AZ.

1945a   *The Excavation of Los Muertos and Neighboring Ruins in the Salt River Valley, Southern Arizona.* Papers of the Peabody Museum of American Archaeology and Ethnology 24(1). Harvard University, Cambridge, MA.

1945b   *Painted Cave, Northeastern Arizona.* Amerind Foundation Technical Report No. 3. Amerind Foundation, Dragoon, AZ.

1950   *The Stratigraphy and Archaeology of Ventana Cave, Arizona.* University of Arizona Press, Tucson.

1976   *The Hohokam: Desert Farmers and Craftsmen.* University of Arizona Press, Tucson.

1985   *Mogollon Culture in the Forestdale Valley East-Central Arizona.* University of Arizona Press, Tucson.

Hawkey, Diane E.

1988   Use of Upper Extremity Enthesopathies to Indicate Habitual Activity Patterns. Unpublished M.A. thesis, Department of Anthropology, Arizona State University, Tempe.

Hawley, Florence

1940   Squash Blossom Headdress in Basket Maker III. *American Antiquity* 6(2):167.

Hawley, Fred G.

1953   The Manufacture of Copper Bells Found in Southwestern Sites. *Southwestern Journal of Anthropology* 9(1):99–111.

Hays-Gilpin, Kelley

2002   Wearing a Butterfly, Coming of Age: A 1500 Year Old Puebloan Tradition. In *Children in the Prehistoric Southwest*, edited by K. A. Kamp, pp. 196–210. University of Utah Press, Salt Lake City.

Hays-Gilpin, Kelley A., Ann C. Deegan, and Elizabeth A. Morris

1998   *Prehistoric Sandals from Northeastern Arizona: The Earl H. Morris and Ann Axtell Morris Research*. The Anthropological Papers of the University of Arizona 62. University of Arizona Press, Tucson.

Headrick, Annabeth

2007   *The Teotihuacán Trinity: The Sociopolitical Structure of an Ancient Mesoamerican City*. University of Texas Press, Austin.

Hefner, Joseph T.

2009   Cranial Nonmetric Variation and Estimating Ancestry. *The Journal of Forensic Sciences* 54(5):985–995.

2011   Macromorphoscopics. In *Osteoware Software Manual*, Vol. 1, edited by C. Wilczak and C. Dudar, pp. 66–78. Smithsonian Institution, Washington, D.C.

Hefner, Joseph T., M. Kate Spradley, and Bruce Anderson

2014   Ancestry Assessment Using Random Forest Modeling. *The Journal of Forensic Sciences* 59(3):583–589.

Hegmon, Michelle

2002   Recent Issues in the Archaeology of the Mimbres Region of the North American Southwest. *Journal of Archaeological Research* 10(4):307–357.

Hegmon, Michelle, and Margaret C. Nelson

2007   In Sync, but Barely in Touch. In *Hinterlands and Regional Dynamics in the Ancient Southwest*, edited by A. P. Sullivan and J. Bayman, pp. 70–96. University of Arizona Press, Tucson.

Henderson, Junius, and John P. Harrington

1914   *Ethnozoology of the Tewa Indians*. Bureau of American Ethnology Bulletin No. 56. Government Printing Office, Washington, D.C.

Hendrickson, Carol

1995   *Weaving Identities: Construction of Dress and Self in a Highland Guatemala Town*. University of Texas Press, Austin.

Hershman, P.

1974   Hair, Sex and Dirt. *Man*, New Series 9(2):274–298.

Hibben, Frank C.

1975   *Kiva Art of the Anasazi at Pottery Mound*. KC Publications, Las Vegas, NV.

Hill, Jane H.

2001   Proto-Uto-Aztecan: A Community of Cultivators in Central Mexico? *American Anthropologist* 103(4):913–934.

2007   The Zuni language in Southwestern Areal Context. In *Zuni Origins: Toward a New Synthesis of Southwestern Archaeology*, edited by D. A. Gregory and D. R. Wilcox, pp. 22–38. University of Arizona Press, Tucson.

2008a   Northern Uto-Aztecan and Kiowa-Tanoan: Evidence for Contact between the Protolanguages? *International Journal of American Linguistics* 74(2):155–188.

2008b   Otomanguean Loans in the Proto-Uto-Aztecan Maize Vocabulary? In *In Hot Pursuit of Language in Prehistory: Essays in the Four Fields of Anthropology in Honor of Harold Crane Fleming*, edited by J. D. Bengtson, pp. 309–320. John Benjamins, Philadelphia, PA.

2011a   Linguistic Paleontology and Migration: The Case of Uto-Aztecan. In *Rethinking Anthropological Perspectives on Migration*, edited by G. S. Cabana and J. J. Clark, pp. 175–190. University of Florida Press, Gainesville.

2011b   Borrowed Names and Indexical Function in the Northern Uto-Aztecan Botanical Lexicon. In *Information and Its Role in Hunter-Gatherer Bands*, edited by R. Whallon, W. Lovis, and R. K. Hitchcock, pp. 167–180. Cotsen Institute of Archaeology Press, Los Angeles.

2012   Proto-Uto-Aztecan as a Mesoamerican Language. *Ancient Mesoamerica* 23(1):57–68.

Hinton, Leanne

2001   Introduction to the Pueblo Languages. In *The Green Book of Language Revitalization in Practice*, edited by L. Hinton and K. Hale, pp. 61–62. Academic Press, New York.

Hinton, Thomas

1983   Southern Periphery: West. In *Southwest*, edited by Alfonso Ortiz, pp. 315–328. Handbook of North American Indians, Vol. 10, William C. Sturtevant, general editor. Smithsonian Institution, Washington, D.C.

Hodder, Ian

1982   *Symbols in Action: Ethnoarchaeological Studies of Material Culture*. Cambridge University Press, Cambridge, UK.

Hoebel, E. Adamson

1979   Zia Pueblo. In *Southwest*, edited by Alfonso Ortiz, pp. 407–417. Handbook of North American Indians, Vol. 9, William C. Sturtevant, general editor. Smithsonian Institution, Washington, D.C.

Hoffman, J. Michael

1993   Human Skeletal Remains. In *The Duckfoot Site*, Vol. 1: *Descriptive Archaeology*, edited by R. R. Lightfoot and M. C. Etzkorn, pp. 253–296. Occasional Paper No. 3. Crow Canyon Archaeological Center, Cortez, CO.

Hoijer, Harry, and Edward P. Dozier

1949   The Phonemes of Tewa, Santa Clara Dialect. *International Journal of American Linguistics* 19(2):118–127.

Holland, Dorothy, and William Lochcotte, Debra Skinner, and Carole Cain (editors)

1998   *Identity and Agency in Cultural Worlds*. Harvard University Press, Cambridge, MA.

Hooton, Earnest A.

1930   *The Indians of Pecos Pueblo: A Study of Their Skeletal Remains*. Yale University Press, New Haven, CT.

Hopi Color-Direction Symbolism, web page

n.d.   http://www.as.wvu.edu/~scmcc/colordirections.pdf (accessed March 31, 2016).

Hough, Walter

1914   *Culture of the Ancient Pueblos of the Upper Gila River Region, New Mexico and Arizona*. U.S. National Museum Bulletin No. 87. U.S. National Museum, Washington, D.C.

Howard, Ann V.

1983　The Organization of Interregional Shell Production and Exchange within Southwestern Arizona. Unpublished M.A. thesis, Department of Anthropology, Arizona State University, Tempe.

Howard, Jerry B.

2006　Hohokam Irrigation Communities: A Study of Internal Structure, External Relationships, and Sociopolitical Complexity. Unpublished Ph.D. dissertation, Department of Anthropology, Arizona State University, Tempe.

Howell, Todd L.

1995　Tracking Zuni Gender and Leadership Roles across the Contact Period in the Zuni Region. *Journal of Anthropological Research* 51(2):125–147.

Hrdlicka, Ales

1906　Beauty among the American Indians. In *Boas Anniversary Volume: Anthropological Papers Written in Honor of Franz Boas*, edited by B. Laufer. G. E. Stechert, New York.

1931　Catalog of Human Crania in the United States National Museum Collections. *United States National Museum Proceedings* 78:1–95.

1935　The Pueblos, with Comparative Data on the Bulk of the Tribes of the Southwest and Northern Mexico. *American Journal of Physical Anthropology* 20(3):235–560.

Huckell, Lisa W.

1993　Plant Remains from the Pinaleño Cotton Cache, Arizona. *Kiva* 59(2):147–203.

Huffman, John W.

1925　Turquoise Mosaics from Casa Grande. *Art and Archaeology* 20(2):82–84.

Hull, Sharon, Mostafa Fayek, Frances J. Mathien, Phillip Shelley, and Kathy R. Durand

2008　A New Approach to Determining the Geological Provenance of Turquoise Artifacts Using Hydrogen and Copper Stable Isotopes. *Journal of Archaeological Science* 35(5):1355–1369.

Hull, Sharon, Mostafa Fayek, Frances J. Mathien, and Heidi Roberts

2014　Turquoise Trade of the Ancestral Puebloan: Chaco and Beyond. *Journal of Archaeological Science* 45(May):187–195.

Huntington, Frederick W.

1986　*Archaeological Investigations at the West Branch Site: Early and Middle Rincon Occupation in Southern Tucson Basin.* Anthropological Papers No. 5. Institute for American Research, Tucson, AZ.

Irwin-William, Cynthia, and Phillip H. Shelley (editors)

1980　*Investigations at the Salmon Site: The Structure of Chacoan Society in the Northern Southwest.* Unpublished final report submitted to funding agencies. Eastern New Mexico University, Portales. On file, Salmon Ruins Museum Library, Bloomfield, NM.

Ives, John W., and Sally Rice

2006　Correspondences in Archaeological, Genetic, and Linguistic Evidence for Apachean Prehistory. Paper presented at the International Conference on Languages and Genes, September 6–10, 2006, University of California–Santa Barbara.

Jernigan, E. Wesley

1978　*Jewelry of the Prehistoric Southwest.* University of New Mexico Press, Albuquerque.

Joyce, Rosemary A.

2005   Archaeology of the Body. *Annual Review of Anthropology* 34: 139–158.

Judd, Neil M.

1954   *The Material Culture of Pueblo Bonito.* Smithsonian Miscellaneous Collections Vol. 124. Smithsonian Institution, Washington, D.C.

Kankainen, Kathy (editor)

1995   *Treading in the Past: Sandals of the Anasazi.* Utah Museum of Natural History in association with the University of Utah Press, Salt Lake City.

Keegan, Marcia

1999   *Pueblo People: Ancient Traditions, Modern Lives.* Clear Light Publishers, Santa Fe, NM.

Kelly, Dorothea S.

1937   McEuen Cave Report. Unpublished draft report. Folder A-164, Arizona State Museum Archives, Tucson.

Kelly, Sophia E., and Laurie D. Webster

2010   Asbestos in the Hohokam World. *Journal of Arizona Archaeology* 1(1):60–70.

Kent, Kate Peck

1940   The Braiding of a Hopi Wedding Sash. *Plateau* 12(3):46–52.

1954   Textiles. In *Montezuma Castle Archeology,* Part 2: *Textiles.* Southwestern Monuments Association, Technical Series (3):2. Coolidge, AZ.

1957   *The Cultivation and Weaving of Cotton in the Prehistoric Southwestern United States.* Transactions of the American Philosophical Society, New Series 47(3):457–732. Philadelphia.

1962   An Analysis and Interpretation of the Cotton Textiles from Tonto National Monument. In *Archeological Studies at Tonto National Monument, Arizona,* by C. R. Steen, L. M. Pierson, V. L. Bohrer, and K. P. Kent, pp. 115–155. Southwestern Monuments Association, Technical Series Vol. 2. Globe, AZ.

1983a   *Prehistoric Textiles of the Southwest.* School of American Research Press, Santa Fe, NM.

1983b   *Pueblo Indian Textiles.* School of American Research Press, Santa Fe, NM.

Khera, Sigrid, and Paricia S. Mariella

1983   Yavapai. In *Southwest,* edited by Alfonso Ortiz, pp. 38–54. Handbook of North American Indians, Vol. 10, William C. Sturtevant, general editor. Smithsonian Institution, Washington, D.C.

Kidder, Alfred V.

1924   *An Introduction to the Study of Southwestern Archaeology.* Yale University Press, New Haven, CT.

Kidder, Alfred V., and Samuel J. Guernsey

1919   *Archaeological Explorations in Northeastern Arizona.* Bureau of American Ethnology Bulletin No. 65. Government Printing Office, Washington, D.C.

King, Mary Elizabeth

1965   Appendix C: Prehistoric Textiles from the Gila Bend Area. In *Salvage Archaeology in Painted Rocks Reservoir, Western Arizona,* by W. W. Wasley and A. E. Johnson, pp. 110–114. The Anthropological Papers of the University of Arizona 9. University of Arizona Press, Tucson.

1974   Medio Period Perishable Artifacts. In *Casas Grandes: A Fallen Trading Center of the Gran Chichimeca*, Vol. 8, by C. C. Di Peso, J. B. Rinaldo, and G. J. Fenner, pp. 76–119. Amerind Foundation, Dragoon, AZ.

1979   The Prehistoric Textile Industry of Mesoamerica. In *The Junius B. Bird Pre-Columbian Textile Conference*, edited by A. P. Rowe, E. P. Benson, and A. Schaffer, pp. 265–278. The Textile Museum and Dumbarton Oaks, Washington, D.C.

Kopper, Philip

1986   *The Smithsonian Book of North American Indians: Before the Coming of the Europeans.* Smithsonian Books, Washington, D.C.

Kroeber, Alfred L.

1916   Thoughts on Zuni Religion. In *Holmes Anniversary Volume: Anthropological Essays Presented to William Henry Holmes in Honor of His Seventieth Birthday*, pp. 269–277. J. W. Bryan Press, Washington, D.C.

Kroskrity, Paul V.

1983   Male and Female Speech in the Greater Southwest. *International Journal of American Linguistics* 49(1):89–91

1985   Areal-Historical Influences on Tewa Possession. *International Journal of American Linguistics* 51(4):486–489.

1993   *Language, History, and Identity: Ethnolinguistic Studies of the Arizona Tewa.* University of Arizona Press, Tucson.

2000   Arizona Tewa Kiva Speech as a Manifestation of a Dominant Language Ideology. In *Language Ideologies: Practice and Theory*, edited by B. B. Schieffelin, K. A. Woolard, and P. V. Kroskrity, pp. 103–122. Oxford University Press. New York.

Lachler, Jordan

2006   *A Grammar of Laguna Keres.* Ph.D. dissertation, Department of Linguistics, University of New Mexico. University Microfilms, Ann Arbor, MI.

Lambert, Marjorie F.

1979   Pojoaque Pueblo. In *Southwest*, edited by Alfonso Ortiz, pp. 324–329. Handbook of North American Indians, Vol. 9, William C. Sturtevant, general editor. Smithsonian Institution, Washington, D.C.

Lamphere, Louise

1983   Southwestern Ceremonialism. In *Southwest*, edited by Alfonso Ortiz, pp. 743–763. Handbook of North American Indians, Vol. 10, William C. Sturtevant, general editor. Smithsonian Institution, Washington, D.C.

Langdon, Margaret, and Shirley Silver

1984   California t/ṭ. *Journal of California and Great Basin Anthropology, Papers in Linguistics* 4:139–165.

Lange, Charles H.

1959   *Cochiti: A New Mexico Pueblo, Past and Present.* University of Texas Press, Austin.

1979a   Cochiti Pueblo. In *Southwest*, edited by Alfonso Ortiz, pp. 366–378. Handbook of North American Indians, Vol. 9, William C. Sturtevant, general editor. Smithsonian Institution, Washington, D.C.

1979b   Santo Domingo Pueblo. In *Southwest*, edited by Alfonso Ortiz, pp. 379–389. Handbook of North American Indians, Vol. 9, William C. Sturtevant, general editor. Smithsonian Institution, Washington, D.C.

Leach, Edmund R.

1958   Magical Hair. *The Journal of the Royal Anthropological Institute of Great Britain and Ireland* 88(2):147–164.

Lekson, Stephen H.

1986   *Great Pueblo Architecture of Chaco Canyon.* University of New Mexico Press, Albuquerque.

2002   *Salado Archaeology of the Upper Gila, New Mexico.* The Anthropological Papers of the University of Arizona 67. University of Arizona Press, Tucson.

2009   *A History of the Ancient Southwest.* School for Advanced Research Press, Santa Fe, NM.

Lister, Robert F., and Florence C. Lister

1996   *Aztec Ruins on the Animas: Excavated, Preserved, and Interpreted.* University of New Mexico Press, Albuquerque.

Loftin, John D.

1991   *Religion and Hopi Life.* Indiana University Press, Bloomington.

Lozada, María C.

2011   Marking Ethnicity Through Premortem Cranial Modification Among the Pre-Inca Chiribaya, Peru. In *The Bioarchaeology of the Human Head,* edited by M. Bonogofksy, pp. 228–240. University Press of Florida, Gainesville.

Lumpkin, Charles K., Jr.

1976   A Multivariate Craniometric Analysis of Selected Southwestern Archaeological Populations. Unpublished Ph.D. dissertation, Department of Anthropology, University of New Mexico, Albuquerque.

Mageo, Jeannette Marie

1994   Hairdos and Don'ts: Symbolism and Sexual History in Samoa. *Man,* New Series 29(2):407–432.

Magers, Pamela C.

1986   Weaving at Antelope House. In *Archeological Investigations at Antelope House,* edited by D. P. Morris, pp. 224–276. U.S. Department of the Interior, National Park Service, Washington, D.C.

Malagon, Maria Sprehn

2001   Tattoos, Women, and Rites of Passage: Body Art in the Casas Grandes World. In *From Paquimé to Mata Ortiz: The Legacy of Ancient Casas Grandes,* edited by G. Johnson, pp. 65–72. San Diego Museum Papers No. 40. San Diego.

Malville, Nancy J.

2008   Stature of Ancestral Puebloan Populations: Population Density, Social Stratification, and Dietary Protein. In *Reanalysis and Reinterpretation in Southwestern Bioarchaeology,* edited by A. L. W. Stodder, pp. 105–126. Arizona State University Anthropological Research Papers No. 59. Tempe.

Martin, Debra L.

1998   Owning the Sins of the Past: Historical Trends, Missed Opportunities, and New Directions in the Study of Human Remains. In *Building a New Biocultural Synthesis:*

Political-Economic Perspectives on Human Biology, edited by A. H. Goodman and T. L. Leatherman, pp. 171–190. University of Michigan Press, Ann Arbor.

Martin, Paul S., John B. Rinaldo, Elaine A. Bluhn, Hugh C. Cutler, and Roger Grange Jr.

1952   *Mogollon Cultural Continuity and Change: The Stratigraphic Analysis of Tularosa and Cordova Caves.* Fieldiana: Anthropology Vol. 40. Chicago Natural History Museum, Chicago.

Martinez, Esther

1982   *San Juan Pueblo Téwa Dictionary.* Bishop Publishing, Portales, NM.

Mathien, Frances J.

1981   Neutron Activation of Turquoise Artifacts from Chaco Canyon, New Mexico. *Current Anthropology* 22(3):293–294.

1997   Ornaments of the Chaco Anasazi. In *Ceramics, Lithics, and Ornaments of Chaco Canyon: Analyses of Artifacts from the Chaco Project*, Vol. 3: *Lithics and Ornaments*, edited by F. J. Mathien, pp. 1119–1207. Chaco Studies Publications in Archaeology No. 18G. U.S. Department of the Interior, National Park Service, Santa Fe, NM.

2000   Identifying Sources of Prehistoric Turquoise in North America: Problems and Implications for Interpreting Social Organization. *Beads, Journal of the Society of Bead Research* 12/13:17–37.

Matthews, Washington, Jacob L. Wortman, and John S. Billings

1893   Human Bones of the Hemenway Collection in the United States Army Medical Museum. *Memoirs of the National Academy of Sciences* 6:141–286.

Mattson, Hannah

2011   Ornaments and Individual Identity in the Prehistoric Southwest: The Practice of Personal Adornment. MS on file, Department of Anthropology, University of New Mexico, Albuquerque.

McClelland, John A.

2003   Refining the Resolution of Biological Distance Studies Based on the Analysis of Dental Morphology: Detecting Subpopulations at Grasshopper Pueblo. Unpublished Ph.D. dissertation, Department of Anthropology, University of Arizona, Tucson.

2010   Dental Biodistance. In *Animas-La Plata Project*, Vol. 15: *Bioarchaeology*, edited by E. M. Perry, A. L. W. Stodder, and C. Bollong, pp. 223–238. SWCA Environmental Consultants, Phoenix, AZ.

McGregor, John C.

1931   Prehistoric Cotton Fabric of Arizona. *Museum Notes* 4(2). Museum of Northern Arizona, Flagstaff.

1941   *Winona and Ridge Ruin*, Part 1: *Architecture and Material Culture.* Museum of Northern Arizona Bulletin 18. Flagstaff.

1943   Burial of an Early American Magician. *Proceedings of the American Philosophical Society* 86(2):270–298.

McGuire, Randall H.

1985   The Role of Shell Exchange in the Explanation of Hohokam Prehistory. In *Proceedings of the 1983 Hohokam Symposium* Part II, edited by A. E. Dittert and D. E. Dove, pp. 473–482. Arizona Archaeological Society Occasional Paper No. 2. Phoenix.

1992 *Death, Society, and Ideology in a Hohokam Community*. Westview Press, Boulder, CO.

2012 Pueblo Religion and the Mesoamerican Connection. In *Religious Transformation in the Late Pre-Hispanic Pueblo World*, edited by D. M. Glowacki and S. Van Keuren, pp. 23–48. University of Arizona Press, Tucson.

McGuire, Randall H., and Christopher E. Downum

1982 A Preliminary Consideration of Desert-Mountain Trade. In *Mogollon Archaeology: Proceedings of the 1980 Mogollon Conference*, edited by P. H. Beckett, pp. 111–122. Acoma Books, Ramona, CA.

McGuire, Randall H., and Ann V. Howard

1987 The Structure and Organization of Hohokam Shell Exchange. *Kiva* 52(2):113–146.

McGuire, Randall H., and Michael B. Schiffer

1982 *Hohokam and Patayan: The Prehistory of Southwestern Arizona*. Academic Press, New York.

McGuire, Thomas R.

1983 Walapai. In *Southwest*, edited by Alfonso Ortiz, pp. 25–37. Handbook of North American Indians, Vol. 10, William C. Sturtevant, general editor. Smithsonian Institution, Washington, D.C.

McKusick, Charmion R., and Jon Nathan Young

1997 *The Gila Pueblo Salado*. Salado Chapter, Arizona Archaeological Society, Globe, AZ.

Merbs, Charles F.

1992 A New World of Infectious Disease. *Yearbook of Physical Anthropology* 35:3–42.

Merbs, Charles F., and Ellen M. Vestergaard

1985 The Paleopathology of Sundown, a Prehistoric Site Near Prescott, Arizona. In *Health and Disease in the Prehistoric Southwest*, edited by C. Merbs and R. Miller, pp. 85–103. Arizona State University Anthropological Research Papers No. 34. Tempe.

Merrill, William L.

1983 Tarahumara Social Organization, Political Organization, and Religion. In *Southwest*, edited by Alfonso Ortiz, pp. 290–305. Handbook of North American Indians, Vol. 10, William C. Sturtevant, general editor. Smithsonian Institution, Washington, D.C.

Miller, Arthur G.

1973 *The Mural Paintings of Teotihuacán*. Dumbarton Oaks, Washington, DC.

Miller, Wick R.

1965 *Acoma Grammar and Texts*. University of California Publications in Linguistics Vol. 40. University of California Press, Berkeley and Los Angeles.

Miller, Wick R., and Irvine Davis

1963 Proto-Keresan Phonology. *International Journal of American Linguistics* 29(4):310–330.

Mills, Barbara J.

2008 Remembering While Forgetting: Depositional Practices and Social Memory at Chaco. In *Memory Work: Archaeologies of Material Practices*, edited by B. J. Mills and W. H. Walker, pp. 3–24. School of Advanced Research Press, Santa Fe, NM.

Mitchell, Douglas R.

n.d.   Computerized Inventory of Pueblo Grande Burials and Their Mortuary Goods. On file, Pueblo Grande Museum, Phoenix, AZ.

1994   *The Pueblo Grande Project*, Vol. 7: *An Analysis of Classic Period Hohokam Mortuary Practices*. Soil Systems Publications in Archaeology No. 20. Phoenix, AZ.

Mitchell, Douglas R., and Judy L. Brunson-Hadley (editors)

2001   *Ancient Burial Practices in the American Southwest: Archaeology, Physical Anthropology, and Native American Perspectives*. University of New Mexico Press, Albuquerque.

Morgan, Michelle E. (editor)

2010   *Pecos Pueblo Revisited: The Biological and Social Context*. Papers of the Peabody Museum of Archaeology and Ethnology Vol. 85. Harvard University, Cambridge, MA.

Morris, Earl H.

1919   *The Aztec Ruin*. Anthropological Papers of the American Museum of Natural History 26(1). New York.

1921   *The House of the Great Kiva at the Aztec Ruin*. Anthropological Papers of the American Museum of Natural History 26(1):109–138. New York.

1924   *Burials in the Aztec Ruin*. Anthropological Papers of the American Museum of Natural History 26(3). New York.

Morris, Earl H., and Robert F. Burgh

1954   *Basket Maker II Sites near Durango, Colorado*. Carnegie Institution of Washington Publication 604. Carnegie Institution, Washington, D.C.

Morris, Elizabeth A.

1980   *Basketmaker Caves in the Prayer Rock District, Northeastern Arizona*. The Anthropological Papers of the University of Arizona 35. University of Arizona Press, Tucson.

Moulard, Barbara

1984   *Within the Underworld Sky: Mimbres Ceramic Art in Context*. Twelvetrees Press, Pasadena, CA.

Munson, Marit

2000   Sex, Gender, and Status: Human Images from the Classic Period Mimbres. *American Antiquity* 65(1):127–143.

Narez, Jesus

1991   *Casas Grandes: catálogo de las colecciones arqueológicas del Museo Nacional de Antropología*. Insituto Nacional de Antropología e Historia, México, D.F.

Neitzel, Jill E.

2000   Gender Hierarchies: A Comparative Analysis of Mortuary Data. In *Women and Men in the Prehispanic Southwest: Labor, Power, and Prestige*, edited by P. L. Crown, pp. 137–168. School of American Research Press, Santa Fe, NM.

2003   (editor) *Pueblo Bonito: Center of the Chacoan World*. Smithsonian Books, Washington, D.C.

2012   The Magician: An Ancestral Hopi Leader. In *The Bioarchaeology of Individuals*, edited by A. L. W. Stodder and A. M. Palkovich, pp. 11–25. University Press of Florida, Gainesville.

Nelson, Greg C., and Felicia Madimenos

2007 Unusual Cranial Deformation in a Gallina Skeletal Series. Abstract. *American Journal of Physical Anthropology* 132(S44):177.

2010 Obelionic Cranial Deformation in the Puebloan Southwest. *American Journal of Physical Anthropology* 143(3):465–472.

Nelson, Richard S.

1981 The Role of a Pochteca System in Hohokam Exchange. Unpublished Ph.D. dissertation, Department of Anthropology, New York University.

1986 Pochtecas and Prestige: Mesoamerican Artifacts in Hohokam Sites: In *Ripples in the Chichimec Sea: New Considerations of Southwestern-Mesoamerican Interactions*, edited by F. J. Mathien and R. H. McGuire, pp. 154–182. Southern Illinois University Press, Carbondale.

Neuman, Georg K.

1952 Archaeology and Race in the American Indian. In *Archaeology of Eastern United States*, edited by J. B. Griffin, pp. 13–34. University of Chicago Press, Chicago.

Newcomb, William W., Jr.

1983 Karankawa. In *Southwest*, edited by Alfonso Ortiz, pp. 359–367. Handbook of North American Indians, Vol. 10, William C. Sturtevant, general editor. Smithsonian Institution, Washington, D.C.

Newman, Stanley

1958 *Zuni Dictionary*. Indiana University Research Center in Anthropology, Folklore, and Linguistics Publication 6. Indiana University Press, Bloomington.

1964 Comparison of Zuni and California Penutian. *International Journal of American Linguistics* 30(1):1–13.

Nicholas, Linda, and Gary M. Feinman

1989 A Regional Perspective on Hohokam Irrigation in the Lower Salt River Valley, Arizona. In *The Sociopolitical Structure of Prehistoric Southwestern Societies*, edited by S. Upham, K. G. Lightfoot, and R. Jewett, pp. 199–236. Westview Press, Boulder.

Nielsen-Grimm, Glenna, and Paul Stavast (editors)

2008 *Touching the Past: Ritual, Religion, and Trade of Casas Grandes*. Brigham Young University Museum of Peoples and Cultures Popular Series 5. Provo, UT.

Northrop, Stuart A.

1975 *Turquoise and Spanish Mines in New Mexico*. University of New Mexico Press, Albuquerque.

Nusbaum, Jesse L.

1922 *A Basket-Maker Cave in Kane County, Utah*. Indian Notes and Monographs 29. Museum of the American Indian, Heye Foundation, New York.

Odegaard, Nancy, and Kelley Hays-Gilpin

2002 Technology of the Sacred: Painted Basketry in the Southwest. In *Traditions, Transitions, and Technologies: Themes in Southwestern Archaeology*, edited by S. H. Schlanger, pp. 307–331. University Press of Colorado, Boulder.

O'Hara, Michael

2008 The Magician of Ridge Ruin: An Interpretation of His Social, Political, and Ritual Roles Represented. Paper presented in the symposium "Beyond Status: Meaning,

Metaphor, and Identity in the New World Mortuary Record," 73rd Annual Meeting of the Society for American Archaeology, Vancouver.

O'Neale, Lila M.

1948   *Textiles of Pre-Columbian Chihuahua.* Contributions to American Anthropology and History No. 45, Carnegie Institution of Washington Publication 574. Carnegie Institution, Washington, D.C.

Opler, Morris E.

1983a   The Apachean Cultural Pattern and Its Origins. In *Southwest*, edited by Alfonso Ortiz, pp. 368–392. Handbook of North American Indians, Vol. 10, William C. Sturtevant, general editor. Smithsonian Institution, Washington, D.C.

1983b   Mescalero Apache. In *Southwest*, edited by Alfonso Ortiz, pp. 419–439. Handbook of North American Indians, Vol. 10, William C. Sturtevant, general editor. Smithsonian Institution, Washington, D.C.

Ortiz, Alfonso

1969   *Tewa World: Space, Time, Being and Becoming in a Pueblo Society.* University of Chicago Press, Chicago.

1979a   (editor) *Southwest. Handbook of North American Indians*, Vol. 9. William C. Sturtevant, general editor. Smithsonian Institution, Washington, D.C.

1979b   San Juan Pueblo. In *Southwest*, edited by Alfonso Ortiz, 278–295. Handbook of North American Indians, Vol. 9, William C. Sturtevant, general editor. Smithsonian Institution, Washington, D.C.

1983   (editor) *Southwest. Handbook of North American Indians*, Vol. 10. William C. Sturtevant, general editor. Smithsonian Institution, Washington, D.C.

Ortman, Scott G.

2012   *Winds from the North: Tewa Origins and Historical Anthropology.* University of Utah Press, Salt Lake City.

Osborne, Carolyn M.

2004   *The Wetherill Collections and Perishable Items from Mesa Verde.* Self-published volume distributed by www.lulu.com.

O'Shea, John M.

1984   *Mortuary Variability: An Archaeological Investigation.* Academic Press, New York.

Palkovich, Ann M.

1980   *The Arroyo Hondo Skeletal and Mortuary Remains.* Arroyo Hondo Archaeological Series Vol. 3. School of American Research Press, Santa Fe, NM.

Palmer, J. W., M. G. Hollander, P. S. Z. Rogers, T. M. Benjamin, C. J. Duffy, J. B. Lambert, and J. A. Brown

1998   Pre-Columbian Metallurgy: Technology, Manufacture, and Microprobe Analyses of Copper Bells from the Greater Southwest. *Archaeometry* 40(2):361–382.

Parsons, Elsie Clews

1925a   A Pueblo Indian Journal, 1920–1921. Memoirs of the American Anthropological Association No.32. Menasha, WI.

1925b   *The Pueblo of Jemez.* Yale University Press, New Haven, CT.

1933a   *Hopi and Zuni Ceremonialism.* Memoirs of the American Anthropological Association No. 39. Menasha, WI.

1933b   Some Aztec and Pueblo Parallels. *American Antiquity* 35(4)611–631.

1936 (editor) *Hopi Journal of Alexander M. Stephen*. Columbia University Press, New York.

1939 *Pueblo Indian Religion*. University of Nebraska Press, Lincoln.

Pascalis, Olivier, and Slater, Alan (editors)

2003 *The Development of Face Processing in Infancy and Early Childhood*. Nova Science Publications, New York.

Pasztory, Esther

1976 *The Murals of Tepantitla, Teotihuacán*. Garland Publishing, New York.

1997 *Teotihuacán: An Experiment in Living*. University of Oklahoma Press, Norman.

Pecos, Regis, and Rebecca Blum-Martinez

2001 The Key to Cultural Survival: Language Planning and Revitalization in the Pueblo de Cochiti. In *The Green Book of Language Revitalization in Practice*, edited by L. Hinton and K. Hale, pp. 75–82. Academic Press, New York.

Penn Museum

2010 Making Piki Bread, video https://www.youtube.com/watch?v=JnjwLzVr5qM.

Pennington, Campbell W.

1983a Tarahumara. In *Southwest*, edited by Alfonso Ortiz, pp. 276–289. Handbook of North American Indians, Vol. 10, William C. Sturtevant, general editor. Smithsonian Institution, Washington, D.C.

1983b Northern Tepehuan. In *Southwest*, edited by Alfonso Ortiz, pp. 306–314. Handbook of North American Indians, Vol. 10, William C. Sturtevant, general editor. Smithsonian Institution, Washington, D.C.

Pepper, George H.

1906 Human Effigy Vases from Chaco Cañon, New Mexico. In *Boas Anniversary Volume: Anthropological Papers Written in Honor of Franz Boas*, 320–334. G. E. Stechert, New York.

1909 The Exploration of a Burial Room in Pueblo Bonito, New Mexico. In *Putnam Anniversary Volume*, by his friends and associates, pp. 320–334. G. E. Stechert, New York.

1920 *Pueblo Bonito*. Anthropological Papers of the American Museum of Natural History No. 27. New York.

Philips, David A., Jr., and Christine S.

2009a Casas Grandes Effigy Pots: Portraits of Individuals? Individual Potters? PowerPoint lecture for the Albuquerque Archaeological Society.

2009b Seeking the Individual in Casas Grandes Pottery: A Progress Report. *Pottery Southwest* 28(3):10–16.

Pilles, Peter J., Jr.

2000 The Pueblo III Period along the Mogollon Rim: The Honanki, Elden, and Turkey Hill Phases of the Sinagua. In *The Prehistoric Pueblo World, AD 1150–1350*, edited by M. A. Adler, pp. 29–47. University of Arizona Press, Tucson.

Piper, Claudette

2002 The Morphology of Prehispanic Cradleboards. In *Children in the Prehistoric Puebloan Southwest*, edited by K. A. Kamp, pp. 41–70. University of Utah Press, Salt Lake City.

Plog, Fred, Steadman Upham, and Phil C. Weigand

1982 A Perspective on Mogollon-Mesoamerican Interaction. In *Mogollon Archaeology:*

Proceedings of the 1980 Mogollon Conference, edited by P.H. Beckett, pp. 227–238. Acoma Books, Ramona, CA.

Plog, Stephen

2003   Exploring the Ubiquitous through the Unusual: Color Symbolism in Pueblo Black-on-White Pottery. *American Antiquity* 68(4):665–695.

2008   *Ancient Peoples of the American Southwest*. 2nd ed. Thames and Hudson, New York.

Potter, James M.

2000   Pots, Parties, and Politics: Communal Feasting in the American Southwest. *American Antiquity* 65(3):471–492.

Potter, James M., and Scott G. Ortman

2004   Community and Cuisine in the Prehispanic American Southwest. In *Identity, Feasting, and the Archaeology of the Greater Southwest*, edited by B. J. Mills, pp. 173–191. University Press of Colorado, Boulder.

Powell, Melissa (editor)

2006   *Secrets of Casas Grandes: Precolumbian Art and Archaeology in Northern Mexico*. Museum of New Mexico Press, Santa Fe.

Powell, Margaret K., and Joseph Roach

2004   Big Hair. *Eighteenth Century Studies* 38(1) 79–99.

Rakita, Gordon F. M.

2001   Social Complexity, Religious Organization, and Mortuary Ritual in the Casas Grandes Region of Chihuahua, Mexico. Unpublished Ph.D. dissertation, Department of Anthropology, University of New Mexico, Albuquerque.

Rakover, Sam S., and Baruch Cahlon

2001   *Face Recognition: Cognitive and Computational Processes*. John Benjamin's Publishing, Philadelphia, PA.

Ravesloot, John C.

1988   *Mortuary Practices and Social Differentiation at Casas Grandes, Chihuahua, Mexico*. The Anthropological Papers of the University of Arizona 49. University of Arizona Press, Tucson.

Reed, Erik K.

1949   The Significance of Skull Deformation in the Southwest. *El Palacio* 56(4):106–119.

Reed, Paul F.

2008   (editor) *Chaco's Northern Prodigies: Salmon, Aztec, and the Ascendancy of the Middle San Juan Region after AD 1100*. University of Utah Press, Salt Lake City.

2011   Chacoan Immigration or Emulation of the Chacoan System? The Emergence of Aztec, Salmon, and Other Great House Communities in the Middle San Juan. *Kiva* 77(2):119–138.

Regan, Marcia H., and Christy G. Turner, II

1997   Physical Anthropology and Human Taphonomy of the Schoolhouse Point Mesa Sites. In *The Archaeology of Schoolhouse Point Mesa, Roosevelt Platform Mound Study: Report on the Schoolhouse Point Mesa Sites, Schoolhouse Management Group, Pinto Creek Complex*, edited by O. Lindauer, pp. 631–667. Roosevelt Monograph Series No. 9, Anthropological Field Series No. 37. Arizona State University, Office of Cultural Resource Management, Tempe.

Reid, J. Jefferson, and Stephanie M. Whittlesey

1982   Households at Grasshopper Pueblo. *American Behavioral Scientist* 25(6):687–703.

Renfrew, Colin

1974   Beyond a Subsistence Economy: The Evolution of Social Organization in Prehistoric Europe. In *Reconstructing Complex Societies: An Archaeology Colloquium*, edited by C. B. Moore, pp. 69–95. Bulletin of the American Schools of Oriental Research, Supplementary Studies No. 20. Cambridge, MA.

Retzius, Gustav

1893   Human Remains from the Cliff Dwellings of the Mesa Verde. In *The Cliff Dwellers of the Mesa Verde, Southwestern Colorado: Their Pottery and Implements*, by G. Nordenskiöld, appendix pp. i–xi. P. A. Norstedt & Söner, Stockholm.

Rice, Glen E.

2016   *Sending the Spirits Home: The Archaeology of Hohokam Mortuary Practices*. University of Utah Press, Salt Lake City.

Riley, Carroll L.

1976   *Sixteenth Century Trade in the Greater Southwest*. Mesoamerican Studies No. 10. University Museum and Art Galleries, Southern Illinois University, Carbondale.

1982   *The Frontier People: The Greater Southwest in the Protohistoric Period*. Center for Archaeological Investigations Occasional Paper No. 1. Southern Illinois University, Carbondale.

Roediger, Virginia M.

1941   *Ceremonial Costumes of the Pueblo Indians: Their Evolution, Fabrication, and Significance in the Prayer Drama*. Reprint 1991. University of California Press, Berkeley.

Rohn, Arthur H.

1971   *Mug House, Mesa Verde National Park, Colorado*. U.S. Department of the Interior, National Park Service, Washington, D. C.

Rood, David S.

1973   Swadesh's Keres-Caddo Comparison. *International Journal of American Linguistics* 39(3):189–90.

Rosenthal, Angela

2004   Raising Hair. *Eighteenth Century Studies* 38(1):1–16.

Ruff, Christopher B.

2006   Environmental Influences on Skeletal Morphology. In *Environment, Origins, and Population*, edited by D. H. Ubelaker, pp. 685–693. Handbook of North American Indians, Vol. 3, William C. Sturtevant, general editor. Smithsonian Institution, Washington, D.C.

2010   Structural Analyses of Postcranial Skeletal Remains. In *Pecos Pueblo Revisited: The Biological and Social Context*, edited by M. Morgan, pp. 93–108. Papers of the Peabody Museum of Archaeology and Ethnology Vol. 85. Harvard University, Cambridge, MA.

Sando, Joe S.

1979   Jemez Pueblo. In *Southwest*, edited by Alfonso Ortiz, pp. 418–429. Handbook of North American Indians, Vol. 9, William C. Sturtevant, general editor. Smithsonian Institution, Washington, D.C.

Sapir, Edward

1931 Southern Paiute Dictionary. *Proceedings of the American Academy of Arts and Sciences* 65(3):537–730.

1936 Internal Linguistic Evidence Suggestive of the Northern Origin of the Navajo. *American Anthropologist* 38(2):224–235.

Sayles, E. B.

1937 Perishable Materials. In *Excavations at Snaketown I: Material Culture*, by H. S. Gladwin, E. W. Haury, E. B. Sayles, and N. Gladwin, pp. 159–162. Gila Pueblo, Medallion Papers No. 25. Globe, AZ.

Schaafsma, Polly

1999 Tlalocs, Kachinas, Sacred Bundles, and Related Symbolism in the Southwest and Mesoamerica. In *The Casas Grandes World*, edited by C. F. Schaafsma and C. L. Riley, pp. 164–192. University of Utah Press, Salt Lake City.

2007 (editor) *New Perspectives on Pottery Mound Pueblo*, University of New Mexico Press, Albuquerque.

2010 *Kachinas in the Pueblo World*. University of Utah Press, Salt Lake City.

Schevill, Margot B., Janet C. Berlo, and Edward B. Dwyer (editors)

1996 *Textile Traditions of Mesoamerica and the Andes: An Anthology*. University of Texas Press, Austin.

Schillaci, Michael A.

1999 A Case of Coccidioidomycosis from the Prehistoric American Southwest. *Journal of Paleopathology* 11(1):41–52.

Schollmeyer, Karen G., Steve Swanson, and Margaret C. Nelson

2009 Mimbres Sites and Settlements: Southwest New Mexico, Southeast Arizona, and Northwest Chihuahua, Mexico. In *Archaeology in America: An Encyclopedia*, Vol. 3: *Southwest and Great Basin/Plateau*, edited by Francis P. McManamon, pp. 171–176. Greenwood Press, Westport, CT.

Schroeder, Albert H.

1979 Pueblos Abandoned in Historic Times. In *Southwest*, edited by Alfonso Ortiz, pp. 236–254. Handbook of North American Indians, Vol. 9, William C. Sturtevant, general editor. Smithsonian Institution, Washington, D.C.

Schwartz, Douglas W.

1983 Havasupai. In *Southwest*, edited by Alfonso Ortiz, pp. 13–24. Handbook of North American Indians, Vol. 10, William C. Sturtevant, general editor. Smithsonian Institution, Washington, D.C.

Scott, G. Richard, and Christy G. Turner, II

1997 *The Anthropology of Modern Human Teeth: Dental Morphology and Its Variation in Recent Human Populations*. Cambridge University Press, Cambridge, UK.

Secakuku, Alph H.

1995 *Following the Sun and Moon*. Northland Publishing, Flagstaff, AZ.

Sekaquaptewa, Emory

1976 Hopi Indian Ceremonies. In *Seeing with a Native Eye*, edited by W. H. Copps, pp. 35–43. Harper and Row, New York.

Sekaquaptewa, Emory, Kenneth C. Hill, and Dorothy K. Washburn

2015 *Hopi Katsina Songs*. University of Nebraska Press, Lincoln.

Seltzer, Carl C.

1936   New Light on the Racial Prehistory of the Southwest Area. Abstract. *American Journal of Physical Anthropology* 21(2):17.

1944   *Racial Prehistory of the Hawikuh Zunis*. Papers of the Peabody Museum of American Archaeology and Ethnology Vol. 23(1). Harvard University, Cambridge, MA.

Seymour, Deni J.

1988   An Alternative View of Sedentary Period Hohokam Shell Ornament Production. *American Antiquity* 53(4):812–829.

Shafer, Harry J.

2003   *Mimbres Archaeology at the NAN Ranch Ruin*. University of New Mexico Press, Albuquerque.

Shaul, David Leedom

1980   A Preliminary Analysis of the Pueblo Culture Area as a Linguistic Area. Manuscript on file, Department of Anthropology, University of Arizona. Tucson.

1982   Glottalized Consonants in Zuni. *International Journal of American Linguistics* 48(1):83–85.

1985   Azteco-Tanoan *-l/r-. *International Journal of American Linguistics* 51(4):584–586.

2014   *A Prehistory of Western North America: The Impact of Uto-Aztecan Languages*. University of New Mexico Press, Albuquerque.

Shaul, David Leedom, and Jane H. Hill

1998   Tepimans, Yumans, and Other Hohokam. *American Antiquity* 63(3):375–396.

Sieber, Roy, and Frank Herreman

2000   Hair in African Art and Culture. *African Arts* 33(3):54–69, 96.

Sigleo, Anne

1975   Turquoise Mine and Artifact Correlation for Snaketown Site, Arizona. *Science* 189(4201)459–460.

Simms, Steven R., and Francois Gohier

2010   *Traces of Fremont: Society and Rock Art in Ancient Utah*. University of Utah Press, Salt Lake City.

Simpson, Georgina K.

1999   *A Guide to Indian Jewelry of the Southwest*. Western National Parks Association, Tucson, AZ.

Sims, Christine P.

2001   Native Language Planning: A Pilot Process in the Acoma Pueblo Community. In *The Green Book of Language Revitalization in Practice*, edited by L. Hinton and K. Hale, pp. 63–74. Academic Press, New York.

Sims, Christine P., and Hilaire Valiquette

1990   More on Male and Female Speech in (Acoma and Laguna) Keresan. *International Journal of American Linguistics* 56(1):162–166.

Slater, Alan, and Paul C. Quinn

2001   Facial Recognition in the Newborn Infant. *Infant and Child Development* 10(1–2): 21–24.

Slobodin, Richard

1981   Alexander Hunter Murray and Kutchin Hair Style. *Arctic Anthropology* 18(2): 29–42.

Smith, Heather F.

2009 Which Cranial Regions Reflect Molecular Distances Reliably in Humans? Evidence from Three-Dimensional Morphology. *American Journal of Human Biology* 21(1):36–47.

Smith, Michael E.

2011 *The Aztecs*. 3rd ed. Wiley-Blackwell, Malden, MA.

Smith, Watson

1952 *Kiva Mural Decorations at Awatovi and Kawaika-a*. Papers of the Peabody Museum of American Archaeology and Ethnology Vol. 37. Harvard University, Cambridge, MA.

Snead, James E., Clark L. Erickson, and J. Andrew Darling (editors)

2009 *Landscapes of Movement: Trails, Paths, and Roads in Anthropological Perspective*. University of Pennsylvania Press, Philadelphia.

Snow, David H.

1973 Prehistoric Southwestern Turquoise Industry. *El Palacio* 79(1):33–51.

Snow, Meradeth H., Kathy R. Durand, and David G. Smith

2010 Ancestral Puebloan mtDNA in Context of the Greater Southwest. *Journal of Archaeological Science* 37(7):1635–1645.

Speirs, Randall H.

1966 *Some Aspects of the Structure of Rio Grande Tewa*. Ph.D. dissertation, Department of Linguistics, State University of New York at Buffalo. University Microfilms, Ann Arbor, MI.

Spencer, Robert F.

1946 The Phonemes of Keresan. *International Journal of American Linguistics* 12(4): 229–236.

Spielmann, Katherine A.

2004 Communal Feasting, Ceramics, and Exchange. In *Identity, Feasting, and the Archaeology of the Greater Southwest*, edited by B. J. Mills, pp. 210–232. University Press of Colorado, Boulder.

Sprague, Roderick

1963 Inventory of Prehistoric Southwestern Copper Bells. *Kiva* 28(1):1–20.

Spranz, Bodo

1973 *Los dioses en los códices mexicanos del grupo Borgia: una investigación iconográfica*. Fondo de Cultura Económica, México, DF.

Stanislawski, Michael B.

1979 Hopi-Tewa. In *Southwest*, edited by Alfonso Ortiz, pp. 587–602. Handbook of North American Indians, Vol. 9, William C. Sturtevant, general editor. Smithsonian Institution, Washington, D.C.

Steen, Charlie R., Lloyd M. Pierson, Vorsila L. Bohrer, and Kate Peck Kent

1962 *Archeological Studies at Tonto National Monument, Arizona*. Southwestern Monuments Association Technological Series Vol. 2. Globe, AZ.

Stephen, Alexander M.

1936 *Hopi Journal of Alexander M. Stephen*, edited by E. C. Parsons. 2 vols. Columbia

University Contributions to Anthropology 23. Columbia University Press, New York.

Stevenson, Matilda C.

1904 *The Zuni Indians: Their Mythology, Esoteric Fraternities, and Ceremonies.* Twenty-third Annual Report of the Bureau of American Ethnology for the Years 1901–1902, pp. 3–634. Government Printing Office, Washington, D.C.

1915 *Ethnobotany of the Zuni Indians.* Thirtieth Annual Report of the Bureau of American Ethnology for 1908–09, pp. 31–102. Government Printing Office, Washington, D.C.

1987 Dress and Adornment of the Pueblo Indians, edited by Richard V. N. Ahlstrom, and Nancy J. Parezo. *Kiva* 52(4):275–312.

Stewart, Kenneth M.

1983 Mohave. In *Southwest*, edited by Alfonso Ortiz, pp. 55–70. Handbook of North American Indians, Vol. 10, William C. Sturtevant, general editor. Smithsonian Institution, Washington, D.C.

Stewart, T. D.

1937 Different Types of Cranial Deformity in the Southwest. *American Anthropologist* 39(1):169–171.

Stodder, Ann L. W.

1990 Paleoepidemiology of Eastern and Western Pueblo Communities in Protohistoric New Mexico. Unpublished Ph.D. dissertation, Department of Anthropology, University of Colorado, Boulder.

2006 Skeletal Biology: Southwest. In *Environment, Origins, and Population*, edited by D. H. Ubelaker. Handbook of North American Indians, Vol. 3, pp. 557–580. Smithsonian Institution, Washington, D.C.

Stodder, Ann L. W., and Ann M. Palkovich (editors)

2011 *The Bioarchaeology of Individuals.* University Press of Florida, Gainesville.

Strathern, Andrew

1989 Flutes, Birds, and Hair in Hagen (PNG). *Anthropos* 84 (1–3):81–87.

Stubbs, Stanley A.

1959 Prehistoric Woven Asbestos Belt Fragment. *El Palacio* 66(2): inside back cover.

Sutton, Logan

2012 Personal communication (December 16, 2012)

2014 Kiowa-Tanoan: A Synchronic and Diachronic Study. Unpublished Ph.D. dissertation, Department of Linguistics, University of New Mexico, Albuquerque.

Swadesh, Morris

1967 Linguistic Classification in the Southwest. In *Studies in Southwestern Ethnolinguistics*, edited by D. H. Hymes and W. Bittle, pp. 281–309. Mouton, the Hague.

Tainter, Joseph A.

1978 Mortuary Practices and the Study of Prehistoric Social Systems. In *Advances in Archaeological Method and Theory*, Vol. 1, edited by M. B. Schiffer, pp. 105–141. Academic Press, New York.

Taylor, Allan R.

1976 Words for Buffalo. *International Journal of American Linguistics* 42(2):165–166.

Teague, Lynn S.

1996   Textiles from the Upper Ruin. In *Archeological Investigations at the Upper Ruin, Tonto National Monument. Part 1: Salvage Excavations at the Upper Ruin, AZ U:8:48(ASM)—1995*, edited by G. L. Fox, pp. 157–176. Publications in Anthropology 70, Western Archeological and Conservation Center. U.S. Department of the Interior, National Park Service, Tucson, AZ.

1998   *Textiles in Southwestern Prehistory*. University of New Mexico Press, Albuquerque.

Tedlock, Dennis

1979   Zuni Religion and World View. In *Southwest*, edited by Alfonso Ortiz, pp. 499–508. Handbook of North American Indians, Vol. 9, William C. Sturtevant, general editor. Smithsonian Institution, Washington, D.C.

Tiller, Veronica E.

1983   Jicarilla Apache. In *Southwest*, edited by Alfonso Ortiz, pp. 440–461. Handbook of North American Indians, Vol. 10, William C. Sturtevant, general editor. Smithsonian Institution, Washington, D.C.

Titiev, Mischa

1937   A Hopi Salt Expedition. *American Anthropologist* 39(2):244–258.

Tower, Donald B.

1945   The Use of Marine Mollusca and Their Value in Reconstructing Prehistoric Trade Routes in the American Southwest. *American Anthropologist* 49(3):466–467.

Townsend, Richard F.

2005   (editor) *Casas Grandes and the Ceramic Art of the Ancient Southwest*. Yale University Press, New Haven, CT.

2009   *The Aztecs*. 3rd ed. Thames and Hudson, London.

Trager, George L.

1946   An Outline of Taos Grammar. In *Linguistic Structures of Native America*, edited by C. Osgood and H. Hoijer, pp. 184–221. Viking Fund Publications in Anthropology No. 6. New York.

Turner, Christy G., II

1999   The Dentition of Casas Grandes with Suggestions on Epigenetic Relationships among Mexican and Southwestern U.S. Populations. In *The Casas Grandes World*, edited by C. F. Schaafsma and C. L. Riley, pp. 229–236. University of Utah Press, Salt Lake City.

Turner, Christy G., II, and Steven A. LeBlanc

2010   The Pecos Dentition: Discrete Morphological Traits. In *Pecos Pueblo Revisited: The Biological and Social Context*, edited by M. Morgan, pp. 57–70. Papers of the Peabody Museum of Archaeology and Ethnology No. 85. Harvard University, Cambridge, MA.

Underhill, Ruth M.

1938   *Singing for Power*. University of California Press, Berkeley.

1946   *Papago Indian Religion*. Columbia University Press, New York.

Vajda, Edward

2010   A Siberian Link with Na-Dene languages. In *The Dene-Yeniseian Connection*, edited by J. Kari and B. Potter, pp. 33–99. Anthropological Papers of the University of

Alaska, New Series 5(1–2). Department of Anthropology and Alaska Native Language Center, Fairbanks.

VanPool, Christine S., and Todd L. VanPool

2006   Gender in Middle Range Societies: A Case Study in Casas Grandes Iconography. *American Antiquity* 71(1):53–75.

2007   *Signs of the Casas Grandes Shamans.* University of Utah Press, Salt Lake City.

Vargas, Victoria D.

1995   *Copper Bell Trade Patterns in the Prehispanic U.S. Southwest and Northwest Mexico.* Arizona State Museum Archaeological Series No. 187. University of Arizona, Tucson.

Vint, James M.

2000   Variation in Whole Vessel Attributes. In *Tonto Creek Archaeological Project Artifact and Environmental Analysis, Vol. 1: A Tonto Perspective on Ceramic Economy*, edited by J. M. Vint and J. M. Heidke, pp. 147–222. Anthropological Papers No. 23. Center for Desert Archaeology, Tucson, AZ.

Vivian, R. Gwinn, Dulce N. Dodgen, and Gayle H. Hartmann

1978   *Wooden Ritual Artifacts from Chaco Canyon, New Mexico: The Chetro Ketl Collection.* The Anthropological Papers of the University of Arizona 32. University of Arizona Press, Tucson.

Vokes, Arthur W.

1998   Shell Artifacts. In *Archaeological Investigations of Early Village Sites in the Middle Santa Cruz Valley: Analyses and Syntheses*, edited by J. B. Mabry, pp.437–470. Anthropological Papers No. 19, Part 1. Center for Desert Archaeology. Tucson, AZ.

Vokes, Arthur W., and David A. Gregory

2007   Exchange Networks for Exotic Goods in the Southwest and Zuni's Place in Them. In *Zuni Origins: Toward a New Synthesis of Southwestern Archaeology*, edited by D. A. Gregory and D. R. Wilcox, pp. 318–357. University of Arizona Press, Tucson.

Von Bonin, Gerhardt

1936   Skeletal Material from the Lowry Area. In *Lowry Ruin in Southwestern Colorado*, edited by P. S. Martin, pp. 143–193. Field Museum of Natural History Publication No. 356, Anthropological Series Vol. 23(1). Chicago.

Walt, Henry

1978   An Effigy Cache from the Cliff Valley, New Mexico. Unpublished M.A. thesis, Department of Art History, University of New Mexico, Albuquerque.

Washburn, Dorothy K. (editor)

1980   *Hopi Kachina: Spirit of Life.* California Academy of Sciences, San Francisco.

Wasley, William W.

1962   A Ceremonial Cave on Bonita Creek, Arizona. *American Antiquity* 27(3):380–394.

Wasley, William W., and Alfred E. Johnson

1965   *Salvage Archaeology in Painted Rocks Reservoir, Western Arizona.* The Anthropological Papers of the University of Arizona 9. University of Arizona Press, Tucson.

Waters, Frank

1963   *Book of the Hopi.* Viking Press, New York.

Webster, Laurie D.

1997   Effects of European Contact on Textile Production and Exchange in the North

American Southwest: A Pueblo Case Study. Unpublished Ph.D. dissertation, Department of Anthropology, University of Arizona, Tucson.

2000   Economics of Pueblo Textile Production and Exchange in Colonial New Mexico. In *Beyond Cloth and Cordage: Archaeological Textile Research in the Americas*, edited by P. B. Drooker and L. D. Webster, pp. 179–204. University of Utah Press, Salt Lake City.

2001   An Unbroken Thread: The Persistence of Pueblo Textile Traditions in the Postcolonial Era. In *The Road to Aztlan: Art from a Mythic Homeland*, edited by V. M. Fields and V. Azmudio-Taylor, pp. 274–289. Los Angeles County Museum of Art, Los Angeles.

2006   Worked Fiber Artifacts from Salmon Pueblo. In *Thirty-Five Years of Archaeological Research at Salmon Ruins*, Vol. 3: *Archaeobotanical and Other Analytical Studies*, edited by P. F. Reed, pp. 893–1012. Center for Desert Archaeology, Tucson, AZ, and Salmon Ruins Museum, Bloomfield, NM.

2007a   Ritual Costuming at Pottery Mound: The Pottery Mound Textiles in Regional Perspective. In *New Perspectives on Pottery Mound Pueblo*, edited by P. Schaafsma, pp. 167–206. University of New Mexico Press, Albuquerque.

2007b   Mogollon and Zuni Perishable Traditions and the Question of Zuni Origins. In *Zuni Origins: Toward a New Synthesis of Southwestern Archaeology*, edited by D. A. Gregory and D. R . Wilcox, pp. 270–317. University of Arizona Press, Tucson.

2008   An Initial Assessment of Perishable Relationships among Salmon, Aztec, and Chaco Canyon. In *Chaco's Northern Prodigies: Salmon, Aztec, and the Ascendancy of the Middle San Juan Region after AD 1100*, edited by P. F. Reed, pp. 167–189. University of Utah Press, Salt Lake City.

2011   Perishable Ritual Artifacts at the West Ruin of Aztec, New Mexico: Evidence for a Chacoan Migration. *Kiva* 77(2):139–171.

2012   The Perishable Side of Early Pueblo Style and Identity: Textiles, Sandals, and Baskets. In *Crucible of Pueblos: The Early Pueblo Period in the Northern Southwest*, edited by R. H. Wilshusen, G. Schachner, and J. R. Allison, pp. 159–184. Cotsen Institute of Archaeology Press, Los Angeles.

Webster, Laurie D., Kelley Hays-Gilpin, and Polly Schaafsma

2006   A New Look at Tie-dye and the Dot-in-a-Square Motif in the Prehispanic Southwest. *Kiva* 71(3):317–348.

Webster, Laurie D., and Micah Loma'omvaya

2004   Textiles, Baskets, and Hopi Cultural Identity. In *Identity, Feasting, and the Archaeology of the Greater Southwest*, edited by B. J. Mills, pp. 74-92. University Press of Colorado, Boulder.

Weigand, Phillip C., and Garman Harbottle

1993   The Role of Turquoise in the Ancient Mesoamerican Trade Structure. In *The American Southwest and Mesoamerica: Systems of Prehistoric Exchange*, edited by J. E. Ericson and T. G. Baugh, pp. 159–177. Plenum, New York.

Weigand, Phillip C., Garman Harbottle, and E. V. Sayre

1977   Turquoise Sources and Source Analysis: Mesoamerica and the Southwestern U.S.A.

In *Exchange Systems in Prehistory*, edited by T. K. Earle and J. E Ericson, pp. 15–34. Academic Press, New York.

Weiner, Annette B., and Jane Schneider (editors)

1989   *Cloth and Human Experience*. Smithsonian Institution Press, Washington, D.C.

Weinreich, Peter, and Wendy Saunderson (editors)

2013   *Analysing Identity: Cross-Cultural, Societal and Clinical Contexts*. Routledge, Cambridge, UK.

Weisensee, Katherine E.

2008   Reassessing Sex in the Pecos Pueblo Population: New Analyses of Hooton's Data. In *Reanalysis and Reinterpretation in Southwestern Bioarchaeology*, edited by A. L. W. Stodder. Arizona State University Anthropological Research Papers No. 59, pp. 185–196. Tempe.

Weisensee, Katherine E., and Richard L. Jantz

2010   Rethinking Hooton: A Reexamination of the Pecos Cranial and Postcranial Data Using Recent Methods. In *Pecos Pueblo Revisited: The Biological and Social Context*, edited by M. Morgan, pp. 43–55. Papers of the Peabody Museum of Archaeology and Ethnology Vol. 85. Harvard University, Cambridge, MA.

Weitz, Rose

2001   Women and Their Hair: Seeking Power through Resistance and Accommodation. *Gender and Society* 15(5):667–686.

Whalen, Michael E.

2013   Wealth, Status, and Marine Shell at Casas Grandes, Chihuahua, Mexico. *American Antiquity* 78(4):624–639.

White, Leslie A.

1942   *The Pueblo of Santa Ana, New Mexico*. Memoirs of the American Anthropological Association No. 60. Menasha, WI.

1944   A Ceremonial Vocabulary among the Pueblos. *International Journal of American Linguistics* 10(4):161–167.

Whittaker, John C., and Kathryn A. Kamp

1992   Sinagua Painted Armbands. *Kiva* 58(2):177–182.

Whittlesey, Stephanie M.

1978   Status and Death at Grasshopper Pueblo: Experiments Toward an Archaeological Theory of Social Correlates. Unpublished Ph.D. dissertation, Department of Anthropology, University of Arizona, Tucson.

1984   Uses and Abuses of Mogollon Mortuary Data. In *Recent Research in Mogollon Archaeology*, edited by S. Upham, F. Plog, D. Batcho, and B. Kaufmann, pp. 276–284. University Museum Occasional Paper No. 10. New Mexico State University, Las Cruces.

Whittlesey, Stephanie M., and J. Jefferson Reid

2004   Mortuary Ritual and Organizational Inferences at Grasshopper Pueblo, Arizona. In *Ancient Burial Practices in the American Southwest: Archaeology, Physical Anthropology, and Native American Perspectives*, edited by D. R. Mitchell and J. L. Brunson-Hadley, pp. 68–96. University of New Mexico Press, Albuquerque.

Whorf, Benjamin Lee, and George L. Trager

1937   The Relationship of Uto-Aztecan and Tanoan. *American Anthropologist* 39(4): 609–624.

Wilcox, David R.

1979   The Hohokam Regional System. In *An Archaeological Test of Sites in the Gila Butte-Santan Region, South-Central Arizona*, by G. Rice, D. Wilcox, K. Rafferty, and J. Schoenwetter, pp. 77–116. Arizona State University Archaeological Research Papers No. 18. Tempe.

1987   *Frank Midvale's Investigation of the Site of La Ciudad.* Arizona State University Anthropological Field Studies No. 19. Tempe.

Williamson, Margaret Holmes

1979   Powhatan Hair. *Man,* New Series 14(3):392–423.

Witherspoon, Gary

1983   Navajo Social Organization. In *Southwest*, edited by Alfonso Ortiz, pp. 524–535. Handbook of North American Indians, Vol. 10, William C. Sturtevant, general editor. Smithsonian Institution, Washington, D.C.

Wobst, H. Martin

1977   Stylistic Behavior and Information Exchange. In *For the Director: Research Essays in Honor of James B. Griffin*, edited by C. Cleland, pp. 317–342. University of Michigan, Museum of Anthropology Anthropological Papers No. 61. Ann Arbor.

Woodward, Arthur

1931   *The Grewe Site, Gila Valley, Arizona.* Occasional Papers of the Los Angeles Museum of History, Science and Art 1. Los Angeles.

Woolf, Charles M.

2005   Albinism (OCA2) in Amerindians. *Yearbook of Physical Anthropology* 48:118–140.

Wyman, Leland C.

1983   Navajo Ceremonial System. In *Southwest*, edited by Alfonso Ortiz, pp. 536–557. Handbook of North American Indians, Vol. 10, William C. Sturtevant, general editor. Smithsonian Institution, Washington, D.C.

Yoder, David T.

2010   Plain-Weave Sandals from Antelope Cave, Arizona. *Kiva* 75(3):327–350.

Yumitani, Yukihiro

1998   *A Phonology and Morphology of Jemez Towa.* Ph.D. dissertation, Department of Linguistics, University of Kansas. University Microfilms, Ann Arbor, MI.

Figure Sources and Permissions

I.3.   Haury 1950: Plate 59c, Arizona State Museum, University of Arizona, ASM photo #352, Oscar F. Davisson, sculptor, Emil W. Haury, photographer.

I.4.   Jernigan 1978: Fig. 27, courtesy of the artist, E. Wesley Jernigan.

2.1.   Adapted from Kent 1983a: Fig. 24f.

2.2.   (*a*) Adapted from Kent 1983b: Fig. 20a. (*b*) Drawn by Robert Schultz. (*c*) Adapted from Kent 1983a: Fig. 105a. (*d*) Kent 1983a: Fig. 108b, drawing of cat. #29.1/5508, courtesy of the Division of Anthropology, American Museum of Natural History. (*e*) Kent 1983a: Fig. 86a, drawing of cat. #MOCA3259, courtesy of the National Park Service. (*f*) Kent 1983a: Fig. 77c, drawing of cat. #MOCA 3259, courtesy of the National Park Service.

2.3.   Kent 1983a: Pl. 14, courtesy of Telluride Historical Society.

2.4.   Courtesy of Penn Museum, cat. #29-43-183, image #151952.

2.5.   Haury 1945b: Pl. 11, reconstruction of Amerind cat. #PC39/36, courtesy of the Amerind Foundation, Inc., Dragoon, Arizona, Florence Shipek, illustrator.

2.6.   Arizona State Museum, University of Arizona, ASM cat. #20511, photo #C-3919, Helga Teiwes, photographer.

2.7.   Drawn by Harriet ("Hattie") Cosgrove, courtesy of the Cosgrove Collection and Carolyn O'Bagy Davis.

2.8.   (*a*) Arizona State Museum, University of Arizona, ASM cat. #25982, E. B. Sayles, photographer. (*b*) Haury 1934: Pl. XLa, courtesy of the Arizona State Museum, University of Arizona.

2.9.   (*a*) Arizona State Museum, University of Arizona, ASM cat. #2983, Helga Teiwes, photographer. (*b*) Adapted from Kent 1983a: Fig. 102a4.

2.10. From Watson Smith 1952, *Kiva Mural Decorations at Awatovi and Kawaika-a with a Survey of Other Wall Paintings in the Pueblo Southwest*, Fig. 52a, left, Papers of the Peabody Museum of Archaeology and Ethnology 37. Reproduced courtesy of the Peabody Museum of Archaeology and Ethnology, Harvard University.

2.11. Hibben 1975: Fig. 72, courtesy KC Publications, *Kiva Art of the Anasazi* ©1975 by Frank C. Hibben.

2.12. Detail from Plate I, Watson Smith, *Kiva Mural Decorations at Awatovi and Kawaika-a with a Survey of Other Wall Paintings in the Pueblo Southwest*, Papers of the Peabody Museum of Archaeology and Ethnology 37. Reproduced courtesy of the Peabody Museum of Archaeology and Ethnology, Harvard University.

2.13. Hibben 1975: Fig. 75, courtesy KC Publications, *Kiva Art of the Anasazi* ©1975 by Frank C. Hibben.

2.14. (*a*) Adapted from Kent 1983a: Fig. 137g. (*b*) Arizona State Museum, University of Arizona, ASM cat. #13400.

2.15. © President and Fellows of Harvard College, Peabody Museum of Archaeology and Ethnology, PM #24-15-10/94584, digital file #60740393.

2.16. (*a*) Haury 1934: Pl. XLIa, Arizona State Museum, University of Arizona, ASM cat. and photo #GP17150, Janelle Weakly, photographer. (*b*) Courtesy of the Division of Anthropology, American Museum of Natural History, cat. #29.0/7654. (*c*) Courtesy of the Division of Anthropology, American Museum of Natural History, cat. #29.0/5289. (*d*) Fulton 1941: Fig. 4, cat. #WIN/101a, courtesy of the Amerind Foundation, Inc., Dragoon, Arizona, Laurie Webster, photographer. (*e*) Arizona State Museum, University of Arizona, ASM cat. #ASM GP-6439, photo #77504.

2.17. Jernigan 1978: Fig. 59, courtesy of the artist, E. Wesley Jernigan.

2.18. Detail from Plate I, Watson Smith, *Kiva Mural Decorations at Awatovi and Kawaika-a with a Survey of Other Wall Paintings in the Pueblo Southwest*, Papers of the Peabody Museum of Archaeology and Ethnology 37. Reproduced courtesy of the Peabody Museum of Archaeology and Ethnology, Harvard University.

2.19. Hibben 1975: Fig. 74, courtesy KC Publications, *Kiva Art of the Anasazi at Pottery Mound* ©1975 by Frank C. Hibben.

3.1. Courtesy National Geographic Society, NGS image #606419, Charles Martin/ National Geographic Creative, photographer.

3.2. Courtesy the American Southwest Virtual Museum, http://swvirtualmuseum.nau .edu, Dan Boone/Ryan Belnap, photographers.

3.3. Private collection, drawn by Robert Schultz, Mimbres Pottery Images Digital Data Base #10281.

3.4. Arizona State Museum, University of Arizona, ASM photo #C-1443, Helga Teiwes, photographer.

3.5. Arizona State Museum, University of Arizona, ASM photo #C-1452, Helga Teiwes, photographer.

3.6. (*a*) Haury 1976: Fig. 11.10b, left, Arizona State Museum, University of Arizona, ASM photo #41461, Helga Teiwes, photographer. (*b*) Haury 1976: Fig. 13.18, left, Arizona State Museum, University of Arizona, ASM photo #2942e, E. B. Sayles, photographer.

3.7. (*a*) and (*b*) Morris 1919: Fig. 73. Both images courtesy of the Division of Anthropology, American Museum of Natural History.

3.8. Courtesy of Museum of Northern Arizona ©2015, NA1785.9, Eleanor Bareiss, illustrator.

3.9. Courtesy of Museum of Northern Arizona ©2015, NA1785.10, Eleanor Bareiss, illustrator.

3.10. Courtesy of Museum of Northern Arizona ©2015, NA1785.10, Eleanor Bareiss, illustrator.

3.11. Jernigan 1978: Fig. 30, courtesy of the artist, E. Wesley Jernigan.

3.12. Arizona State Museum, University of Arizona, ASM photo #C-1456.

3.13. Di Peso 1974: Fig. 240-2, courtesy of the Amerind Foundation, Inc., Dragoon, Arizona, Nita Rosene, photographer.

3.14. Private Collection, the Art Institute of Chicago, Photography © The Art Institute of Chicago.

3.15. Di Peso 1974: Fig. 236-2, top, courtesy of the Amerind Foundation, Inc., Dragoon, Arizona, Nita Rosene, photographer.

3.16. Di Peso 1974: Fig. 242-2, top right, Amerind cat. #3415, courtesy of the Amerind Foundation, Inc., Dragoon, Arizona, Eric Kaldahl, photographer.

3.17. Hibben 1975: Fig. 38, courtesy KC Publications, *Kiva Art of the Anasazi at Pottery Mound* ©1975 by Frank C. Hibben.

3.18. Hibben 1975: Fig. 14, courtesy KC Publications, *Kiva Art of the Anasazi at Pottery Mound* ©1975 by Frank C. Hibben.

4.1. Pl. 19, Samuel James Guernsey and Alfred Vincent Kidder, *Basket-Maker Caves of Northeastern Arizona*, Papers of the Peabody Museum of American Archaeology and Ethnology 8:2, 1921. Reproduced courtesy of the Peabody Museum of Archaeology and Ethnology, Harvard University.

4.2. (*a*) Private collection, drawn by Robert Schultz, Mimbres Pottery Images Digital Data Base #780. (*b*) ©President and Fellows of Harvard College, Peabody Museum of Archaeology and Ethnology, PM# 26-7-10/95879, digital file #60740373.

4.3. Courtesy Anthropology Department, Natural History Museum of Los Angeles County.

4.4. Private Collection, Art Institute of Chicago, Photography ©The Art Institute of Chicago.

4.5. Hibben 1975: Fig. 99, courtesy KC Publications, *Kiva Art of the Anasazi at Pottery Mound* ©1975 by Frank C. Hibben.

4.6. Hibben 1975: Fig. 17, courtesy KC Publications, *Kiva Art of the Anasazi at Pottery Mound* ©1975 by Frank C. Hibben.

4.7. Smith 1952: detail from Pl. F, Watson Smith, *Kiva Mural Decorations at Awatovi and Kawaika-a with a Survey of Other Wall Paintings in the Pueblo Southwest*, Papers of the Peabody Museum of Archaeology and Ethnology 37. Reproduced courtesy of the Peabody Museum of Archaeology and Ethnology, Harvard University, Louie Ewing, illustrator.

4.8. (*a*) Private collection, drawn by Robert Schultz, Mimbres Pottery Images Digital Data Base #10702. (*b*) Courtesy of the Division of Anthropology, Peabody Museum of Natural History, Yale University, YPM ANT.24914, peabody.yale.edu. (*c*) Drawn by Harriet ("Hattie") Cosgrove, courtesy of the Cosgrove Collection and Carolyn O'Bagy Davis. (*d*) The Collection of the Frederick R. Weisman Art Museum, transfer from Department of Anthropology, University of Minnesota, 1992.22.757.

4.9. Museum of Indian Arts and Culture, Laboratory of Anthropology, Santa Fe, NM, cat. #8315/11, Christine VanPool, photographer.

4.10. Museum of Indian Arts and Culture, Laboratory of Anthropology, Santa Fe, NM, cat. #8321/11, Blair Clark, photographer.

4.11. Hibben 1975: Fig. 64, courtesy KC Publications, *Kiva Art of the Anasazi at Pottery Mound* ©1975 by Frank C. Hibben.

4.12. Hibben 1975: Fig. 39, courtesy KC Publications, *Kiva Art of the Anasazi at Pottery Mound* ©1975 by Frank C. Hibben.

4.13. All figures redrawn by Robert Schultz from Jernigan 1978: Figs. 29, 62–64, 67, 87, 91.

4.14. Courtesy of Museum of Northern Arizona ©2015, NA1785.8, Eleanor Bareiss, illustrator.

4.15. Courtesy of Museum of Northern Arizona ©2015, C1333, Virgil Hubert, sculptor.

4.16. Arizona State Museum, University of Arizona, ASM photo #9554, Douglas Lindsay, photographer.

4.17. Francois Gohier and University of Colorado Museum of Natural History, ©2005.

5.1. (*a*) Private collection, Mimbres Pottery Images Digital Data Base #9339. (*b*) The Collection of the Frederick R. Weisman Art Museum, transfer from Department of Anthropology, University of Minnesota. 1992.22.349. (*c*) Private collection (Moulard 1984: Pl. 93), courtesy of the photographer, John Bigelow Taylor. (*d*) Image courtesy Saint Louis Art Museum, Museum Purchase 118:1944.

5.2. Pepper 1909: Plate XXIX, Fig. 2.

5.3. *Left two*, Pepper 1909: Figs. 13b–c; *right four*, Judd 1954: Figs. 62a, c–e. Courtesy of the Division of Anthropology, American Museum of Natural History (Pepper) and Smithsonian Institution Scholarly Press (Judd).

5.4. (*a*) Pepper 1909: Plate XXVIII, Fig. 2; courtesy of the Division of Anthropology, American Museum of Natural History, cat. # H/5243. (*b*) Arizona State Museum, University of Arizona, ASM photo #112689, Helga Teiwes, photographer.

5.5. Redrawn by Robert Schultz from Fig. 29a, Emil W. Haury, *The Excavation of Los Muertos and Neighboring Ruins in the Salt River Valley, Southern Arizona*, Papers of the Peabody Museum of American Archaeology and Ethnology 24:1, 1945. Reproduced courtesy of the Peabody Museum of Archaeology and Ethnology, Harvard University.

5.6. Gift of Mary T. Hemenway. ©President and Fellows of Harvard College, Peabody Museum of Archaeology and Ethnology, PM#46-73-10/52018 (digital file# 99260011).

5.7. Gift of Mary T. Hemenway. ©President and Fellows of Harvard College, Peabody Museum of Archaeology and Ethnology, PM#46-73-10/44320 (digital file# 99260013).

5.8. (*a*) Private collection (Moulard 1984: Pl. 93). (*b*) Private collection (Moulard 1984: Pl. 97). Both images courtesy of the photographer, John Bigelow Taylor.

5.9. Courtesy Logan Museum of Anthropology, Beloit College.

5.10. Private collection, the Art Institute of Chicago. Photography © The Art Institute of Chicago.

5.11. Courtesy Centennial Museum at the University of Texas at El Paso. Cat. #A36.2.22. Scott Cutler, photographer.

5.12. Courtesy of the Museum of Peoples and Cultures, Brigham Young University. Cat. #1986.18.57.1.

6.2. Fred Kabotie, *Hopi Tashaf Kachina Dance,* Museum purchase, 1946.15, ©2014 Philbrook Museum of Art, Inc., Tulsa, Oklahoma.

6.3. Edward S. Curtis Collection, Library of Congress.

6.4. Edward S. Curtis Collection, Library of Congress.

Contributors

Jane Hill
Departments of Anthropology
and Linguistics
University of Arizona
Tucson, AZ

Jill E. Neitzel
Department of Anthropology
University of Delaware
Newark, DE

Ann L. W. Stodder
Office of Archaeological Studies
Museum of New Mexico
Santa Fe, NM
and
Department of Anthropology
University of New Mexico
Albuquerque, NM

Laurie Webster
Department of Anthropology
University of Arizona
Tucson, AZ

Index

Numbers in *italics* indicate material contained in figures, tables, and illustrations.

Adair, John, 210n57
Adams, F. Charles, 219n38
agriculture, and impact of labor
  on femur robusticity, 25;
  See also beans; corn; feasts;
  pumpkin; squash
Akins, Nancy J., 200n8, 200n11,
  202n21, 207n3, 207n5
albinism, frequency of in
  historic-period pueblos, 31;
  See also skin color
Alfred Herrera site (New
  Mexico), 27, *181*, *182*
Alkalai Ridge (Utah), *181*, *182*,
  183
Anawalt, Patricia R., 206n59
Ancestral Puebloans (Arizona,
  New Mexico, Utah, Colo-
  rado): and clothing, 37, 38, 39,
  40, 41, 44, 45, *46*, 48–51, *52*–
  54, 55–57, 59–60, 62–66, 68;
  and dual-gender identity, 174;
  and facial features, 21, *22*, 23,
  180, *181*; and femur robusticity, 25, *26*; hairstyles and hair
  decorations of, *54*, *64*, *96–97*,
  109, *111–13*, 114, *118–19*, *120*,
  122, *192–93*; and head shape,
  28, 29, *183–84*; and indicators of identity to outside
  observers, 176; and jewelry,
  52, *64–65*, 89–100, *112*; and
  nonresidential architecture,

210n55; skeletal assemblages
  and mortuary practices of,
  199n6; and skin color, 31;
  and stature, *16*, 17, *18*, *20*, *179*,
  180; and textiles, *184*, *185*; and
  time periods, *8*, 198n10. *See
  also* Chaco Canyon; Kayenta;
  Mesa Verde; Pueblo I; Pueblo
  II; Pueblo III; Pueblo IV
Anderson, Keith M., 204n22
animals: depictions of birds, in
  murals, *52*, *97*, *112*, *120*; depictions of, on jewelry, *77*, *85*, *90*,
  98–99; and head adornments,
  116; as sources of weaving
  materials, 38. *See also* bighorn
  sheep; bison; deer; elk; feasts;
  feathers; meat; pronghorn
  antelope; rabbits; turkeys
anthropology. *See* archaeology,
  cultural anthropology; forensic anthropology; physical
  anthropology
Antieau, John M., 208n12
Anyon, Roger, 208n17
Apachean language family, 154,
  159, *196*, 217n4, 219n25
aprons, and women's garments,
  48–50, *108*
archaeology: historic-period
  Native groups and interpretation of remains in Southwest,
  215–16n24; and identity

studies of prehistoric Southwest, 3–5, 178. *See also* burials;
  ceramics; textiles; jewelry
areal linguistics, 155–59
Arroyo Hondo (New Mexico),
  91, 93, 95, 98, 99–100, *191*,
  210n53, 210n55
asbestos, in woven fabrics, 38
Atakapa, 168
Athapaskan language family, 154
Auerbach, Benjamin M., 201n15
Awat'ovi (Arizona), *53*, *57*, *63*,
  64, 66, 109, *113*, *115*, *192*, *193*,
  211n11, 212n19
Aztec Ruins (New Mexico), 57,
  58, 82, *83*, 87, 88, 187, 199n3,
  209n26, 209n34, 210n42
Aztecs (State of Mexico): and
  historic-period Pueblo religions, 146–47; and symbolism of facial designs, *195*

Baca site (New Mexico), *108*
backstrap loom, 40
Barnes, Ethne, 200n11, 202n21
Barth, Fredrik, 197n1
Bassman, Theda & Michael,
  210n57
Basketmakers: and clothing, 50,
  57, 59, 60, 68, 69; and fabric
  decoration, 44; and facial features, 21, *180*, *181*; and femur
  robusticity, 27; and hairstyles,

261

107, 121; and head shape, 28, *183*; and jewelry, 81

batik, and decoration of fabrics, 41, 204n20

Bayman, James M., 86, 91, 208n14, 208n16, 209n35, 209n37, 209n39

beans, words for in Southwest languages, 166

Bear Village site (Arizona), 29, *184*

Bedinger, Margery, 210n57

Bell, Willis H., 203n8

belts, and clothing, 57. *See also* sashes

Bennett, Kenneth A., 29, 202n21, 202n23

Benson, S. L., 197n4

Berrin, Kathleen, 216n34

Bessels, Emil, 201n16–17

bighorn sheep, 38

"Big View of Identity and Interaction: Macro-Regional Cultural Variation in the U.S. Southwest" (Society for American Archaeology 2009), xv–xiv

bison, 167, 168

bizygomatic breadth, and facial features, 21

Black Mesa (Arizona), *181, 182*

blankets, and clothing, 45–48, 60–61, 62, *65*, 66, 67, *113*, *163–64*, 205n36, 206n53

Blanton, Richard E., 81, 208n20

Blum-Martinez, Rebecca, 221n64

boarding schools, and hairstyles, 128, 213n32

Bohrer, Vorsila L., 203n7

boiling, as cooking method, 165

Bowen, Thomas, 211n4, 214n4

Bowern, Claire, 219n22

Bradley, Rona J., 208n14, 210n50

braiding, and weaving techniques, 39–40, 57, 59

Brand, Donald D., 208n14

breechcloths, and men's garments, 50–51, 60, 62, *136*, 205n37 Bright, William, 218n17

Brody, J. J., 202n4

Brunson-Hadley, Judy I., 197n4, 207n3

Bunzel, Ruth L., 216n26

Burgh, Robert F., 203n9, 205n46

burials: and jewelry of Chacoans, Mimbres, and Hohokam in AD 900–1150 time period, 73–82, *185–86*, *189*; and jewelry of Chacoans, Hohokam, and Sinagua in AD 1150–1300 time period, 82–89, *187–88*; and jewelry of Hohokam, Casas Grandians, Mountain Mogollon, and Ancestral Puebloans in AD 1300–1450 time period, 89–100, *187*, *189–91*; mortuary practices of Ancestral Pueblo and Hohokam and skeletal assemblages from, 199n6; and role of social status in mortuary practices, 207n3; of multiple individuals, 207n4, 209n26

Cahlon, Baruch, 202n27

Campbell, Lyle, 216n1, 217n5, 217n12

Canyon de Chelly (Arizona), 21, 32, 56, 114, *180, 181, 183*

Canyon Creek Pueblo (Arizona), *49, 58*

caps. *See* hats

Casa Buena site (Arizona), *180*

Casas Grandes (Chihuahua): and clothing, 66; and facial

decorations, *94*, *109–10*, *117–18*, 135, 140, *141*, 142, *143–44*, 145, *194*, 214n14, 215n19–20; hairstyles and hair decorations of, 107, *109*, *110*, 114, 115, 117, *118*, 121, *191*, *193*, 211n9, 212n17, 215n18; and indicators of identity to outside observers, 176; and jewelry, 89–100, 210n45; and time periods, *8*, *9*. *See also* Paquime

Castetter, Edward F., 203n8

ceramics, and artistic representations: of facial decorations, 133, *136–40*, 214n6, 214n11; of hairstyles and hair decorations, 107, *108*, 109, *110–13*, 114–15, *116–17*, 117, *118–20*, 121

Chaco Canyon (Chacoans) (New Mexico): cultural characteristics of, 5, 8; and facial decorations, 135, *137–38*, 140, 142, 144, 214n8, 214–15n15, 215n19; and facial features, *181*; hairstyles and hair decorations of, 121, *122*, 123, *138*; and head shape, 29, *183*; and indicators of identity to outside observers, 176; and jewelry, 73–89, *185*; morphology and physical appearance of, 32, 33; and stature, 19, *179*, *180*. *See also* Pueblo Bonito

Chaves Pass (Arizona), *180, 181*

Christman, Ernest H., 146, 212n17, 216n33

Clark, Geoffrey A., 198n6, 207n3

climate. *See* environment

clothing: and complete outfits, 60–67; and garment types, 45, 47–60; and identity, 10, 37, 41, 68–69; raw materials and weaving techniques for, 37–45 coccidioidomycosis (valley fever), 33

Cochiti site (New Mexico), *181, 182*

Cocopa (Arizona, California), 106

color: ancestral connections and symbolism of in Southwest and Mesoamerica, 175; and decoration of fabrics, 41, 44–45, *185*, 204n19; and religious symbolism of jewelry, 80, 88, 98. *See also* dyes; skin color

Colorado River Quechan (Arizona, California), 106

Colton, Harold S., 208n14, 216n25

communities: identities within, 173–74; variation of personal characteristics within and between, 1

copper bells, *74*, 78, 80, 81, 87

Cordell, Linda S., 198n10

corn, words for in Southwest languages, 166.

Coronado, Francisco Vásquez de, 9

Cosgrove, C. Burton, 205n46

cotton, and fabrics, 38, 57, 69. *See also* raw materials

Cowgill, George L., 216n34

cradleboards, and head shape, 27–28, 29, 201n16–18

cranial modification. *See* head shape

Crotty, Helen K., 86, 209n33–34, 209n36, 210n49

Crown, Patricia L., 197n4, 207n2–3, 216n28

cultural anthropology, and theoretical perspectives on identity, 3

culture: and association of distinctive physical appearance with particular groups, 33; and clothing, 61–62, 68; and concept of culture areas in history of Southwest archaeology, 3; and hairstyles, 114, 121; and identities in relation to outsiders, 174–75; jewelry and contemporary tribal affiliations, 100; list of attributes included in analysis, 1; maps of culture areas, *6–7*; and regional chronologies for Southwest, 5–9; and weave structures, 40–41

Curtis, Edward S., *164*

Cushing, Frank H., 209n29, 219n39, 220n40

Darkmold site (Colorado), *183*

Davies, Nigel, 216n30

Davis, Irvine, 220n47–49, 221n56

Dayley, Jon, 220n42

Dean, Jeffrey S., 210n43

Debenport, Erin, 221n64

decoration: of fabrics, 41, 44–45, *46*, 63, 66, 67, *185*, 204n20; of hair, 114–15, *116–17*, 117, *118–120*, 121–28, *192–93*. *See also* facial decorations

deer, 168

Dennis, Arthur E., 203n7

Dennis, Wayne & Marsena G., 201n17

designs. *See* color; decorations; motifs

dialects, and language families, 153, 216n2

Di Peso, Charles C., 208n8, 211n10, 213n28

DNA analysis, 15, 198n1. *See also* genetics

Dolores sites (Colorado), *181, 182, 183*

Douglas, Michele T., 200n11, 202n21

Downum, Christopher F., 208n14

Dozier, Edward P., 220n46

Drennan, Robert D., 208n20

dresses, blankets worn as, 50, *65, 66, 164*, 205n36. *See also* garment types

Duckfoot site (Colorado), 21, *180*

Dutch Ruin site (New Mexico), 215n18

Dutton, Bertha P., 202n4, 205n39, 206n55, 206n58

dyes, and fabric decoration, 44, 204n19. *See also* tie-dyeing

Earle, Edwin, 216n25

elk, 167, 168

El-Najjar, Mahmoud Y., 200n11, 202n21

Emery, Irene, 203n12, 203n17

environment: droughts and social upheaval in AD 1300–1450 time period, 9; and femur robusticity, 24, 27; influence of on stature, 17

Eriacho, Wilfred, Sr., 220n40, 220n51

ethnography, and studies on travel in prehistoric Southwest, 197n1

eye orbit and width, and facial features, 21, *22*

Ezell, Paul H., 204n35

Ezzo, Joseph A., 29–30, 202n23

fabrics. *See* textiles

facial decorations: artistic representations of as evidence of prehistoric, *48, 54, 76, 79,*

90, 94, 109–10, 117–18, 133,
134–45, 213n2, 214–15n6–15,
215n17–23; and contem-
porary artist's depiction of
Sedentary-period Hohokam,
4; design and frequency of by
cultural group, 193–94; and
historic period, 133–34; and
identity, 10, 133, 140, 142–45,
147; and religious symbolism,
145–47, 195
facial features: average metrics
by cultural group and time
period, 180–81; morphology
and physical variation in,
21–24; multivariate studies of,
200n10; sources of information on, 15, 17
feasts, and words for foods,
161–70
feathers: and blankets, 206n53;
and clothing, 38, 39, 48; and
hair decorations, 115, 192, 193;
as ornaments, 92, 120, 206n52
Feinman, Gary M., 208n22
femur robusticity: averages by
cultural group, gender, and
time period, 181–82; formula
for measurement of, 201n14;
and physical variation in
morphology, 24–27; sources
of information on, 15, 17
Ferguson, T. J., 209n30
Fewkes, Jesse W., 209n29, 212n15,
216n25
finger weaving techniques, 39
Fish, Suzanne K., 197n4,
207n2–3
footgear, and leg coverings,
57–59, 158. See also leggings;
sandals
Ford, Richard I., 216n29
forensic anthropology, 200–
201n13

Fowler, Catherine S., 167, 217n9,
221n55
Frank, Larry, 210n57
Frantz, Donald G., 220n43
Fremont (Utah), 126
Fulton, William S., 205n49

Gal, Susan, 219n34
Galaz Ruin (New Mexico),
75–77, 80, 81, 116, 136, 186,
208n9
galena crystals, 87
Gallina (New Mexico), 29, 30,
32, 184
garment types, and clothing,
45, 47–60. See also aprons;
blankets; breechcloths;
dresses; footgear; kilts;
leggings; sandals; sashes;
shirts; special-occasion outfits
gauze weaves, 40, 41, 43, 184
gender: and clothing, 37, 48–56,
59–62, 66, 68; and facial decorations, 144–45; and facial
features, 180–81; and femur
robusticity, 25, 26, 27, 181–82;
festive cuisine and travel by
women, 170; and hair decorations, 115; and hairstyles, 106;
and identities within communities, 173–74; and indicators
of identity to outside observers, 176; and language, 218n19;
and preparation of stews, 168;
and rapid spread of paper
bread among Pueblos, 164–65,
170; and sandals, 205n46; and
stature, 16, 17, 20, 179–80
genetics: and femur robusticity,
24; and head shape, 27; and
height of Chaco elite, 19; and
nonmetric trait data, 198n2;
and skin color, 31. See also
DNA analysis

Genovés, Santiago, 17, 199n6
Gila River Pima (Arizona), 106
Gilman, Patricia, 208n11
Gladwin, Winifred & Harold S.,
197n2
glide hardening, and language
areas, 156, 218n16
Glycymeris bracelets, 77, 79–80,
81, 85, 86, 95, 208n15, 210n47
Gohier, Francois, 213n26
Gonzales, Rena, 220n40,
220n51
Gourd Cave (Arizona), 50
Grand Canal Ruin (Arizona),
181, 182, 184
Grand Gulch (Utah), 21, 180, 181
Grasshopper Pueblo (Arizona),
29, 30, 91, 95, 98, 184, 190,
202n23, 210n52
Gray, Russell, 217n9
great houses, and relationship
between stature and social
status, 19. See also Pueblo
Bonito; Chaco Canyon
Gregory, David A., 208n13–14,
208n19
Guernsey, Samuel J., 203n5,
205n46, 213n29

hairpins, 90, 121, 122, 126, 127–28,
213n31
hairstyles: artistic depictions
of styles and decorations on
ceramics, 53–54, 64–65, 79,
96–97, 107, 108, 109, 110–13,
114–15, 116–17, 117, 118–20,
121, 136, 138; and cranial
modification, 30; data on by
cultural group, 191–93; in
historic period, 105–6, 163,
211n2–3; and identity, 10,
105, 114, 117, 121, 127–29; and
preserved prehistoric hair
decorations, 121–28. See also

decoration; hats; headbands; headdresses; human hair; kiva murals

Hale, Kenneth L., 220n43, 220n50

Hall, Robert L., 203n7

Hammond, George P., 202n26

Handbook of North American Indians (Ortiz 1979a, 1983), 211n2, 213n3, 213n32

Harbottle, Garman, 208n13

Harrington, John P., 163, 221n53

Haspelmath, Martin, 219n22

hats, and hair decorations, *62*, *76*, *108*, 115, 123, *124*, *125*, 127, 128. *See also* headbands; headdresses

Haury, Emil W., 197n2, 198n8, 202n22–23, 203n5–6, 203n9–10, 205n46, 205n49–50, 206n59, 208n12–13, 211n7

Hawikku site (New Mexico), 33, 126, *183*

Hawkey, Diane E., 197n4

Hawley, Florence, 212n15

Hawley, Fred G., 208n8

Hays-Gilpin, Kelley, 127, 202n24, 203n5, 205n48, 212n14, 212n23

headbands, *48*, *108–9*, *142*, *144*, *192*, *193*

headdresses, *54*, *65*, *96–97*, 115, *116*, 117, *118–19*, 121, 126, *192*, *193*, 212n18

Headrick, Annabeth, 216n34

head shape: and ambiguity in definitions of cranial modification, 201–2n20; and cranial modification by cultural group and time period, *183–84*; and physical variation in morphology, 27–31; sources of information on, 15, 17. *See also* cradleboards

Hefner, Joseph T., 24, 200n13

Hegmon, Michelle, 209n24, 215n16

Henderson, Junius, 221n53

Hendrickson, Carol, 202n1

Hero Twins, clothing in depiction of, *48*

Hibben, Frank C., 202n4, 205n39, 205n42, 206n55, 206n58

Hidden House (Arizona), *47*

Hill, Jane H., 11, 217n4, 217n6, 217n8–10, 218n13, 218n15, 219n23–24, 219n32, 219n35, 220n49, 221n57

Hinton, Leanne, 221n63

historical linguistics, 151, 170, 171, 216–17n4

historic period: and analysis of language, 1; and cranial modification, *183–84*; and cultural upheaval, 9; and facial decorations, 133–34; and hairstyles, 105–6, *163*, 211n2–3; and jewelry, 100–101; Native groups of Southwest and interpretation of archaeological remains, 215–16n24; and skin color, 31. *See also* Hopi; Pueblo (contemporary); Zuni

Hoffman, J. Michael, 200n11, 202n21

Hohokam (Arizona): artist's depictions of, *4*, *90*; and jewelry, *4*, 73–100, *125*; and clothing, 37, 38, 40, 41, 44, 47, 48, 50, *58*, 59, 61, 66–67, *90*; cultural characteristics of, 8, 9; and facial decorations, *4*, *79*, *90*, 135, *138–39*, 140, 142, 143, 144, 214n10, 215n19; and facial features, *22*, 23, *180–81*; and femur robusticity, 25, *26*;

hair decorations and hairstyles of, *79*, 121, *122*, 123, *125*, 126–27; and head shape, 29, *184*; and indicators of identity to outside observers, 176, 177; morphology and physical appearance of, 32; mortuary practices of and preservation of skeletal assemblages, 199n6, 201n15; and stature, *16*, *17*, *18*, *19*, *20*, *179*, *180*; and textiles, *184*, *185*; and time periods, 8. *See also* Los Muertos; Snaketown

Hoijer, Harry, 220n46

Holland, Dorothy, 197n1

Hooton, Ernest A., 23, 198–99n3, 200n12

Hopi (Arizona): and albinism, 31; and blankets, 47, *163–64*; and braiding, 40, 57; and clothing, 63, 66, 67, *163–64*; and cranial modification, 29, 30, *183*; and hairstyles, 105–6, 114, *164*; and dialects, 216n2; and loan words, 159, 160, 161; and paper bread, 161–65; and religious symbolism of facial decorations, 145–46, *195*; and travel, 197n1; words for foods in language of, 165, 166, 167, 168, 169, 220n43; and Zuni language, 218n18, 218n21

Hough, Walter, 203n9, 204n22, 205n38

Howard, Ann V., 208n14

Howard, Jerry B., 208n22, 209n23, 209–10n41, 210n56

Howell, Todd L., 197n4, 207n3

Hrdlicka, Ales, 198n3, 201n17

Huckell, Lisa W., 203n8

Hull, Sharon, 208n13

Humanas pueblos (New Mexico), 134

human hair, and raw materials for fabrics, 38, 60. *See also* hairstyles

identity: and clothing, 10, 37, 41, 68–69; and cranial modification, 30; and facial decorations, 10, 133, 140, 142–45, 147; and hairstyles or hair decorations, 10, 105, 114, 117, 121, 127–29; and jewelry, 10, 73, 101; and language, 11, 151, 171, 172; morphological and cultural attributes included in analysis, 1; observation of by travelers, 175–77; in relation to outsiders, 174–75; and synthesis of conclusions drawn from studies of variation in personal characteristics, 11; theoretical concept of and place in Southwest archaeology, 3–5; within communities, 173–74

immigrants and immigration: and cranial modification, 30; and Proto-Uto-Aztecan language, 155; strontium isotope analysis and presence of at Grasshopper Pueblo, 202n23; studies of enclaves in Southwest archaeology, 3, 5; and variation in facial features, 23

Indo-European languages, 153

Irvine, Judith T., 219n34

Italian language, 156

Ives, John W., 217n7

Jantz, Richard, 23, 200n12

Jémez Pueblo (New Mexico), 31, 160, 161

Jernigan, Wesley, 5, 207n1, 208n10, 212n21–22, 213n27

jewelry: from burials and artistic depictions of Chacoans, Hohokam, and Sinagua in AD 1150–1300 time period, *62*, 82–89, *124*, *187–88*; from burials and artistic depictions of Hohokam, Casas Grandian, Mountain Mogollon, and Ancestral Puebloan in AD 1300–1450 time period, *52*, *64*, *65*, 89–100, *112*, *187*, *189–91*; from burials of Chacoans, Mimbres, and Hohokam during AD 900–1150 period, 73–82, *185–86*, *189*; and contemporary artist's depiction of Hohokam, *4*; and contemporary Puebloans and Navajos, 100–101; and identity, 10, 73, 101; interpretation of from multiple burials, 207n4; and kachina ceremonies, *158*; Mimbres ceramics and depictions of, *48*; and Salado, *141*; and social status, 73, 75, 81, 88–89, 99–100. *See also Glycymeris* bracelets; shell; turquoise

Jewelry of the Prehistoric Southwest (Jernigan 1978), 5

Johnson, Alfred F., 208n12

Joyce, Rosemary A., 198n7

Judd, Neil M., 207n5

Kabotie, Fred, *158*

kachina religion: historic-period artist's depiction of, 158; and loan words, 159–61; and Mimbres hair decorations, *116*; and symbolism of facial decorations, 145–46, *195*, 216n27

Kamp, Kathryn A., 209n32

Kankainen, Kathy, 205n46

Kawaika'a site (Arizona), 63, *192*, *193*, 211n11, 212n19

Kayenta (Arizona): and facial features, *180*, *181*; and jewelry from burials, 85, 89, *189*

Keegan, Marcia, 206n61

Kelly, Sophia E., 203n11, 206n51

Kent, Kate Peck, 202n3, 203n5–7, 203n9–12, 203n15, 204n18–23, 204n30, 204n34, 205n37, 205n42–43, 206n51, 206n55, 206n59 206n61

Keresan language family, 154, 160, 166, 167, 168, *196*, 217n4, 218n18, 218n20

Kidder, Alfred V., 197n2, 203n5, 205n46, 213n29

kilts, and men's garments, 51–55, 63, 67, *90*, *119–20*, *158*, 206n57

King, Mary Elizabeth, 203n9, 205n39, 205n49–50, 206n59

Kiowa language, 155, 167

Kiowa-Tanoan language family, 154–55, *196*, 217n4

kiva murals, 202n4, 206n54; as sources of information on facial designs, 147, *195*, 213n2, 214n6; as sources of information on feathers and headdresses, 115, 117, *119–120*; as sources of information on garments, 51, *52–54*, 56–57, 62–63, *64–65*, 66, 205n36; as sources of information on hairstyles, 109, *111–13*, *192*, *193*, 212–13n11, 212n19–20; as sources of information on jewelry and ornaments, 95, *96–97*, 98

Kopper, Philip, 210n46

Kroskrity, Paul V., 157, 159, 218n19, 219n25, 219n29

Kuaua site (New Mexico), 63, 109, 115, *192*, *193*, 212n11, 212n19 labor, and femur robusticity, 25, 27; and jewelry, 86

La Ciudad site (Arizona), 77–78, 80, *186*

lambdoidal cranial modification, 28

Langdon, Margaret, 218n17

Lange, Charles H., 220n40, 220n46

language: analysis of based on historic-period data, 1; and areal linguistics, 155–59; contemporary status of small, indigenous forms of in Southwest, 171–72; and historical linguistics, 151, 170, 171, 216–17n4; and identity, 11, 151, 171, 172; and language families in Southwest, 151–54, *196*, and loan words, 157, 159–61, 169, 219n25–26, 219n29, 219n37; and phylogenetic linguistics, 151–55; and words for foods, 161–70

La Plata sites (New Mexico, Colorado), *180, 181, 182, 183*

Largo Gallina site (New Mexico), *184*

Las Acequias (Arizona), *139*

LA 3333 (New Mexico), *181, 182*

Leach, Edmund R., 210n1

LeBlanc, Steven A., 208n17

leggings, and clothing, *48, 56,* 59–60, 61, 66, *76*

Lekson, Stephen H., 198n10, 208n21, 215n16

Lister, Robert F. & Florence C., 209n41

Lizard Man site (Arizona), *184*

Llaves Valley sites (New Mexico), *184*

loan words, 157, 159–61, 169, 219n25–26, 219n29, 219n37

Loma'omvaya, Micah, 204n28, 206n60, 209n30

looms, weaving techniques and introduction of, 40

Los Muertos (Arizona), *139, 140, 180, 181,* 198n3

Lowry Ruin (Colorado), *181, 182, 183*

Lumpkin, Charles K., Jr., 200n8

Madimenos, Felicia, 201n20

Magers, Pamela C., 203n7, 203n9–10, 206n51

Magician of Ridge Ruin: clothing of, *62*; and hair decorations, 123, *124,* 127, 212n24; and jewelry, 83–85, 86–88, 89, *124, 188*; stature of, 19, 32. *See also* Ridge Ruin

Malagon, Maria Sprehn, 145, 215n22

Malville, Nancy J., 200n8

Mancos Canyon site (Colorado), *183*

Maricopa (Arizona), 106

Martin, Paul S., 203n6

Mathien, Frances J., 207n6, 208n13, 208n19

Matthews, Washington, 201n16

Mattson, Hannah, 208n19, 209n34

McBrinn, Maxine E., 198n10

McGregor, John C., *62, 124,* 197n4, 200n9, 204n22, 209n34, 212n24

McGuire, Randall H., 127, 207n2–3, 208n14, 213n31, 216n31

meat, and words for foods in Southwest languages, 167–68. *See also* animals

men. *See* gender

Merbs, Charles F., 197n4, 202n26

Mesa Verde (Colorado): and blankets, 206n53; and clothing, 56; and facial features, *180, 181*; and femur robusticity, 27, *181, 182*; and head shape, 29, *183*

Mesoamerica: ancestral connections and symbolism of color and design in, 175; copper bells and contacts with, 80; and Hohokam clothing, 68; and introduction of cotton to Southwest, 38; and religious symbolism of facial decorations, 146–47; and weave structures in southern Southwest, 41, 68–69. *See also* Aztecs; Casas Grandes; Mexico; Paquime; Teotihuacan; Toltecs

Mexico: and introduction of loom to Southwest, 40; jewelry and direct contacts with, 87; and kilts as men's garments, 51. *See also* Mesoamerica

Miller, Wick R., 220n40, 220n48–49, 221n56

Mills, Barbara J., 208n17

Mimbres (New Mexico): and clothing, *48,* 51, 56, 66, *108, 136*; cultural characteristics of, 8; and facial decorations, *48,* 134–35, *136,* 140, 142, *193,* 214n7, 214–15n15, 215n19–20; and facial features, 21, *181*; and hair decorations, 115, *116,* 117, 121, *122, 192–93,* 212n16; and hairstyles, 107, *108,* 114, *136, 191,* 211n8; and head shape, 29, *184*; and indicators of identity to outside observers, 176; and jewelry, *48,* 73–82, 208n10; and stature, *16, 17, 18, 20, 179, 180*

Mitchell, Douglas R., 88, 197n4, 207n3, 209n34, 209n38, 209n40

Mogollon (New Mexico, Arizona): and clothing, 38, 39, 45, 48, 51, 57, 59, 61, 66–67, 68; and facial features, 22, *180*, *181*; and femur robusticity, 25, *26*, *181*, *182*; and head shape, 29, *184*; and textiles, *184*, *185*; and time periods, *8. See also* Grasshopper Pueblo; Mimbres; Mountain Mogollon; Point of Pines

Mohave (Arizona, New Mexico), 106

morphology: list of attributes included in analysis, 1; skin color and variation in, 31; sources of information on, 15, 17; study of regional differences in, 9–10. *See also* facial features; femur robusticity; head shape; stature

Morris, Earl H., 209n26–27, 209n41

Morris, Elizabeth A., 203n5, 203n9, 205n46, 206n51

mortuary studies, and history of Southwest archaeology, 3. *See also* burials

motifs: ancestral connections between Southwest and Mesoamerica and symbolism of, 175; and fabric decoration, 44, *185*; and religious symbolism of jewelry, 80. *See also* zoomorphic forms

Mountain Mogollon (Arizona, New Mexico): cultural characteristics of, 8; and facial features, 22, 23; and femur robusticity, 25; and hair decorations, *122*, 126–27; and head

shape, 29; and indicators of identity to outside observers, 176; and jewelry, 89–100; and nonresidential architecture, 210n55; and social differentiation, 9; and stature, *16, 17, 18*, 19, *20*, *179*, *180. See also* Mogollon

Munson, Marit, 207n2

museums, and presentations on appearance of prehistoric Southwesterners, 5

Na-Dene language family, 154

NAN Ranch Ruin (New Mexico), *184*

nasal cavity breadth/height and nasal index, and variation in facial features, 21, *22*.

Neitzel, Jill F., 10, 11, 200n9, 207n3, 208n21, 209n30

Nelson, Margaret C., 215n16

Nelson, Richard S., 201n20, 208n8, 208n13–14, 209n29

Neuman, Georg K., 199n3

Newman, Stanley, 217n6, 221n59

Nicholas, Linda, 208n22

Northern Tepehuan (Chihuahua), 106

Northrop, Stuart A., 208n13

nose skewers, 95, 98

Numic languages, 159, 218n18

Nusbaum, Jesse L., 203n9

obelionic and occipital cranial modification, 28, 29, 30

Odegaard, Nancy, 127, 212n23

O'Hara, Michael, 209n30

Oñate expedition, 33

O'Neale, Lila M., 203n5

O'odham (Arizona), 50, 197n1. *See also* Pima

orbital index, and variation in facial features, 21, *22*

ornaments. *See* jewelry

Ortman, Scott G., 167, 170, 200n11, 219n23, 219n36, 220n44, 220n52

Osborne, Carolyn M., 203n7, 203n9, 204n32, 205n42, 213n29

Paa'ko site (New Mexico), *180*, *181*

Pacific Coast, as source of shell for jewelry, 79

Painted Cave (Arizona), *46*, *55*, 206n53

painting: and fabric decoration, 41, 44, *46*, *185*; and facial decorations, 134

Paiute, Southern (Arizona, California, Nevada, Utah), 169

Palkovich, Ann M., 210n53

Palmer, J. W., 208n8

paper bread (*piiki*), 161–65, 169–70, 220n41

Paquimé (Chihuahua), 55, 91, *92–94*, 95, 98, 99, 126, *189*, 210n55. *See also* Casas Grandes

parenting, and cranial modification, 28, 30–31. *See also* cradleboards

Parsons, Elsie Clews, 160, 216n25, 216n31, 219n28, 219n33, 221n53

Pasztory, Esther, 216n34

Peabody Museum of Archaeology and Ethnology, 211n8, 214n7

Pecos, Regis, 221n64

Pecos Pueblo (New Mexico), *22*, 23, 32, *180*, *181*

Pelones (Texas, Coahuila), 106

Pena Blanca (New Mexico), *182*

Pepper, George H., 207n5

Philips, David A., Jr. & Christine S., 212n18

phylogenetic linguistics, 151–55

physical anthropology: and estimates of stature, 17; racism in
early literature of, 15, 199n4
physical variation, speculation
on perception of by prehistoric people, 32–33. *See also*
morphology
piiki. See paper bread
Pima (Arizona), 106. *See also*
O'odham
Piper, Claudette, 28, 201n18
plain-weave textiles, 40, *42, 184*
Plog, Stephen, 80, 198n10,
204n26, 208n8, 208n18, 214n5
Point of Pines (Arizona): and facial features, *180, 181*; and head
shape, 29, *30, 184*; and jewelry,
91, 99, *190,* 210n47; morphology and physical appearance
at, 32; size of, 210n55
Potter, James M., 167, 170,
219n36, 220n44, 220n52
Pottery Mound (New Mexico):
and clothing, *52, 54, 63, 65,*
205n36; hairstyles and hair
decorations at, 109, *111–12,*
115, *119–20, 192, 193,* 212n11,
212n19; and jewelry, *96–97*
pronghorn antelope, 168
Proto-Apachean language, 154
protolanguages, of Southwest,
154–55, 217n4
Proto-Uto-Aztecan language, 155
Pueblo (contemporary): clothing
of and connections with ancestral past, 69; and continu-
ation of crafting and wearing
of jewelry, 100–101; and face
painting, 134; facial decorations and identity of, 147; and
hairstyles, 114, 129. *See also*
historic period; Hopi; Zuni
Pueblo Bonito: and facial
decorations, *138,* 214n8; and

facial features, 21, *181*; grave
goods from burials at, 207n5;
and indicators of identity to
outside observers, 176; and
jewelry, *74,* 75, 80, 81, *185*; and
stature, *18,* 19, *20, 179, 180. See
also* Chaco Canyon
Pueblo Grande (Arizona),
82–83, 88–89, 98, 99, *187,*
209n34, 209n40
Pueblo I: and clothing, 57; and
cotton production, 38; and
facial features, 21; and femur
robusticity, 27; and head
shape, 28, *183*
Pueblo II: cotton cultivation
and weaving by, 38; cultural
characteristics of, 5, 8; and
fabric decoration, 44; and
facial decorations, 135, 140,
142, 144; and head shape,
28–29, *183*; and jewelry, *74*;
and sandals, 59
Pueblo III: and clothing, 59, 60,
68; cotton cultivation and
weaving by, 38; and cranial
modification, *183*; cultural
characteristics of, 8; and
fabric decoration, 44; and
facial decorations, 135, 140,
143, 144, 214n8; and head
coverings, 127; and jewelry,
82, *83,* 88
Pueblo IV: and clothing, 40,
57, 62, 67, 68; and cranial
modification, *183*; emergence
and cultural characteristics of,
9; and fabric decoration, 44;
hairstyles and hair decorations
of, 109, 114, 115, 117, 121, 126,
192, 193; and jewelry, 91, 93
pumpkin, words for in Southwest languages, 167
Puye site (New Mexico), *181*

Quechan (Arizona, California),
106
Quinn, Paul C., 213n1

rabbits: and clothing from fur,
38, 39, 48; vocabulary for in
Southwest language families,
167.
racism, and early literature in
physical anthropology, 15,
199n4
rag-weft blankets, 48
Rakover, Sam S., 202n27
Rarick Canyon (Arizona), *58*
Ravesloot, John C., 207n3
raw materials: for fabrics, 38–39,
48; for jewelry, 78–80, 86–87,
95, 98; for sandals, 57–59. *See
also* cotton; human hair; trade
RB568 site (Arizona), 85, 86, 89,
189, 209n34
Reed, Erik K., 201n19, 202n22
Reed, Paul F., 209n41
Regan, Marcia H., 200n11,
202n21
Reid, J. Jefferson, 127, 210n52,
213n31
religion, and religious beliefs:
and ceremonial headdresses,
121; and fabric decoration,
44–45; and facial deco-
rations, 145–47, *195*; and
hairstyles, 114; and jewelry,
80–81, 87–88, 98–99. *See also*
kachina religion; kivas; ritual
Renfrew, Colin, 208n20
retroflex coronals, and language
areas, 156, 218n16
Retzius, Gustav, 201n16
Rey, Agapito, 202n26
Rice, Glen E., 207n3, 217n7
Ridge Ruin (Arizona), 89, *184,*
209n34, 210n43. *See also*
Magician of Ridge Ruin

Ridges Basin (Colorado), 21, *180,
181, 182, 183
Riley, Carroll L., 197n1
ritual: ceremonial roles and
identities within communi-
ties, 174; and linguistic data,
221n62; styles of contempo-
rary clothing for and connec-
tions with ancestral past, 69.
See also religion
Rocky Point site (Sonora), *181,
182, 184*
Roediger, Virginia M., 206n61
Rohn, Arthur H., 203n10, 206n51
Rood, David S., 217n5
Roosevelt Platform Mound sites
(Arizona), *184. See also* Tonto
Basin Salado
Ruff, Christopher B., 201n4

Salado (Arizona, New Mexico):
and clothing, 38, 41, 44, 45,
47, 48–50, 51, 55, *58,* 59, 61,
66–67, 68; and facial decorations, 135, 140, *141,* 143,
214n12, 215n19; and facial
features, 22, 23, *180, 181;* and
femur robusticity, 25, *26,* 27,
181, 182; and head shape, 29,
184; and indicators of identity
to outside observers, 176; and
jewelry, *141;* morphology and
physical appearance of, 32;
and stature, *16,* 17, *18,* 19, *20,*
179, 180; and textiles, *184, 185;*
and time periods, *8. See also*
Roosevelt Platform Mound
sites; Tonto Basin Salado
San Cristobal (New Mexico), *183*
sandals, and clothing, 57–59, 63,
67, *90,* 205n46–49. *See also*
footgear
San Ildefonso Pueblo (New
Mexico), 106

Santa Domingo Pueblo (New
Mexico), 106
Sapir, Edward, 217n7, 220n41
sashes, and clothing, *48, 51, 52,
53,* 57, 63, 67, *90, 113, 119,* 137
Saunderson, Wendy, 197n1
Sayles, F. B., 205n49, 208n12
Schaafsma, Polly, 216n31, 219n27
Schevill, Margot B., 202n1
Schiffer, Michael B., 208n14
Schillaci, Michael A., 202n26
Schneider, Jane, 202n1
Schoolhouse Point (Arizona),
180, 181. See also Roosevelt
Platform mound sites
Sekaquaptewa, Emory, 160,
219n31
Seltzer, Carl C., 198n3, 200n11,
202n21
Seri (Sonora), 106, 134, *196,*
211n4, 216n2
settlement patterns, and leadership strategies, 81, 88–89, 99,
210n42–43
Seymour, Deni J., 208n14
Shafer, Harry J., 207n2, 209n25
Shaul, David L., 155, 156–57,
161, 217n12, 218n13, 218n15,
218n18, 218n20, 219n35
shell, in burials, 75–78, 80–83,
89–91, *90,* 93; ornaments as
identifiers or status messages,
8, *62,* 78, 95, 175–77; and raw
materials for jewelry, 73, 78,
78, 79, *84,* 86–87, 95, 98; religious symbolism of jewelry
made from, 98–99. *See also*
Glycymeris bracelets; jewelry
shell tinklers, 81, 88
shirts, and men's garments, 55–56,
61, 62
Shoshone, Tumpisa (California,
Nevada) 169
Sigleo, Anne, 208n13

Silver, Shirley, 218n17
silver, and contemporary Pueblo
jewelry, 100–101
Simms, Steven R., 213n26
Simpson, Georgina K., 210n57
Sims, Christine P., 218n19,
221n64
Sinagua (Arizona): and clothing,
38, 41, 44, 45, 47, 48–50, 51,
55, *58,* 59, 61, 66–67, 68; and
facial features, 22, 23, *180, 181;*
hairstyles and hair decorations of, 114, 123, 126–27;
and head shape, 29, *184;*
and indicators of identity to
outside observers, 176; and
jewelry, 79, 82–89; morphology and physical appearance
of, 32; and social differentiation, 9; and stature, *16, 18, 19,
20, 179, 180;* and textiles, *184,
185;* and time periods, *8, 9. See
also* Magician of Ridge Ruin;
Ridge Ruin
site locations, map of, *2*
skin color, and physical variation
in Southwest populations,
15, 31
skirts, and women's garments, 50
Slater, Alan, 213n1
Smith, Michael E., 216n30
Smith, Watson, 202n4, 204n29,
205n39, 205n42, 206n55,
206n58
Snaketown (Arizona), *77, 78, 79*
Snead, James F., 197n1
Snow, David H., 208n13
social status, and differentiation:
and clothing, 38, 41, 62; and
identities within commu-
nities, 174; and jewelry, 73,
75, 81, 88–89, 99–100; and
mortuary practices, 207n3;
and physical appearance of

distinctive kin groups, 33; and
stature, 19
socks, and leg coverings, 60. *See
also* leggings
Southwest: ancestral connections and symbolism of color
and design in, 175; contemporary status of small, indigenous languages in, 171–72;
identity studies in archaeology of, 3–5; and language
families, *152*, 153–54; and
protolanguages, 154–55; and
regional chronologies, 5–9.
See also historic period; Hopi;
Pueblo; Zuni
Spanish language, 153
special-occasion outfits, and
clothing, 62–67
Speirs, Randall H., 220n46
Sprague, Roderick, 208n8
Spranz, Bodo, 216n32
squash, words for in Southwest
languages, 167
stamped designs, on fabrics, 41
Starkweather Ruin (New Mexico), *181, 182*
stature: male and female averages
for cultural groups and
time periods, *16, 20, 179–80*;
mortuary practices and
meta-analysis of, 199n6; and
physical variation in cultural
groups, 17–20; sources of
information on, 15, 17
Steen, Charlie R., 203n6, 203n9,
204n22, 205n46, 205n50
Stephen, Alexander M., 203n8
Stevenson, Matilda C., 203n8
stews, and words for foods in
Southwest languages, 165–66,
168–69, 220n45
Stodder, Ann L. W., 9–10, 197n5,
199n5, 200n11, 201n15, 202n21

Stubbs, Stanley A., 203n11,
205n44
Sutton, Logan, 166, 167, 217n8,
220n50
Swadesh, Morris, 217n5
Swarts Ruin (New Mexico), 21,
56, 181

Tadmor, Uri, 219n22
Tamarron site (Colorado), *182*
Taos Pueblo (New Mexico), 29,
105, *183*
Tarahumara (Chihuahua), 134
tattoos, 133–34. *See also* facial
decoration
Taylor, Allan R., 221n58
Teague, Lynn S., 202n3, 203n5–7,
203n9, 203n11–13, 203n15,
204n18, 204n20, 204n22–23,
205n43, 206n59
Teotihuacán (State of Mexico):
and religious symbolism
in prehistoric Southwest,
146–47; and Southwest facial
designs, *195*
Tewa (New Mexico), 159, 160,
162, 163, 165, 166, 167, 168
textiles: and fabric decoration by
cultural group, *185*; distribution of types by cultural
group, *184*; identity-based
perspective on, 10. *See also*
clothing; decoration; weaving
techniques
three-dimensional scanning, of
facial features, 24
tie-dyeing, of fabrics, 41, 44, *46,
185*
Tijeras Pueblo (New Mexico),
93, *191*, 210n55
time periods: and facial metrics,
180–81; and femur robusticity,
181–82; range of included
in analysis, 1; and regional

chronologies in Southwest,
5–9, 198n10; and stature, *18,
179–80*
Tiwa (New Mexico), 63, 66, 115,
162, 163, 166, 167, 168, 212n20,
220n43
Tohono O'odham (Arizona),
197n1. *See also* O'odham
Toltecs (State of Mexico), and
religious symbolism in prehistoric Southwest, 146, 147
Tonto Basin Salado (Arizona),
9, 127, *181, 182*. See also
Roosevelt Platform Mound
sites; Salado
Tonto Creek site (Arizona), *184*
Tonto Ruins (Arizona), *50, 55*
Towa (New Mexico), 162, 166,
167, 168, 218n21, 220n43
Tower, Donald B., 208n14
Townsend, Richard F., 216n30
trade: and diffusion of loan
words, 159; in shell and shell
jewelry, 79, 95, 208n15. *See
also* raw materials; travel
Trager, George L., 217–18n12
travel, and travelers: clothing
and observation of identity
messages by, 37, 73, 175,
176, 177; facial decorations
and observation of identity
messages by, 133, 147, 177;
hairstyles/hair decoration and
observation of identity messages by, 105, 128, 175, 176–77;
languages/linguistic patterns
in Southwest and cultural
affiliation, 11, 151, 171, 173;
observation of differences in
physical characteristics by, 11,
15, 32–33, 173, 176; ornaments
and observation of identity
messages by, 73, 100, 175, 177;
and recognition of cultural

identity of individuals by morphological and cultural attributes, 1, 11; by women and patterns in festive cuisine and food-related language across Southwest, 170; by prehistoric Southwesterners, 197n1. *See also* trade

Treasure Hill (New Mexico), *48*

tribal affiliation: and boarding schools, 128; and jewelry, 101

turkeys, words for in Southwest languages, 167. *See also* feathers

Turner, Christy G., II, 200n11, 202n21

turquoise: found in burials, 75–78, 80, 82–83, 87, 89, 91, 93; and mosaics, 87, *90*, 127, 175; ornaments as identifiers or status messages, 8, 78, 79–80, 95, 98, 101, 128, 175, 176; as raw material for jewelry, 62, *74*, 75–76, 78–79, *83*, *85*, 86, 95, 98; religious symbolism of jewelry made from, 80; sources of, 86, 208n13; and trade, 175

twill weaves, 40, 41, *42*, 44, *184*

Underhill, Ruth M., 197n1

Uto-Aztecan language family, 154–55, 159, *196*, 217n4, 217n9, 217n11, 219n26

Vajda, Edward, 216n3

Valiquette, Hilaire, 218n19

Van Liere site (Arizona), *79*

VanPool, Christine S. and Todd L., 145, 212n18, 215n20, 215n23

Vargas, Victoria D., 208n8

vegetables, and words for foods in Southwest languages, 166–67.

Vestergaard, Ellen M., 197n4

Vivian, R. Gwinn, 204n26

Vokes, Arthur W., 208n13–14, 208n19

Von Bonin, Gerhardt, 201n16

Walt, Henry, 204n22

warp-faced weaves, 40

Wasley, William W., 204n22, 208n12

weaving, techniques of, 39–41, *42–43*, 44, 56, 57, 184

Webster, Laurie D., 10, 114, 202n3–4, 203n5, 203n7, 203n9, 203n11, 203n14, 203n16, 204n20, 204n22, 204n25–29, 205n39, 205n48, 205n50, 206n51, 206n55, 206n59–60, 212n13

weft-wrap openwork weaves, 40, 41, *43*, 56, *184*

Weigand, Philip C., 208n13

Weiner, Annette B., 202n1

Weinreich, Peter, 197n1

Weisensee, Katherine E., 23, 200n11–12, 202n21

West Branch site (Arizona), *138*

Whalen, Michael E., 98, 210n51

White, Leslie A., 160, 219n30

Whittaker, John C., 209n32

Whittlesey, Stephanie M., 127, 207n3, 210n52, 213n31

Whorf, Benjamin Lee, 217–18n12

Wilcox, David R., 197n3, 209n29

Winchester Cave (Arizona), *58*

Winona site (Arizona), *184*

women. *See* gender

Woodward, Arthur, 208n12

Woolf, Charles M., 202n25

Yavapai (Arizona), 106, 134

Yellow Jacket site (Colorado), 27, *181*, *182*, *183*

Yeneseic language family (Siberia), 154

Yoder, David T., 205n46

yucca: and fabrics, 38, 39, 48; and sandals, 57–59

Yuman language family, 154–55, 159, *196*, 217n4, 219n26

zoomorphic forms, and religious symbolism of Hohokam, 98–99. *See also* animals

Zuni (New Mexico): and albinism, 31; and braiding, 40; and hairpins, 126–27; and language families, 154, *196*, 217n4, 218n18, 219n20–21, 219n26, 219n37; and loan words, 160, 161; population movement and distribution of coccidioidomycosis, 33; words for foods in language of, 162–63, 165, 166, 167, 168